RAMÓN GRIFFERO: YOUR DESIRES IN FRAGMENTS
AND OTHER PLAYS

T0314875

Ramón Griffero

YOUR DESIRES IN FRAGMENTS AND OTHER PLAYS

translated by Adam Versényi

OBERON BOOKS
LONDON

WWW.OBERONBOOKS.COM

For Robin

First published in 2016 by Oberon Books Ltd
521 Caledonian Road, London N7 9RH
Tel: +44 (0) 20 7607 3637 / Fax: +44 (0) 20 7607 3629
e-mail: info@oberonbooks.com
www.oberonbooks.com

Collection copyright © Ramón Griffero, 2016

Translation copyright © Adam Versényi, 2016

Introduction copyright © Catherine Boyle, 2016

Ramón Griffero is hereby identified as author of these plays in
accordance with section 77 of the Copyright, Designs and Patents
Act 1988. The author has asserted his moral rights.

Adam Versényi is hereby identified as translator of these plays in
accordance with section 77 of the Copyright, Designs and Patents
Act 1988. The translator has asserted his moral rights.

All rights whatsoever in this play are strictly reserved and
application for performance etc. should be made before
commencement of rehearsal to the author c/o Oberon Books. No
performance may be given unless a licence has been obtained,
and no alterations may be made in the title or the text of the play
without the author's prior written consent.

You may not copy, store, distribute, transmit, reproduce or
otherwise make available this publication (or any part of it) in
any form, or binding or by any means (print, electronic, digital,
optical, mechanical, photocopying, recording or otherwise),
without the prior written permission of the publisher. Any person
who does any unauthorized act in relation to this publication may
be liable to criminal prosecution and civil claims for damages.

A catalogue record for this book is available from the British
Library.

PB ISBN: 9781783197279
E ISBN: 9781783197286

Visit www.oberonbooks.com to read more about all our books
and to buy them. You will also find features, author interviews and
news of any author events, and you can sign up for e-newsletters
so that you're always first to hear about our new releases.

Contents

Acknowledgements   viii

Foreword   ix

Introduction   xvii

———

Your Desires in Fragments   1

Cups of Wrath   39

Midday Lunches or *Petit Dejeuner du Midi*   59

Sebastopol (Desert Times)   81

Downstream (Río Tormentoso)   123

Ecstasy or *Steps to Sainthood*   171

Long Live the Republic: The Three Antonios   229

Gorda   265

The Opera Cleaners   279

Legua's Gynaecologist   295

Acknowledgments

The best work in the theatre is the result of putting the most creative and collaborative people you can find into a room and then allowing that hard-won creativity to meet serendipity. First and foremost my thanks go to Ramón Griffero who serendipitously handed me these plays one night in Santiago, and for creating these works whose worlds it has been my pleasure to enter and to translate. I am extremely pleased that these plays are finally being published and made accessible to an English-speaking audience. As any translator for the theatre knows, translating the words themselves is the least of your task. Much more important is the creation of speakable, theatrically vibrant language for the stage. That task cannot be done alone and I am grateful for my friends and colleagues Julie Fishell, Ray Dooley, Jeff Cornell, Elisabeth Corley, Bonnie Gould, Hope Alexander, Joseph Megel, Kathy Williams, and Caroline Strange who have gathered in my living room to help me hear these plays. My thanks as well to the members of The FENCE who helped me hear *Sebastopol (Desert Times)* during the Trans (Re)lation Convening at the O'Neill Theatre Center in Connecticut. George Spender has been a joy to work with at Oberon Books, shepherding everything through the publication process with care. I hope these translations have captured the aurality, orality, and theatricality Ramón created and all of you have helped me hear. Any faults are my own.

Foreword

Images: inside the fragments of a brain, a shepherd boy in Portugal, salmon in large, narrow fish tanks, flowers cultivated in the Atacama desert, an apartment building dancing, egg whites slipping down the skin of an arthritic body, a woman desperately rolling about in her lover's books, another woman lovingly touching every object in the room before committing suicide, a gynecologist encouraging complicity as he whispers in an audience member's ear, a cleaning woman *zapateando* and singing *cante jondo* on the stage of the Opera.

Yearning: for another, to believe, for happiness, to be free from fear, for reincarnation, for death, for home, for sex, for friendship, for release, for escape, for passion, for martyrdom, for maternal love, for liberty, for complicity, for the realization of dreams.

These were just a few of the images and feelings washing over me as I read *Ramón Griffero: Diez Obras de Fin de Siglo*, a collection of ten plays that Griffero had given me, on a flight back to the United States from Chile. Captivated by the theatrical energy, poetry, humor, and multiplicity of forms I found in these plays I contacted Griffero virtually as soon as I returned home and expressed my desire to translate them. What you are reading is the result of several years of collaboration between Griffero and myself to bring his work into English translation. Doing so has proved to be challenging, immensely satisfying, and always exhilarating.

I first met Ramón Griffero in 1991 when the Artistic Director of PlayMakers Repertory Company where I am Dramaturg, David Hammond, and I took a trip sponsored by the United States Information Agency and the International Theatre Institute to Mexico City, Buenos Aires, Montevideo, and Santiago de Chile. In thirteen days we saw fifteen productions and met with theatre professionals in each location from early in the morning until late at night. In Santiago I was impressed by the work Griffero was doing both with his own company, Teatro de Fin de Siglo, and with 'El Trolley', a cultural space he ran in the former meeting hall of the Trolley Workers Union. Our paths crossed again several years later when the Artistic Director of City Theatre in Pittsburgh, Marc Masterson, asked me to join a grant application for a project that never came to fruition in which I would translate a Calderón de la Barca play that Griffero would then direct at City Theatre. We met once again in Santiago in 2011 when I was investigating how former sites of torture under the military dictatorships in the Southern Cone during the 1970s and 1980s were now being turned into 'sites of memory'. That dinner in Santiago laid the groundwork for this collection, which has finally come together around each of our busy schedules.

Theatrical translation always goes beyond the words. Just as the playwright's work becomes a pre-text for the production, so too does the source text become a pre-text for the translated text in the target language. When working in the same language director, designers, dramaturg, actors, and audience all collaborate with the playwright, creating something new as they engage with the pre-text, something that is both the playwright's work and much more. The production is simultaneously the playwright's work and the confluence of the work of all those who collaborate with him or her. Frequently much of that combined work is largely invisible in reading the text of a play. As theatrical translator it is doubly important for me to convey what is not there in the source text since those encountering it in the target language will, by and large, not have access to the source text itself. Consequently, theatrical translation is for me a process of donning and discarding a series of hats as I work through the source text: translator as dramaturg, translator as director, translator as designer, translator as actor, translator as adaptor, translator as playwright, translator as audience member. Wearing all of these hats is how I strive to capture the essence of the original and create it anew in my translation. It is also always my intention to avoid the all too common tendency in translation to 'explicate' the text, eliminate ambiguity, and remove the unknown or unfamiliar. For me the crux of translation is to convey the excitement, the confusion, and the dawning comprehension that working in the source language brings me and to give those reading in the target language the same access to a cultural way of being distinct from their own. A 'seamless' translation, then, one in which the translated text can be assumed to have been written in the target language itself, is a failure. I want the collaborators on my translated pre-text to experience the same process in dealing with the play as I experienced in the process of translating it. I want directors, actors, and audiences to inhabit the worlds of these plays precisely because those worlds are different from their own, not because those worlds are familiar.

Translating these ten plays has been a constant process of negotiation carried out in collaboration with Griffero and with his full consent. Griffero typically directs the first production of each of his plays and writes attuned to how his texts will work in performance. This presented a challenge in translating The Forgotten's monologue in *Cups of Wrath* where the text's punctuation creates a particular rhythm in Spanish that provides a tool for the actor to use in developing characterization. My initial impulse was largely to retain the Spanish punctuation in the English version, but working with actors and conferring with Griffero led me to abandon that impulse and instead search for English punctuation that would create an English rhythm different from, but analogous to, the Spanish rhythm in performance.

Other aspects of translation were also thoroughly discussed: What does the slang in a Chilean gay Internet chat room in *Your Desires in Fragments* mean? What is the cultural ambience experienced when entering that space? How would Chilean Nobel Laureate poet Gabriela Mistral's return to Chile be perceived in *Midday Lunches or Petit Dejeuner du Midi*? What led to the formation of workers theatres in the nitrate mines run by the British in late nineteenth century Chile? What are the differences between the various musical styles employed in *Downstream (Río Tormentoso)*? What do they say about the characters who sing or listen to them? How were the scenes in *Ecstasy or Steps to Sainthood* involving electrical shocks performed? What do the allegories called for in *Long Live the Republic* portend for performance? How is the gesture with the letter done in *Gorda*? Are there cultural equivalents elsewhere to the use of the *zapateando* and *cante jondo* in *The Opera Cleaners*? Who is The Gynaecologist speaking to in *Legua's Gynaecologist?* The translations in this collection contain my answers to these questions and my solutions to these problems. My intention has always been to create performable translations that capture Griffero's own voice and his particular theatrical approach.

In his book *The Dramaturgy of Space* Griffero posits that, human society conceives of space primarily in terms of squares and rectangles but those forms don't occur naturally in the non-human environment. As both playwright and director Griffero incorporates the circle not the square. In *Your Desires in Fragments* thoughts, emotions, relationships are constantly fragmented yet simultaneously fluid. For Griffero theatrical discourse is multi-layered and multivalent. Past, present, and future exist simultaneously, not as a linear progression. Ideas, dreams, and desires are actualized by scenic images that provide a visual counterpoint to the words that are spoken. As we move through the galleries in You's 'Internal Museum' we encounter a world where both characters and locations are constantly circling back on each other, reconnecting and recapitulating what has gone before as a spur to both present and future action. Words and phrases spoken by one character in one context are repeated by another character in a different context.

In *Cups of Wrath* a prophet cycles through time adopting the guises of The Young Pharaoh, The Shepherd Boy of Fatima, The Forgotten, and The Officer each of whom in their own way delivers a message of impending apocalypse. Their prophecies are frequently compared to the military coup of 1973 and the repression carried out during the subsequent years of Pinochet's regime. Past, present, and future combine to paint a picture of a particularly Chilean apocalypse.

In *Midday Lunches or Petit Dejeuner du Midi*, a play that premiered just as Pinochet was placed under house arrest in London in 1998, we encounter Esteban, a prisoner condemned to death who writes a novel to leave as his legacy. In a series of scenes the novel is alternately about Socrates, the Chilean poet and Nobel Laureate Gabriela Mistral, a psychopathic killer, and a woman in a garden. Esteban exists condemned to death while simultaneously embodying a disappeared prisoner who receives no trial, is ignorant of both the means and the place where he will die, will never be able to say goodbye, and who knows that his face will soon fade from memory. Socrates, then, is Esteban's historical antecedent, each of their societies fears what they have to say, and each of them drinks the hemlock in order to sear into social memory the supreme importance of free and unfettered discourse.

Where *Your Desires in Fragments, Cups of Wrath*, and *Midday Lunches or Petit Dejeuner du Midi* each in various ways places us in both the present and during the Pinochet regime, *Sebastopol (Desert Times)* takes us further back in Chilean history to the late nineteenth century when the British developed and ran the nitrate mines in the desert as if they were an extension of the United Kingdom. When two lovers, Cristina and Luis, run carelessly through the abandoned Sebastopol mine in 1997, she falls down a mine shaft and finds herself the daughter of the mine's nineteenth-century English administrator who looks upon Chile as nothing more than a territory to be exploited and the Chileans themselves as savages. While struggling against the borrowed existence thrust upon her Cristina develops relationships with two young men: Sidney, the British chemist her father Humber has employed, and Luis, a worker in the mine. With Luis she performs the role of The Future in a workers' theatre production and searches for magical beings that might help her return to her own time. With Sidney, who reminds her of her own circle in Santiago, she engages in sexual ecstasy and then bids him goodbye. As Luis and the other striking workers are gunned down by the army Cristina is returned to the Luis in her own time.

The combination of the sensual and the social that characterizes *Sebastopol (Desert Times)* appears once more in *Downstream (Río Tormentoso)* where Waldo befriends the river that flows in front of his apartment building as he and the other young people his age attempt to define themselves in a world still heavily marked by the enmities and alliances forged before and after the coup in 1973. In haunting, humorous, and poetic ways Griffero imbues *Downstream (Río Tormentoso)* with a series of images culminating in Waldo's death at the hands of drug traffickers, his mother Eugenia (who still sings the songs of

Allende's Unidad Popular) killing her neighbor Willy (a former torturer for the Pinochet regime), while the ghost of a drowned boy stands over Waldo's corpse, and Waldo's friend Lorena deliberately snaps the pencil with which she was writing in her diary in two. This simple final gesture in the play is emblematic of the ways in which each of its characters leads broken lives.

Long Live the Republic: The Three Antonios continues Griffero's combination of past, present, and future. The play tells the story of two Frenchmen, Antoine Gremey and Antoine Gramusset, and one Chilean, Antonio de Rojas, who wrote 'The Polpaíco Manifesto' in 1785, a document that both predated 'The Declaration of the Rights of Man' published in France in 1789 and shared its goals. The action continually shifts between the Colony of Chile, aboard ship, and Spain as the three Antonios conspire to liberate Chile from Spanish rule and establish a republic. Betrayed by members of the Creole (born in Chile but educated in Spain) elite, Antonio de Rojas escapes while the two Frenchmen are condemned and sent to the Viceroy in Lima for execution. Threaded throughout are brief scenes in which a Boy reads from a book about 'The Three Antonios' to his aunt Juliana as they listen to demonstrations in the streets by the early twentieth-century Chilean leftwing Frente Popular movement. Juliana is also Gramusset's lover in the eighteenth-century portion of the play and her presence in different time periods serves to connect Griffero's audience to the events taking place in 1785, the 1930s, and the present as the goals of the Three Antonios and the Frente Popular become connected to those of Salvador Allende's Unidad Popular whose electoral victory was crushed by the military coup in 1973, the repercussions of which are still being felt in Chile today.

The collection concludes with three one-acts from the 1990s: *Gorda, The Opera Cleaners,* and *Legua's Gynecologist.* Each one is a small jewel the facets of which reflect individual aspects of Griffero's prismatic approach to presenting the world. The theatre distinguishes itself by the use of embodied performance. It takes place live, in front of us, immediately present. Griffero's plays may not always be instantaneously comprehensible but they are always theatrically rich, vibrating with the human being in process. These are plays supremely *of* the theatre, conceived and constructed for the stage, not for any other art form. Combining poetic meditation, acute insight into the human condition, and powerful theatrical imagery, they come alive in performance.

It is my pleasure to provide English-speaking audiences with this collection and the access it gives to Griffero's work. I hope that you will approach Griffero's work on its own terms, rather than expect immediate accessibility or complete familiarity. If you do so you will experience the same depth of design, rich artistry, and moments of surprise that I encountered in translating these plays.

Adam Versényi

Introduction

Ramón Griffero has been a major presence in Chilean theatre since his first production in the country in 1982, *Recuerdos de un hombre con su tortuga* (*Memories of a Man with his Tortoise*). His theatre is now seen as foundational of new dramatic languages in Chile in the 1980s, distrustful of the primacy of the word and determined to introduce a complex theatre aesthetic to challenge from the stage the repressive realities of the Pinochet regime (1973-90). Born in 1954, Ramón Griffero began a degree in Sociology at the University of Chile in 1971 during the Salvador Allende Popular Unity government (1970-73). As a student in this effervescent political period he was active in political and social movements, and, after the military coup led by General Augusto Pinochet in September 1973 and the closure of the School of Sociology he left the country, part of an exodus of the left repressed and prohibited under the Pinochet regime. He continued his degree in Sociology in England at the University of Essex, and in the late 1970s moved to Belgium to study first cinema and then dramaturgy and directing at the University of Leuven. It was in Belgium that Griffero produced his first play, *Opera pour un naufrage* (1980). Working with the Belgian scenographer and designer Herbert Jonckers (1953-96), Griffero set out, from very early in his career, to create a dramaturgy of space – an approach to the production of theatre that would, in the words of Jonckers, interweave scenography, text and performance. From his return to Chile in 1982, Griffero established himself as someone who would bring a new voice to the Chilean stage, new ways of contesting the dominant political order through the theatre.

In 1983, with his newly formed Teatro de Fin de Siglo, Griffero established the cultural centre El Trolley, in a disused warehouse of the union of trolley bus drivers. It was situated, as Griffero has said, in an unfashionable part of town 'between a brothel and a prison'. Productions were funded by parties, gigs, art events, which became a kind of alternative haven for young people in search of new forms of community and contestation.

El Trolley became an environment in which theatre could be produced in the context of a loyal and largely young audience in search of varied political and artistic responses to the complex realities of living in a repressive regime. Griffero prized the autonomy of this precarious independent theatre, what he has called its pre-capitalist marginality, which in fact constituted its freedom, the site from which he established his political poetics and his dramaturgy of space. In 2000, Griffero remembered how El Trolley was regularly visited by the 'guardians of public order', who he would assure that the participants were artists and not communists, to be met with the chilling response, 'of course you're not communists. If you were we wouldn't be asking you what you're doing here'. It was in the provocative space of El Trolley, and with the plays *Historias de un galpón abandonado* (*Stories of an Abandoned Warehouse*, 1984), *Cinema Utoppia* (1985) and *Morgue-99* (1986), that Griffero began to put into practice his 'dramaturgy of space'. In essence this is a language for the stage that recognises its creative and demanding multiplicity and uses this idea of writing for the imagined stage as the motor for theatrical performance.

Ramón Griffero was not alone in using the stage as a place from which to defy the dictatorship. From early in the regime dramatists and theatre groups had fought to create a strong voice that would represent what was being silenced in the country. Groups like the collectives Teatro Ictus and the Taller de Investigación Teatral, dramatists like Juan Radrigán, Isidora Aguirre and Marco Antonio de la Parra, directors like Jaime Vadell and Raúl Osorio (to name a few) had all written and produced works that denounced the extreme social cost of the repressive neo-liberalism of the Pinochet regime. The regime saw theatre as a minority art speaking to a very small proportion of the liberal elite and so occupying a relatively benign space. As such, it suffered less direct censorship than the mass media; for example, many actors who were on stage every night were blacklisted from appearing on television, where their presence could be much more pernicious. It was to this space that Ramón Griffero returned from exile, bringing a theatrical voice that invited audiences into scenic spaces where innovation and adventure opened up new possibilities in the dramatic imagination and in a new venue, one that was a type of place of residence rather than only accessible for the time of the performance. Teatro Fin de Siglo and El Trolley announced that there were ways of subverting the social codes that had effectively silenced the multiple voices in Chile, unrepresented in the brutally narrow definitions of 'normality'. This was the great success of *Cinema Utoppia*, which has become a point of reference, a 'mini legend' in the memory of the Chilean stage of the 1980s, in the words of theatre critic Juan Andrés Piña.

In *Cinema Utoppia* Griffero asked his audience to engage with different timeframes, spatial perspectives and themes. The play takes place in a neighbourhood cinema in the fifties where a group of lonely misfits watch a type of futuristic serialised film set in Paris in the 1980s where Chilean exiles live the loss of disappeared loved ones, drug addiction, poverty and exclusion in their new country, prostituting themselves to pay their rent. In this context, there is only one tragic end possible. It is a tragic end that is in violent contrast with the romance and escapism that the 1950s viewers go to the cinema to seek, and it is a tragic reality in which they become implicated as they become one with the film and witness the violent end of the protagonist. In its inventiveness and playfulness, *Cinema Utoppia* was characteristic of the work of Teatro Fin de Siglo. It posed questions of the awareness in Chile of the internal and external impact of the dictatorship; it asked questions of the languages and codes that had developed to disguise reality; and it suggested painful, tragic and uncomprehending complicity when these languages and codes are accepted and repeated without challenge. Challenge was what El Trolley provided. And here, too, was a theatre that forcefully confronted problems that were both Chilean and not Chilean–drug addiction, homosexuality, legality and repression, love—a subversive way of taking Chile out of its isolation.

Throughout the 1980s Griffero received national and international prizes for his work, and this recognition has been the basis for his continued presence as a major dramatist, theorist and educator in Chile. His work is never still, but it always returns to the same questions of the creation of a coherent language system on stage, one that is robust enough to resist the processes of rehearsal, performance and engagement with the audience. His key question has always been about how to speak *from* the theatre, using languages formed in the air from reality to create a stage world that gives new form to that reality. For Griffero, the problem for dramatists during the dictatorship was not 'from where to write', for this was almost a given: it was the traditional place of Chilean theatre, a place of social commentary and political contestation. The question for him was 'how to write', how to use the same language as them and make it belong elsewhere, speaking from the dramatist for others. In the years following the return to democracy, from 1990–94, Griffero did not write theatre, turning instead to prose (a book of short stories, *Yo soy de la Plaza de Italia / I'm from the Plaza Italia*, 1992) and to writing on his theories of drama and cultural practice. The question of 'how to write' had become more problematic. For Griffero it was imperative to go beyond the simplistic narrative of the transition, in which the fragile democracy sought forgetting and a new type of public order over the troubling and disruptive power of remembering. Again Griffero turned to the dramaturgy of space to explore this new reality. He has sought to find 'places of fight', places of resistance to capture thinking that is at odds with dominant narratives, to find out how not to 'talk as they do and see as they see or represent as they represent'.

The plays that mark his dramaturgy since the 1990s seek to revitalise the space of the individual imagination, of those who are not represented in dominant collective structures, delving into realities that take him far beyond the dictatorship, deep into structures of being in Chilean society. In plays like *Río abajo* (*Downstream*, 1995), *Brunch* (1999), *Tus deseos en fragmentos* (*Your Desires in Fragments*, 2003), Griffero forcefully remodels for the stage places that are both enclosed and multiple: the marginal intimacy of the block of flats by the river in *Downstream* ; in *Brunch*, the terrible moment of realization by an imprisoned detained-disappeared man, in a setting of long narrow fish tanks and multiple mirrors, that he will fade into unremembered nothing, a fate multiplied over and again in the historic reality of repression; and in the 'conceptual eruptions' of *Your Desires in Fragments* a series of abstract 'rooms' provide multi-layered experiences and systems of movement between the myriad spaces in which we perform our being in the past and present, the internal and the external selves, the intimate and the public.

Griffero's is a dramatic imagination that sees all the elements of the production together, to be embodied onstage in a complex accumulation of his language of textual, visual, physical and conceptual signs. In this there is a profound sense of what he calls 'scenic memory', a history of the stage that contains all its actors in each dense moment. In a world where an increasing lack or defiance of historical consciousness threatens us all, Ramón Griffero's insistence on the creation of scenic languages that provide the possibility of performing the complex historic multiplicity of our individual and collective being is worth the effort of recreating.

Catherine Boyle

YOUR DESIRES IN FRAGMENTS:
CONCEPTUAL IRRUPTIONS
TEXTUAL POETICS FOR A POETICS OF SPACE

Characters

The Speakers:

YOU

SHE

ONE (FEMALE)

HE

THAT ONE (MALE)

Concerning the characters: they are speakers, each body assumes different voices ... there are voices that emerge again from a forgotten body, others that are other peoples' memories that speak through your body, there are voices that are registers-recordings. There are disemboweled characters that contain other characters. There are speakers in the present – from the past and others of desire.

WHERE TO READ FROM

From inside the fragments of a brain. Actions are presented
linearly on the page, but happen simultaneously on the stage.

They occur where the situations interconnect read
spatially, by means of the mechanisms of the visual
narrative.(Objects, projections).

These texts should be visualized for the stage from the
perspective of an archeologist, behind the ideas(concepts)
lie cities ... Temples to disembowel

SCENIC INSTALLATIONS

These texts are written for multiple installations that form
and disappear, producing the feeling of a mental labyrinth,
where ideas, dreams, desires, intersect with a world of plastic
and conceptual images, or points of reality that deliver a
parallel perception to that of the verbal action described.

A BEGINNING

The Internal Museum

YOU: I knew exactly who I wanted to seduce when I bought the lilac shirt with black borders, I looked at myself in the dressing room, thinking that someone else observed me. That was the reason it took me so long to choose between the distressed jeans and the hip-hugger slacks. Yes, I said to myself, I like this. And what about the dark green shirt with the cuffed pants … ?

And that's how I was dressed … not as you see me now, these are the residue, the fragments of outfits destined for different lovers.

She would have smiled at my alpaca sweater. He, passed his hand over the orange quadrilles.

I would love to speak after death …

Crimes surround me, not the ones in the papers, not the ones done with knives. I know that you understand …

How many times did I sing my siren's song? How many people, because of me, killed themselves with weapons that aren't punished by any law?

Nurse, nurse … pick up your pen, I've got something to tell you. False, I won't be able to, besides she'd only think I'm raving. She would just ring the bell.

I'll never know if, when I caressed them, this was pleasure, this was love …

I'm not sick, depressed, blue, or anything with evident existential …

I'm passing the time … whiling away the time … a tourist in this city. Visiting, entertaining myself … a tourist in my life.

Detained in front of every man and woman, visiting as if in a museum, they are what attract me this time round … So, there are museums I never went through, places … I'm going to write you this … "You went to a museum full of embalmed animals" …

You took me to the room that least interested you, you knew beforehand that you took me to the gallery of forgetting ...

I'm certain ... that in those, those where I stopped ... I never got to the main exhibition, I saw the temporary ones ... there wasn't time, I tell you ...

I could have stayed in someone forever, enjoying their details, their walls ... their eternal kisses.

I'm submerged in my own museum ... You're in luck today, the exhibition is open, you can stroll through the galleries where the pictures are already hung, the sculptures made, the inscriptions on the walls. The album of my mind in motion ... There are forbidden rooms, others that have been demolished already ... some that we don't wish to visit.

Nurse ... the brochures ... we have visitors ... they need the brochures ... the headphones with the self-guided tour. The slides, the post cards ...

Nurse ... I want to saturate myself in your white skirt and disappear.

GALLERY ONE

The Mistake

HE: I got this video ... they're takes, I recognize a few faces ... the places ...

YOU: Well, tell me ... What's the mystery?

HE: You're in one part ...

YOU: Great.

HE: Has to be edited, you were never in Egypt ... Were you?

YOU: What's wrong with you, relax ...

HE: It's you, sailing the Nile ... In black and white.

YOU: I don't know what you're talking about, it must be a montage ... something creative, a gift.

HE: Yes, but on the bank, between the papyri, there's an Arab embracing someone and that someone is me ... and I talk to you, speaking with my voice ... and I shout at you ... Andrés! ... Andrés! ... you on the Nile ... and I run along the bank and you don't look at me ... I'm so happy, it's where I've always wanted to be with you. It's the place where I would be able to tell you what without wanting to I'm saying now, here on this frozen floor ... Andrés, the video's my dream, it's my face suffused with the happiness with which I see myself, but never have. My body in the sun, burnt, looking beautiful like it never is ... It's the Sahara in the background and the palm trees on the bank, it's the place she promised but where I wanted to be, there, with you, but it's no longer possible, because by that point you were already dead ... Andrés.

It's what's left of my nightmare. After images of the video.

From the Beginning

YOU: Nurse ... the brochures are upside down, we've come in the wrong way, through the last door. We should have used the one on the right ... The one from the beginning.

GALLERY TWO

ONE: You shouldn't donate organs, donating organs is a terrible thing, they can't resuscitate you ... No reason anymore to go to wakes and wait for them to revive ... Don't let them do an autopsy! Don't give them your eyeballs! You don't have to be afraid that they'll bury you alive today, you don't have to build the coffin that opens from the inside, or ask them not to close up the hole until the third day ... There aren't any people beating the coffins from inside now, no vapor on the stained glass of the urns.

And I was frightened for so long, worrying about a last mistake, believing that even though I was gone, I still was ... the best thing would be to wake up during the Mass ...

7

such panic and happiness at the same time ... I don't fear today anymore.

THAT ONE: I'm no longer afraid either. I want to go dancing now, Zeba. I'm no longer interested in going out with sluts in their senior year of high school, or with the cashiers from Walmart. Besides, I never dared tell them to show me their clitoris, or what you said was the best ... "fuck her in the ass" ... Even when I did it was by mistake, she said to me ... "Oh, that hurts a lot and it isn't great" ... I hate fucking in the car. Besides, when you took me to whores, she didn't take off her clothes, neither did I and you, on the bed, to one side, even less ... so it was the same as rubbing yourself in high school, you didn't see anything ... "Take your hand away", she told me, "Leave it to me, I'll guide you" ... I didn't see anything more than her wide mouth and her teeth stained with rouge ... Besides, you only called me because I've got a car, so you could fill it with your friends and take off for a party in Puente Alto that was sure to be full of secretaries ... Why bother ...

Maybe I'll head for the beach, I might see her go by ... I hope it rains. She likes walking in the rain ... smiling and picking flowers ...

YOU: Why didn't we have a child who would walk in the rain and pick flowers?

THAT ONE: Hi, do you want to go to Chiloé?

SHE: What's there?

THAT ONE: Rain, canals, we'll take the train ...

SHE: How? There isn't a train.

THAT ONE: I've got chocolate. Want some?

SHE: No, I don't want you to see me eat, it deforms my face, I don't want you to see how it disfigures me.

THAT ONE: Me neither, then. Let's take the train.

SHE: But those canals are in Venice. It's late.

THAT ONE: We'll sleep there. On the steps of the church.

How good it is to wake up, here, cold and hungry, how good to wake up ... In Venice ... full of canals and museums that I don't have the cash to enter or want to see ... I'm more interested than I can tell you ... that's the way it was, with the hot chick, making love on the steps of Santa Sofía, putting my hand inside her jacket, feeling her wet ... eating a pizza, dead from the heat, feet soaking on the shore, then throwing ourselves into it right there. And then in Greece, nude on the beach, lying across the rocks ... sleeping in another church, Orthodox, white ... looking down towards the cliffs of the Santorini volcano ... *(To the audience.)* Ever done it?

YOU: But it was on the cliffs of Ios that hate appeared, where we began to kill each other. Then ...

HE: Better to talk to a Dane: My country is very beautiful ... lots of nature ... good wine ... come sometime ... I want to show it to you ... no, it's not like here, people so alone, no family ... old people dying alone ... There, if someone sleeps in the street, they'll pick them up, take them to shelter, give them hot coffee ... If there's an accident everyone helps ... people are cultured, even a laborer will recite you Neruda ... People get together in their homes ... friends invite you ... you don't have to warn them like here, ask if there's room in their schedule ... there ... everyone's friendly, you'll like it ... Sun all year round, here, you're stuck with clouds, there aren't any clouds, the sky's like pavement ... there you ski for a while, and when you get bored, you're already at the beach. A sea with waves, not like here where all you get is pluf ... pluf ... and people don't live squeezed into places without bathrooms, where you can't even fit a computer ... No, houses with patios, big apartments with a view of the mountains ... Come see.

From the Beginning II

YOU: Nurse, you wash me, you rinse my eyes with alcohol ... you watch me and don't talk to me, you smile ... you read

the chart ... take my temperature, toss the syringes, cover
yourself in green ... close the curtains ... dim the light,
even when it isn't dark ... look at your small gold watch ...
take my pulse, write ... Nurse, please open your lips ...

SHE: You don't recognize me, you never recognize me, even
if I let down my hair and shake out the coif I don't wear.
I'm sure you see me wearing a white apron, you don't see
my silhouette walking on the wet cobblestones, you don't
see me bringing flowers ... You picked up the feathers in
the parks ... I harvest winds, it's me with the pink nipples
and hair down to my shoulder ... Look, I'm the one with
blue eyes ... we're like we were on the rocky shores on
the island of Ios ... What did we argue about? It deformed
your face, mine, and how we showed our teeth ... It was
going to be a beautiful trip ... as beautiful as postcards
written while contemplating the acropolis ... we stole
grapes from the fields and I taught you what an olive was
... We were two transparent silhouettes lying nude across
the stones ... I, submerging myself between the rocks ...
coming back to see: my house between the eucalyptus
under the sea ... my mother's sad eyes ... the melancholy,
beautiful days ... We're the ones that escaped from the tv
stars on Sábados Gigantes ... those who didn't look at the
mountain range like it was a wall ... We're the ones who
believed that to write would destroy our daily dialogue.
I'm the one who felt that my clothes stank of urine and the
man I loved was a fallen angel ... I'm the one who now
shines in a star, so that you'll see me as a nurse ... I've
come to love you anew, not to fill the table with flavors,
nor make the bed with embroidered sheets ... I came
back to find us ... you pushed me through an underwater
channel and you went by yourself on the Aegean Sea ...
And now ...

GALLERY THREE

I'm Happy

HE: I comb my hair, I take a shower, it's three in the afternoon
... I'm nervous, I just talked to him ... I'm happy ... this
is what it's like to be happy, waiting until seven arrives ...
Thinking four hours left ... washing yourself for someone
... taking a good look at yourself in the mirror and finding
yourself handsome ... imagining the encounter, yearning
for his gaze again ... yearning for them to see you, to see
him ... I'm happy. And if he doesn't come ... and if he
calls to say that he can't right now ... I should go out and
make some photocopies ... he might not come, he forgot
... I'll call him from a payphone ... I'll remind him ... No,
obsession ... how wonderful it is to exist ... Santiago's so
beautiful, I love its traffic jams, please let me get there on
time ... Who will get there first ... he will, sitting with his
back to me ... I'll surprise him ... or nobody will be there
... and I'll have to pretend ... with a newspaper or a beer
... It's five, two hours left ... he'll be as happy ... smiling
... or maybe he's already had second thoughts and he'll tell
me that he just came for five minutes, then he has to go,
he forgot about a friend's birthday ... Then I'll go type his
name into a chat room, looking for/ someone cool, green
eyes, one meter seventy, who wants to now ... / hello,
where are you? ... / Ñuñoa / I'm here in Bella ... / do you
want to get together? ... / what do you like? / ... thinking
it's him answering ... Been here long?

THAT ONE: Just got here.

HE: Where should we go?

THAT ONE: Wherever you'd like.

HE: I'm happy ...

GALLERY FOUR

I love Him

ONE: I love him, I love him, I love him ... I don't want to
suffer ... Look, Cristián, I love you ... but I don't want
to suffer, I don't want to see you hugging someone else
tomorrow, smiling at her like you smile at me, turning
your tender cheeks to each other with me greeting you as
I pass by ... I don't want you to tell me you don't have
time ... that you'll call me later ... I don't want to wake up
in a cold bed ... or on someone's arm that's not you ... I
can't be happy thinking this is over ... I don't want you to
shout at me "possessive, hysterical" ... Nor do I want to
spend an entire night saying goodbye ... Listening to your
reasons ... internal ... your doubts, all under the cover
of something uncertain ... And me feeling mature, even
giving you advice: "Do what's best for you" ... "Do what
you need you need to do" ... So that I remain dignified
and fierce in front of you, because I don't know what else
to do and you thanking me for my friendship. Me, filling
the glass with wine, trying to make a longing surface that's
already gone up in smoke ... but always with hidden desire
... You turn your head and flash, you look at me with the
same love ... telling me it was all to see how I would react.
And I hit you with the pillow, and you take me by the
wrists and remove my clothes with your teeth ... and we
sweat screaming ... I don't want to think about all of that
and never have it happen ... That's why I don't love you,
Cristián.

THAT ONE: Yes, I understand, you've been great for me, but
I'm not ready ...

ONE: We've always told each other everything ... it's great that
you're so clear.

THAT ONE: It's just that ... I've still got so much to live for,
and I don't want to trick you ... That's fundamental, it's
important to be truthful, with me, with you ...

ONE: You've met someone else?

THAT ONE: No, that's not it ... I don't want to hurt you, but I can't tell you ... I'm leaving because I love you so much that, if we were to see each other in another life I would be born and buried with you ...

ONE: Well, if you need anything, call me ... Wait ... *(showing a tattoo on her shoulder)* It's a butterfly right where you always bite me ... It was a surprise.

THAT ONE: I'll bite it ... then I'll go.

ONE: I'll turn on the radio, I'll dance and sing ... until dawn ... I want to make love to a Palestinian suicide bomber ...

I saw him last night, with his black lock of hair, his come hither look, kissing his Kalashnikov, I'm going, I'll buy a ticket to Ramallah or Belen ... With him, I'll finally be able to love someone.

GALLERY FIVE

A Strange Retelling

THAT ONE: Hi, I'm Cristián, my friend Cristina wanted to meet you, but couldn't get tickets; I want to spend the night preparing for your suicide with you, if you want.

HE: I like Chileans; I've got an uncle in Llay Llay ...

THAT ONE: Listen, how much time do we have? ... Your eyes, if I could only have those eyes.

HE: I have to wash them, my feet too. I turned them in already; they're no longer mine.

THAT ONE: I'll help you ... I'll wash mine too ... they're very dirty ... the sand, I could give you a massage, oil your body. Eh?

HE: Since you're here, do what you have to do ...

THAT ONE: I don't dare ...

HE: I do.

THAT ONE: Don't kiss me, I can't, I feel awful, as if I'm taking advantage of you ... Tomorrow you're offering yourself for something I don't believe in ... everything will be the same, except you won't be here and I'll be all alone, desiring you ... this is what it means to be frivolous. Trembling ...

HE: It's the tank treads. I'm a martyr and tomorrow I'll be in paradise, I'm happy.

THAT ONE: I came because I want to be your lover ... and I won't have to kill you because you'll already be dead tomorrow and I'd like to say ... I slept with a Palestinian kamikaze ... and be a bit of a hero ... I saw you on TV ... and said to myself: There's someone I want to meet. No, it's not because you were on TV ... How can I explain? Do what you want with me ... put the explosives belt on me ... We'll go get a pizza and when I kiss you ... Pow, we'll go to heaven together ... But first, I'll shave your chest ... cover you with oil ... I'll wallow in your body ... just give me your semen. OK?

GALLERY SIX

Events

SHE: I was going to go out this evening, but I saw you go by and this time I said ...

HE: Shall we dance?

SHE: Let's dance hard, and talk about everything, he studied film ... it's a good thing I'd just gone for the weekend ... And I told him: I love going to the movies, I cry a lot, I believe the stories. It seemed like I liked him more ... I couldn't believe it when he began to hug me, he was hot. And when I felt his tongue, it washed everything away ...

HE: I don't like it here, let's go someplace else.

SHE: So, I told him ... You're a good kisser, he said.

HE: I caught a glimpse of you before; I'd already seen you ...

SHE: You asked me: where's the bathroom? ... Behind the bar, I told you.

HE: Yes, the bathroom ... I came back but you were with someone else.

SHE: A friend, nothing more. Just as we got in the car his friends arrived saying:

"Don't go yet ... don't run out on us ... "

I smiled ... acting cool, smart ... He stopped the car ... how that bummed me out ... and they talked and talked ... and that hot chick took my picture ... "Let's get out of here," he said ... As he drove he began to play with his fingers between my legs ... He loosened his jeans and guided my hand toward ...

HE: Squeeze it hard. It's yours ...

SHE: We hit a red light.

HE: Relax, they can't see anything.

SHE: I didn't want to contradict him ... just then someone honked ... it was Lucas and Susana ... They lowered the window ...

"You're having a good time" (they said to me).

"A classmate, nothing more" (I told them).

Uff, he was hard and dripping ...

HE: Look what you did ... go on

SHE: "No, not here". He stroked my hair and lowered my head

HE: Don't worry about it, let's have a good time.

SHE: Don't let it end, please ... the last thing I saw was the metallic reflection of the snaps on his jeans. The gearshift buried itself in my skull. He lay across the dash ... Telephones began to ring

– Hello, Susana, did you know ... Angela had an accident ... yes ... I'm telling you ... she died" ... "They're sure it's my girl, they're sure. Please tell me it's not true ... "

"Hi, it's Cristián, bad news, Angela ... yes, the wake's tomorrow ... They don't know where yet."

SHE: That's what went through my head.

HE: Hey, what's going on? You fell asleep.

SHE: But you ... You're done?

HE: Sorry, I couldn't last and since you were still there ...
Where are you going? I'll drop you off.

SHE: And you don't have anything ...

HE: Nothing ... So, where to?

SHE: To my house, I'd tell him ... I was going to go out this
evening but no one called and I started to cry.

From the Beginning III

YOU: Nurse, stop crying, and don't keep standing there,
staring out the window ... Leave the room, go somewhere
where there's only happiness. Don't you see that the halls
will get longer and the exhibition of sadness greater until it
will never end ... Nurse, enough, dry your tears.

GALLERY SEVEN

Events

THAT ONE: They told me to call her, that Angela gave great
head, and I believed them. I believed everything ... that
Christ might appear suddenly ... and ask me things ...
Why not? ... even orders to pass my exams, so my mother
wouldn't get cancer ... On my knees at Lourdes ... I
believed it all ... thought the Pope was a saint and when
I saw him go by ... I really choked up ... when others
were sad, I embraced them, and told them about myself
... Besides that I believed that I'd go to hell ... Purgatory
was the worst, I also believed that I had to help the poor,
gave them alms ... I volunteered for good works, building
houses, singing to the old people in the Hogar de Cristo
... I believed them when I entered university ... they
congratulated me, good job, they told me ... I believed
it was just a matter of applying yourself and everything

would come … I believed my friends when they talked
about their lives and how well everything went, now I
listen to them all … and all I hear is lies … How happy
they are with the new jeep … how the girl is golden,
they're going to get married; they're leaving the country
because it's cool … I also believed it was time to go away
… believed that their vacations were better than mine …
believed them that you had to make love in a threesome,
and took it when they screwed me while I was screwing
the chick touching the ceiling … I did it and believed them
… now I only listen to them … I'm a good listener … if
you don't believe in something, you'll never get anywhere,
you have to believe … I believed it was best … When we
robbed Pedro's digital camera, I still believed, in rebellion,
the rest … I got a piercing and weaved my hair … then
they told me I was goth … and I believed it … shouted in
the streets for the Minister, the President, the General to
get out … I believed in the new candidate … I believed in
the TV … the Emcees … the commercials, in them above
all, I even believed in video clips and tried to become a
rock star … I believed there was no future, and if there
were, when I worked, I believed myself fortunate. I've
been waiting a long time for someone to tell me something
to believe in … but I'm stranded …

THAT ONE: Listen, believe me, I really love you.

HE: You better be serious, you bastard, or I'll …

THAT ONE: And he believed it.

GALLERY EIGHT

From Her

SHE: Don't worry, I'm not crying for any particular reason,
I'm crying because nothing's going on in my life, so I think
about it and cry, it's the way I get ready for something to
happen.

I cry thinking about all those who've died, whose names I have to erase from my calendar, my email, my computer, whose photos I put in frames, smiling on the lakeshore. I cry thinking about those who were killed, how they were alone in their homes in the middle of Santiago ... while other people made love, they had a pistol pointed at their skull ... I cry because life goes on and what I'm doing doesn't matter ... I'm crying because I ought to be stupid and happy and laugh just because birds fly. I ought to be playing guitar by the fire, happy when you cover me with your parka and tell me how much you'd like a house, happy about the child we'd have with my nose and his mouth. Happy to see the dawn, the sun lighting up the fields ... I ought to be happy like a television model, suffering because she'll make less, because she doesn't look good on the cover, because they don't call her a star, worrying because they caught her with her makeup running ... I'm crying because I can't take advantage of the happiness I could have ... No, I'm not crying, I'm just letting water swaddle my face so it won't get wrinkled.

GALLERY NINE

YOU: Bring Petunias and cover up this shit with flowers, I want my bed in the midst of a garden of Petunias, surrounded by water and filled with black necked swans. And in the distance, have them plant a forest of birches, tall enough to reach the lookouts and wave at me with red handkerchiefs, so I'll see them in the distance ... . so that we'll get bigger from farther and farther away ... I want them to see me only from far away.

NURSE, FILL THIS BLOODY LAGOON WITH YOUR WAILS.

GALLERY TEN

From the Afraid

ONE: Yes, I'm easily scared.

THAT ONE: Me too.

ONE: Dogs scare me.

THAT ONE: I'm afraid they know.

ONE: The dark makes me shit myself.

THAT ONE: I'm afraid to kill you.

ONE: I'm afraid of people at night.

THAT ONE: You imagine thieves, slicing your face.

ONE: Silhouettes scare me.

THAT ONE: No, they frighten you.

ONE: No, spirits frighten me. … you believe in spirits.

THAT ONE: Why not, since you're a spirit.

ONE: How touching.

THAT ONE: I don't scare you.

ONE: When you look like that, yes.

THAT ONE: How do you know? … I like to do things passionately.

ONE: Passionately … how so?

THAT ONE: Let me tie you up.

ONE: You've seen too many videos … .

THAT ONE: We won't be alone; I've invited some friends.

ONE: Someone's knocking.

THAT ONE: It's them.

ONE: That's enough, Cristián, stop it.

THAT ONE: Keep quiet; there are four of them … you'll like them. It's a fantasy, or are you too uptight to fantasize? You don't like it when they stick things in

ONE: Cristián, let me go … I'll scream.

THAT ONE: Scream and scream again, it'll excite them. Don't you love me? Or do you think that love is like eating popcorn at the movies in the mall?

SECOND NEXUS

GALLERY ONE

The Children's Room

YOU: Which room are we in? I can't see you, you're not here
yet, it's the little boys' room, the little girls' ... the one
with the toys, the electric trains that don't go anywhere,
the talking dolls, your teddy bear, *(To the audience.)* Didn't
you have teddy bears? Sticks to beat them with and see
how they fall, dolls to be used in autopsies, the place with
sexless dolls, I detest the children's room ... You can hear
the parents' voices; you can hear the sound of false pride
and indestructible love ... Papa ... Papa ... nyah nyah ...
googoo . The little boy, the wished for future never built.
Poor kids, laying bricks on a house already built ... Poor
children, invalids, violated ... Rich kids ... Fat kids. Girls
like their mothers. Boys as ugly as their fathers. Kids as
happy as their aunts, holy kids, hero kids, wicked kids,
hated kids, abandoned kids, autistic kids, cancerous kids,
assassinated kids, kids thrown in rivers. Painted girls, virgin
girls, strong girls, hateful girls, perfect girls, pretty girls,
arrogant girls. Famous kids, spoiled kids. Nervous kids.
I would have liked to have been in nursery school with
Hitler–Mother Teresa–Pinochet and the Pope. With the
psychopathic kids. We'll have to search the kindergartens,
the nursery schools ... get rid of them before they grow up.
This little boy will be the love you'll never have and this
little girl will assassinate you ... How frightening the future
must be. Let's get out of the children's room ... I don't
want to remember that I was a child.

ONE: Don't tickle me anymore ... You know I don't like it.
Here, I brought you this. Put it there, by the whirlpool ...
you've gotten spoiled ... Hit your little finger, such a stupid
little thing ... that's it, leave my skirt alone. You know
what's there ... You're even looking at me as if I were a
toy. Seriously. Don't squeeze me ... Yes, yes, I love you.
Yes, up to the sky ... Yes, more than the firmament ... Yes,

I love you, so that people will see I'm not alone, I love you because when we go to the movies you hold my hand, because I have someone to hug me at parties, and when everyone laughs, I laugh with you, because you stroke my back in the metro and everyone sees there's someone who loves me, because when you're not here I can talk about when you'll come ... and they ask me about you. And I can strip you bare and say that you're a great lover, and everyone envies me ... And say that I have to go because you're waiting for me ... that I have to get some asparagus because you love it ... I love you because I no longer have to wait for someone to love me ... And do you love me? ...

YOU: You're such a child ...

From the Middle I

YOU: Shut the doors ... Lock the windows, close the curtains. Turn off the TV, the radio, the CD player. I don't want to know what they're saying. I don't want them to tell me the story of the day or whose face is famous. I don't want to know who won a prize, or whose head was cut off. I don't want them to tell me what's happening ... which book I have to read, I don't care if stocks are down, or if there are storms in Colorado, I don't care if planes blow up, or bodegas burn to the ground ... the smoke billowing on the screen or the woman screaming. Only about the pain in my back and my lack of memories ... Do stoplights stop when you suffer? The garbage man will still go by my window the morning I breathe my last ... and my death won't be more than a disagreeable tic for people going to the office.

Nurse ... Don't let them close the museums on Mondays ... Have them bring me my webcam ...

Chat Room

HE: I write my profile, read my profile, make up my nickname
... I'm ... modern ... cool ... endowed ... heavy ... ready
for good sex ... now ... already ... place ... interesting ...
professional ... university student ... active ... latino ...
hot ... hard ... dark ... no lunatics ... nobody fat ... no
street hustlers ... no liars ... Your best sex ... creative sex
... looking for 23, 28, 36 year-olds ... trios ... quartets ...
toys ... dildos. Bears, teddy bears. Skinny ones, little dark
skinny ones ... thick legs, muscular, blond ... black ...
serious ... passive ... modern.

You like to suck, you like cum ... great ass ... well
endowed ... no endless conversations, now, downtown ...
at 8 ... I want it now ... you've got big hands ... what do
you like to do ... what's your favorite ... you're sweet ...
where are you ... who do you live with ... what do you do
... do you have a picture ... there you are, hi ... I want it
too ... what are you looking for ... call me ... you've got
a cell ... there you are ... don't lie to me, please ... I'm
at the office ... I'm on the web ... I'm at my place ... I'm
with a friend ... I'm wearing black jeans ... a red shirt ...
short shorts ... carrying a green backpack ... notebooks
in my hand ... 170-172 kilograms dark clean-shaven-virile,
coffee-colored eyes ... 184, 20 centimeters 75 kilograms
great ass ... you like to suck it ... I'm hard and you ...
what're you doing ... what will you do to me, how do you
like it, what's your favorite, there you go, turn and turn, I'll
swallow it, I want to suck, I want you to give it to me, let
me put it, yes, I'm horny, hot, ... yes, it's okay, besides ...
you're discreet ... a cool guy ... you're fun ... I'm friendly
... happy ... what music do you like ... you work out ...
do you have a camera ... let me see it ... show me more ...
take the shirt off ... in twenty minutes ... in an hour, how
will I recognize you ... how you move ... I've got a tattoo
... stripped shirt, gray pants, hang on, my sister's here ...
I'm hanging up, I'm going to lunch, I have to go, what's
your name ... I like your nickname ... let's get together,

see each other, hook up, yes, at the kiosk, the exit from the metro, on the corner, at the gas station, in front of the drugstore, in the square, at the bank, but you're going to come, sure, I'll just wait five minutes, ten minutes, don't leave me standing here, I want to meet you, but you'll come, sure, use a condom, take this condom, well hello hello hi ... hi hi hi ... there you are ... marino 24 left the Chat Room 2030.

Meeting Rooms

YOU: It was great ...

THAT ONE: You had a good time ...

YOU: Yes, relaxed, very ...

THAT ONE: You always chat ...

YOU: When I feel like it.

THAT ONE: You always use Digital as your username ...

YOU: No, sometimes Megapenis ...

THAT ONE: Oh god, I'm still sore ...

YOU: You didn't have any lubricant handy ...

THAT ONE: I like it rough. Not always, with you, yes.

YOU: You're kind of tight ...

THAT ONE: So they say.

YOU: And if you don't like someone,

THAT ONE: When I see them through the window I tell them to kiss off on the intercom ... Shit, ass fucking is great ... Ah ...

YOU: ... And he keeps talking and I realize I screwed up, I should have gone with 180, 21 centimeters, dark, green eyes, passing through Santiago. I'm sure he would have been better ... This asshole is a nerd ... a nerdy little motherfucker, a med student. Maybe I can get back online and green eyes will still be there. I've got to get out of here.

THAT ONE: Why don't you get yourself a beer ... .

YOU: Well ... it's hot and a beer ... Listen, your dogs are barking.

THAT ONE: They're okay ... And you, what're you doing ...

YOU: What can I tell him ... I finished PR but I don't like it ...

THAT ONE: And what are you going to do now ...

YOU: I don't know, there I am, screwing around ...

THAT ONE: I'll give you my number, we can get together again ...

YOU: Sure, write it down for me ...

THAT ONE: The problem with chat rooms is that the bitches lie a lot ...

YOU: Yes, it happens.

THAT ONE: And they stink, I have to tell them to take a shower ... The other day I got a rich hunk ... But I grabbed his ass and he had shit stuck to the hairs ...

YOU: What did you do ...

THAT ONE: Nothing, I kicked him out ...

YOU: Too much.

THAT ONE: I prefer to pick guys up off the street ... It's kinkier ... You look at them, they look at you, you pass them, you stop at a kiosk ... They approach you, you ask for a light ... and pow ... from there to a motel ... it's cooler ... fast, safe.

YOU: He kept running his mouth. I got up to go, but first I scored, grab the door and suck me off for the last time ... "You're still horny". I told him, I'll close the door and turn off the phone ... a nut walked a dog in the street, I stood up to buckle my sandal, I looked at him, he turned, approached ... I didn't like him, I took off ... That's the way it is, it all builds up, the things people say ...

The Room of Sentences

HE: Filthy Indian, asshole nigger, what a shitty bastard, what a lout, tacky little thing, an ordinary old man, a hot chick, your mediocre friend, slippery asshole, poor faggot, crazy social climber, tricky old guy, silly girl, horrible fat woman, wrinkled old prune, feeble horserace, fallen breasts, sunken ass, lack of a waist, a cretin wouldn't go after her.

ONE: What a marvelous bunch, what a handsome child, your son-in-law's so amorous, your son's taking her, I adore the country, I love the beach, what a beautiful family, your house is wonderful, the country's a fright, your dessert's delicious, it's a shame about the poor, misery's atrocious, I love your hair, your garden's great, come over tomorrow, come over this evening, your granny's good people, you have all the luck, mine's a mess, I'm throwing her out tomorrow, school's great, your friend's superfluous, a beautiful mass, the priest's a dear.

SHE: Her husband hit her, they left her pregnant, he was in jail, he sells joints, sleeps with chicks, his house is ugly, child thieves, horrible guy, tightass bitch, doesn't talk to anyone, you'd think she was dead, doesn't have any education. The car's stolen, a bus hit him, locks up the kids, doesn't wash his clothes, pays the soldier, bastard druggies, without direction, badly dressed, screws over the neighbor, runs down the country house, doesn't pay the installments. Stinks of the kitchen.

The Labryinth Room

HE: Flags make the best bags. You take the four corners and all at once you have a "look", you see?

YOU: And what do I have to do to have a "look"? Dye my hair? … Earrings make me panic. I'm afraid of tattoos. Short hair doesn't suit me. Whatever I do … I don't like it a minute later.

HE: Where were you?

YOU: I crossed the Pyrenees on foot to find you … They wouldn't let me through the borders … And you'd be at the café by the Opera at 5 p.m. and I will not arrive … I'm climbing the Pyrenees … They don't see me … I cross the border, see the Spanish sea, run between the goats … There … I arrive.

HE: I waited for you, you didn't arrive, I thought you'd left …

YOU: I went to buy a book. For the trip.

HE: No, you abandoned me. The book was a lie and you left me there in the café, and the hours passed.

YOU: There were lots of books and I didn't find any history …

HE: I had two beers, smoked ten cigarettes … You never came …

YOU: Where was I going to go? I went back to the hotel and your things weren't there.

HE: Yes, you'd already left me.

YOU: I thought you'd taken the boat and I ran along the dock shouting your name. And the boat sailed away. I called to the captain and told him I was looking for you, that surely you were at the railing preparing to dive, thinking about finding me. I described you; they looked for you amongst the passengers. They didn't find you and I saw you drowning. In the middle of nowhere.

HE: No, I was here, with my beers, waiting for you to come. I don't have a bag anymore. Look what happened to the flag. I used it as a towel, something to remember you by.

YOU: I went to the morgue, the police. I searched all the metro stations. I told them what you looked like a hundred times. I climbed a thousand staircases and asked if you'd registered at every boarding house … The city was big.

HE: Come on … Where would I have been, but here? This was the place where we came for the first time … It was the only place I could be … Even now there you are, leaning against the railing. I felt your noise in the bathroom. And there are the same sounds from when we thrashed around in the bed … I didn't leave, I waited for you. Look at the sheets; they're soaked with piss. There's shit on the floor. I couldn't leave because you could come ... I haven't eaten in three days. Moreover, they're talking about you on the radio, listen ... Don't stick your head out the window, the cars going by ... It's them, the ones who are looking for us.

YOU: I'm the one looking for you ... stupid. Here I am. And on the ship you know what's going to happen ... we can't get on board.

HE: It's getting late; we're already on board ... look how the lights from the port slip away. It's hot ... and the sea is thick like gasoline. There's the island on the horizon.

YOU: It's a trick; this boat isn't taking us to any island. Let me go.

HE: You don't see ... I only want to protect you ... come, let's go. We'll save ourselves; we'll jump. Come.

YOU: Don't let go of my hand.

HE: Save us, Andrés ... they want to kill us ...

YOU: Don't you see it's nighttime. Don't you see those two there down below, in the waves ... We'll disappear and all we'll see is a boat moving away ... we're going to kill ourselves ...

HE: We'll be together ... we'll save ourselves; we'll swim ...

YOU: Please, don't push me and don't let go of me.

HE: They're going to kill us here. Them, the ones in uniform ... they're talking about us ... they want to liquidate us ... they know we're queers ... Come with me, Andrés.

YOU: This place is moving ... this place is turning.

SHE: You didn't want to come towards this side. It seemed to be water, it looked like the sea ... you never understood the signals; you had to look at the sky. You had to think you were an atom. As if we were in the middle of the ocean. As if you didn't know where you were, as if we're part of something twinkling in black space. Look, I'm filming you from someplace you can't see me. Believe me when I tell you I'm in another galaxy and you're no more than a point of light. What can happen to a light submerged in light? We were happy so many times. I'm here, with him. You just let go of my hand.

HE: We're waiting for you ... Nothing's over when you transcend your body ... Your body no longer makes you happy ... let it go ... They'll kill us just the same.

SHE: I would have thrown myself in with him.

YOU: I'm going with my sisters, my mother, the boat's coming on Río Guayas, here come the canoes filled with bananas and little people. The boat breaks the coffee colored water of the Guayas and the mangrove thickets don't let them see the land. I throw them money, they dive for it, they yell at me, I throw another coin. And I go through ... I come up again, with the coin between my teeth ... Now take it from my lips, it's sweet water ... It's tropical ... feel the taste ... Do you like it?

HE: Yes, it's like cacao.

The Room of Being

YOU: I saw them in the distance and I imagined them, they crossed in front of me and I did get to ask them, because they could have been.

ONE: I saw you from afar and I imagined you. You could have been the one who showered with me in the afternoons and soaped my back, the one who spread my legs and licked my pussy for hours with your tongue, you could have been the one who ejaculated in my face, bit my breasts and hit me in the face.

THAT ONE: I imagined you from afar and came closer, you could be the one who took off my clothes, the one who sucked my cock while I sucked yours, you could have been the one who I turned against the wall and penetrated, while I bit your neck.

SHE: I saw you from afar and imagined you, you could be the one to listen to my stories, entertain yourself with my eyes, accompany me on trips, you could be the one I invent each day.

HE: Why can't I bring you a tray full of tostadas and chocolates and we'll go to bed smiling while the kids come running and lie at our feet while we enjoy the stories, the humor and the movies on the screen?

ONE: Why can't we be those who spend whole afternoons looking at cruise brochures, choosing the cities we want to wander on the maps?

HE: Why aren't you the smiling granny who brings me the paper, and refreshes each morning with her ingenuity?

ONE: Why aren't you the crossing guard who tells us to stop and protects our lives with your red stop sign and then turns it to green and greets us as we go by?

HE: Why aren't we the ones who get up each morning to see how the wheat grows in the field, looking at the sky so it won't cloud over, while spreading food on the ground for the geese and ducks?

ONE: Why aren't you the one who drives the subway every day, seeing a light that invades you and fills you with grateful faces in every station?

HE: Why aren't you president and you put me up in your palaces and we greet the people every morning?

YOU: Why isn't everything already in the present, since I won't be here tomorrow?

The Desert Room

YOU: I didn't record it, I didn't film it, we didn't take pictures, I don't have anything with which to fill this space ... there aren't any records, I'd have to invent an installation, put pieces of my body in a juicer alongside his, with neon lights recalling the ones we stopped beneath, with pieces of asphalt where our tracks were imprinted.

THAT ONE: We went to the desert, that's what happened.

YOU: Yes, we went to the desert.

THAT ONE: To see ourselves little … in order not to see ourselves … to be cacti and hug ourselves with our thorns … and it was good … they stuck in well and marked our bodies with tattoos …

YOU: We'll have to fill this room with sand …

THAT ONE: And guanacos … so they can watch us …

Here, there's a letter left, it's not signed, it hasn't been addressed.

– I've got a present in my mouth for you; I can't just give it to you anywhere …

YOU: I feel like putting out the light for a moment.

X's Room Who Dies

YOU: The batteries for the headphones are dead, I open the newspapers, walk through the streets, lie down in the parks, see the people and I don't know, why die?

He–One–She–That One:

Die to get to heaven

Die of pure dignity

Die for ideas that diminish as you go

Die so that you won't see how your body dies

Die so that she can claim the insurance

Die so that your spirit haunts the side of the road.

Die because others also die

Die to become a martyr

Die climbing a hill

Die from being born

Die defending your wallet

Die for tourism

Die because nobody loves you

Die to find the future

Die to keep a secret

Die to save a country

YOU: To die, if only living convinced me.

Room Apart

ONE: I hope he'll come close, to feel his breath. I'm waiting for him, there he comes.

YOU: I approach, but I'll touch her leg to surprise her, to see if she's there.

ONE: I stroke his hair. Squeeze his skull . . .

YOU: I twist her hair. And I'd fall asleep like that … Each of us thinking about the other … about where we are.

ONE: And my eyelids close, so I can see him inside …

YOU: I reply. I open my eyes and smile.

ONE: I see him smile and my lips part, stretch, my teeth appear.

YOU: We laugh … About what?

ONE: His laughing face appears.

YOU: She sees my smile, sees that I am … holds out her arms.

ONE: I hold out my arms, enfold him … My eyes close again … I find his smell, breathe it in.

YOU: I bury her head in my neck and look around us.

ONE: I feel so good that I'm scared.

YOU: I can't tell her: I'm sick, I won't tell her, I'll go away, make it all dissolve, like everything.

ONE: I need his lips, his humid mouth.

YOU: It's too late, I didn't say anything at first, I can't say it now.

31

ONE: Now I know how to die.

YOU: I know she knows I love her, I know she'll know why I left her one day.

Suicide Room

YOU: Don't see the edge ... look at the sky ... Don't see the path, see the clouds, don't think you're falling ... think you're climbing ... running from the bottom. Everything they gave you at parties or you bought in stores, is looking at you. You're already in the air ... Either you use gas, or draw letters with your slit veins, with a pen, a pencil, in envelopes, on math papers, composition sheets, a page from memo books, with the same starting date. What are they saying? ... Nothing ... They've already said it all ... Why don't they leave me a letter?

SHE: I went back to Venice, where you took me. I strolled beneath the bridges and saw how it got orange on the canals as light fell ... I sent you a postcard ... Not the one with the gypsies ... The one that said I'd return ... to the northern roof ... I couldn't stain the waters ... My body was too ugly to float on them ... you were late in arriving.

YOU: We arrived; I stopped before, on the beaches, in the ruins.

SHE: You can't live by the mountains ... it was all a lie ... and the lie wouldn't let me breathe ... It was night and everything was still lit up ... it was summer. Women in bikinis on the beaches, tanned men playing with their little shovels ... I took the train that ran along the seashore ... watching the tracks alongside where we walked ... where we lay happily on the dunes ... They ate ice cream and inflated colored balls ... through the window ... lookouts, barbed wire ... prisoners lined up and they came covering themselves in tanning cream ... how could you think that I could live in this country? ... There, in Valparaíso Street I decided to buy the rope ...

YOU: I arrived ... on the bus to find you weren't there ... I follow, to erase what you wore ... you know. Now I'm on the beach playing with little shovels ...

SHE: I saw you searching the Internet to find out how to do it efficiently.

YOU: Besides, I looked for the doctor in the book that told you how ... I didn't find anything.

SHE: You measured the length of your car, the width of exhaust pipe. You thought about the color of the hose ...

YOU: I parked in the country, tranquil ... with the radio playing.

SHE: You practiced in the kitchen, lying down, with the oven open ... looking fixedly at the greasy light bulb ...

YOU: He was the one who gave me the idea ... I told him you're going to the gym ... And, of course, I believed you, that you'd bought the towels for the bathroom ... I found them rolled up ... soaked, stuffed under the doors ... so the gas wouldn't escape through the cracks ... Professional.

THAT ONE: I know, you don't have to imitate me ...

YOU: I liked it when we made love ... on the floor ... You had good ideas ... Why not copy them? I also heard you when you did it with others. It all ended really well ... Let's leave it there.

The parrot shrieked and I couldn't break down the door and the gas oozed into the pores of the cement ... And there you were, spread out on your bed with the note.

I remembered the first time.

THAT ONE: Where, in the disco?

YOU: No, the first time you turned the knob ... and I hit you so that you'd open your eyes.

THAT ONE: Yes, and I asked you, where am I?

YOU: In heaven, stupid, and I hit you harder.

THAT ONE: But you only wanted to know how it felt, if I didn't change my mind and turn off the gas ... And I told you nothing, only tranquility.

SHE: I said it in the stripes on the walls in my room, I told it to you in letters ... I told you about it when I robbed the supermarkets ... I told you about it next to your photos of them looking at my cadaver.

YOU: I want to go with you ... so you can push me through the underwater cliffs ... to see again through your eyes ... what I can't see any longer today ... So I can feel your skin and do what I never dared to do.

HE: So slow.

YOU: And you ... How crazy, laughing, hugging me ... celebrating the plebiscite like in Roman times ... You, while everyone celebrated. You, laughing with death in your backpack.

HE: Yes, I was laughing ... Stop talking; you're swelling up ... Besides, there's no need to open that door.

YOU: They left her alongside.

SHE: It's dark and you can't see the exhibition.

YOU: Everyone out, don't let anyone in ... the brochures don't explain it well anymore, dust covers the colors, the lighting is insufficient, and we haven't built the exit. There are photos that haven't been developed, people who haven't' arrived, or who enter and disappear, the nurse who never existed, I should go to my display window, there are too many rooms and I'm tired of crossing them, besides, they aren't real and they don't talk about what I feel. Who told you this was a museum? ... There was a history exam yesterday, but ...

1973

ONE: The president's palace no longer white, smoke pours from its windows, the door and the cast iron grills are burnt. There are crushed cars ... thick grease on the

sidewalks and shadows of bodies stamped in the cement.
You can't go downtown.

Don't put the radio on, there's only music you don't like
... run ... and climb the stairs; take the posters down
in your room ... the university's closed, there aren't
classes tomorrow, don't go to the police, don't get near
the detectives, don't ask the patrols for help, don't run to
Congress, don't make denunciations in the courts.

Fill the bathtub with water, cut your hair. No, it isn't New
Year's, don't drink that champagne, smile at those who
smile, don't look at those who are absent ...

Burn your books, your papers, your pictures ... Throw out
the volunteer bracelet; put the Virgin back up over your
bed, the bullets in the night aren't roman candles. Bathe
yourself in the midst of smoke. Don't open the windows or
respond to knocks on the door.

There are people with orifices in their eyes. There are
bullets that cut through brains, bayonets through chests,
there are people lined up along the rivers, against the walls,
alongside their graves ... there are people with broken
hands; teeth pulled out, absent fingernails, there are people
without bodies, or the beauty of the morning.

Let them lock you in the closet and let your impotence
drown you ...

The nights are long and no one sleeps. Grab him, by the
arm, so they don't take him in his pajamas ... Scream;
accept the punches ... . It's the last time you'll touch his
hand. Make the most of it; don't let it go. Don't believe in
his calm, don't believe he'll be back tomorrow, make the
most of it, it's the last time you'll feel his arms.

Don't spend time with those people anymore ... get on
your plane; don't look back ... Don't call on the phone;
don't write sad letters. Don't answer calls ... Don't give
food to the prisoners. Ask them their names and be silent.

Room of Doubt

YOU: I shouldn't be here still; no one should hear me now. Quickly, to the room of forgetting, where everything disappears. The place where the moon returns to only a star, where the Earth is no more than a planet and where people have only recently been born. Because that's what happens and what stops happening.

What Happens and Stops Happening

HE: Why did I have to pick up your body? ... pull back the sheets bathed in alcohol, get mad because the beers had rolled around on the wood floor and you kept sleeping when it was already six in the evening? ... Why did I have to open your closet and cast aside your clothes, empty your drawers that were still in order, when there wasn't anything left in their place? Why did I have to, naively, believe that you were sleeping when, in reality, you were looking at me from death and had stopped talking to me, believing that you were there? ... Why did we insult each other when you already knew that you were saying good-bye? ...

Why did I have to see when the electricity made your body jump? To see if you managed to come back to life for an instant and tell me that you were only scaring me ... . So that I'd live in your absence for a second. Why did I have to take the elevator to the twenty-fifth floor, knock on the door, refuse coffee, to let them know you were dead?

Why did I have to choose your coffin and look for the sunniest spot in the cemetery, choose the shirt, the suit, when you knew I had no taste? Why did I have to see you laid out on a metal slab in the morgue? When I only knew your body lying in the sand.

ONE: That afternoon, I, while I changed my compact and you arranged your things, had to tell you that we should talk, how was I to know that the phone would ring just then, and I only heard the knock on the door, when I came out to look for you you'd already gone, and, so I wouldn't keep stewing in my own rage, I left too. How was I to know that while you strolled the avenue, I walked along the sidewalks and we crossed without seeing each other? Then I went to the movies and felt like it was us, who, hugging, ran to protect ourselves from the bullets. I came back happy to find you, to tell you. But there was only one car parked, and they came out to receive me and hug me knowing that it wasn't my birthday, and they squeezed me so hard that I cried. How was I to know that the last I'd see of you was a noise at the door and your socks thrown at the side of the bed and that this afternoon I'd have to live what I'd never thought? How was I to know that June 24th should have been wiped from the calendar so that we could have met the following day and nothing ever would have existed? How was I to know that I didn't have to answer that call, just stop you before you left, and tell you the trip was going to happen, that I didn't care about the mosquitoes in the jungle? How was I to know that your absence was going to be forever? I'm burning the photographs because I don't dare burn myself.

The Last

SHE: There are days I follow you, see how you roam the streets and places where your mind stops. There are times I stop your hand and seed you with a path of signals. There are afternoons I enter your mind and converse with you in the midst of the reefs. There are nights I accompany you in danger, and detain you in thresholds. That's how I take care of you, not by curing your sadnesses, nor the anguish in your sojourn. There are days I see how you cloud over and don't see the signs along the way. There are times that I seed your ideas with doubts so that you don't realize a single one of them. But there are times you're stronger in your desires and I can't stop what happens to you.

YOU: Close the doors, leave the emergency lights on, the exhibition is over, my feet are frozen and my hands on fire, don't let my family know, I couldn't take my mother's tears on my shoulder, I don't want to hear my brother's quivering voice, nor feel the compassionate caress from my brother-in-law, I don't want to see chattering jaws, nor listen to throats spouting nervous sentences. Don't let my friends know; don't let them bring me their helpful smiles, nor their pupils dilated with courage. Nurse, don't let the earth know. Just you and me.

Tell them, yes, I heard them calling me, yes, I heard the phone ring … Tell them that I sailed the ocean, that, yes, I fell into the waters, tell them tomorrow my nick won't be on the Internet, tell them it was me in the video in the desert and I'm not dead, tell them that's what happens and that's what stops happening. And that my desires are only fragments

SHE: Don't worry; I'll feed the spiders.

THE END

Isla Negra 2003

CUPS OF WRATH

Characters

THE PROPHET

THE YOUNG PHARAOH

THE LITTLE SHEPHERD OF FATIMA

THE FORGOTTEN

THE OFFICER

THE PROPHECIES

THE PROPHET: The instant the Star of Bethlehem burst forth
again it had to be me ... now's the right time. I have to
extract from my remotest coffers what was confided in
me. Now's the time for me to announce what was said,
what has already been seen, but which you don't know
how to spell. They've sent so many emissaries, it's been
announced so often, that the sea no longer knows what it
should do for you mortals to be able to see the signs. My
affection for triangles isn't the reason I built pyramids; my
addiction to cylinders isn't the reason I raised towers. Now
that we're having a birthday I've decided to open a present
for you, not one that was hidden, but the one you've been
sitting on, permit me to ask you to stand, so that I can untie
the ribbons and start to open it.

I adore bundles that presage a good gift. Don't think my
labor is delirious and that my powers cause me to babble
constantly. On the contrary, I'm accustomed to them. Those
who don't understand seem to think I don't realize what I
have. If all this won't be easy, it won't be very difficult either.
I will try to be as pedagogical as I can be, so that you don't
reach potentially catastrophic erroneous interpretations
... or badly understand the signs, which could bring us to
collective suicide. Or have us running through the parks in
the nude. That would truly be a good sign.

It happened once before at the Spanish court, around
1500, they called me to delight a young princess with a
reading of the stars. The poor thing that would become
known to history as Juana la Loca. I hope the same thing
doesn't happen today. Ah, the times when you could relax
in palaces and languish before fields of wheat, observe
the slaves pulling the wagons and the passing swallows
... and the sound of the streams carried on the ululation
of the wind. Bucolic countrysides that didn't last long, the
cardinals' assault was bloody.

Unable to stand the honors showered upon us at court,
nor the wisdom of our words, they accused us of being the

devil's angels. That didn't bother me; we're not going to fixate on the branch of angels. Since the kings depended upon the cardinals' blessing to keep the throne, at least they didn't order us burnt, just pierced by horrible nails – this thick – introduced through the optic hemisphere striking the brain, generating chilling screams and an appallingly unpleasant spectacle.

I have so many stories; we could spend the whole afternoon talking. The Syrians were very agreeable people, cultured, refined, all that's so lacking nowadays. Even I feel a bit frivolous, banal, superfluous, empty inside, as if phrases to make temples shake no longer emerge from my mouth. I feel the need to connect with the profound, with the essential. To be purified. But the conditions aren't right now; it's so difficult to fight against society ... But this isn't the reason for our meeting, I'm not a comedian, I've never been one, it's too easy to be one.

I've come to deliver the gift of prophecies ... which always total seven. The first: ... "The beginning", during the reign of Hakim II, in Luxor.

THE YOUNG PHARAOH: Nubian, pour more oil over my back, the desert wind dries out my skin. I am the son of the son of God, nevertheless, there are signs hidden from me. My father's funeral is tomorrow, and at nightfall I will be able to read the book of the dead ... the same one I will see when I begin my voyage through the darkness and have to cross the river Horus. But that's not what torments me, it's the bearded man's curses, they say that my father's tomb will be buried by water. That this palace will be empty more moons than it will shine with lamps. I've never feared those who come from across the sea, but there are signs that we've buried.

You remember Koroxor, the one who was buried alive in my grandfather's tomb? Bring me his papyri. In the procession to the cold crypt, he said to me: "Prince ... read the omens" ... I fear the sand, it's an ocean that could rise up and there will be nothing to stop it. I fear my brother,

he doesn't stop roaming the terraces and disguising
himself as a slave to be owned in the alleys of Luxor. I see
my great great granddaughter "Cleopatra" handing the
secrets of Isis over to bearded men . . . have you noticed,
Nubian, that a beard always hides uncouthness? In beards
nest all the evils that pursue us ... Shave my head again
... and bring the papyri. Don't open them like that; the
secrets could all go up in smoke ... leave them on the
ground so they recover their strength and so the moonlight
illuminates them ... Prepare for disgrace, since we already
know heavenly bliss and it hasn't weakened our soul.
Who's afraid of happiness?

But evils cause us pain and fear ... and in spite of my being
God ... sometimes the blood in my veins bursts into flame.

Dissemble ... *(Takes the papyri.)* the princesses' cortege
approaches, the smell of the branches they burn precedes
them, it makes me nauseous. They must be going to the
temple to deliver their secrets to the statues. Nubian, they
know more than God's son. Oh, my God, their song surge,
dissimulate, make the kingdom mine ...

(The procession passes.)

Health, daughters of Tebas ... proceed, yes, twenty
sphinxes of pink stone and two obelisks ... But what
horror, they never tire of sacrificing lambs, leaving all the
palace halls covered in blood and that can only attract
more blood.

(He goes towards the palace window.)

Look at the sun, bathing the waters of the Nile orange, and
the wind doesn't ruffle the ships' sails ... it's time for the
God of Gods to rest and for everything to stop so as not to
disturb his sleep. Listen, Nubian, to the silence of the birds.
Tremble before the coming darkness.

It's the shifting of the stars, the time when the priests
clamber over their towers looking to the heavens for curses
on my reign or praises for this land. Tomorrow they will
come, tormented ... begging me to change where I place

my throne, that I procreate at a precise hour or that I go down to bathe beneath the constellations with my retinue. I'll do what they say ... but I'll keep these predictions to myself.

(Reading the hieroglyphs.)

Two eagles, an ellipse, a scribe, a scepter, you don't know how to read?

The force of the infinite will fall upon the kingdom, and the seed will rot in your minds. The hand will cut off the hand that gives you something to drink, the son will stain his sister's sex, feet will crush their friend's heads and exhibit them on spikes across the sands, the time will come when the slave shall be free and will recreate the evils of his masters, there won't be any place on earth that isn't threatened. The man will be afraid of the child; the woman of the elderly and everyone will carry venom in their robes, dagger and fire. Thus will they poison the innocent, nail steel in the heart of any who show signs of clemency, burn villages and from their mounts their flaming lances will destroy the harvests. You will flee looking for an oasis where the water runs clean, you will beg for the shade of a palm tree and the quietude of the horizon. You won't find any of it.

I was afraid that man is no more than the Gods' excrement ... Nubian, make sure that these prophecies are written on the walls of my tomb in the Valley of Kings ... And whoever profanes my sepulcher, on him and his people fall Kororor's predictions.

From me, people of the Nile, expect nothing, my childhood has been disturbed by my father's fantasies, I am deeply bored and now I must cross the river ... My tomb is ready, my golden sarcophagus, bring me the asp that will sink its teeth into my arm and let the sand cover forever the iniquitous monuments of my predecessors. Good-bye, Nubian, I'm sorry you'll have to come with me ...

THE PROPHET: During that time ... I was the Nubian, details, well. It's been seventy years since the German archeologists profaned Hakmir II's tomb, enough looking around us, let's wield a smile, perhaps the young pharaoh's? Let's see how the signs are being fulfilled ... No? Someone doubts? Maybe you've never vacationed in Auschwitz. There's another feverous period in my life, when I was a little peasant boy. The Portuguese shepherd from Fatima ...

THE LITTLE SHEPHERD: Little sister, you're sobbing again, you know how Mother doesn't like tear-stained cheeks ... Look, look how the bull calves are running, come here, I'm going to call this little one Nicolás, like our cousin, but stop crying.

It isn't easy being a shepherd boy in the hills of Portugal. We get up at dawn and have to content ourselves with nothing more than a bowl of milk. If it's a lucky day, the bread crust will come with cheese from the Pyrenees ... we're a poor family.

Enough, stop these big tears, you'll never get a young man that way, and comb your hair ... When do you say she'll visit us?

Yes, Father. We've brought the flock to the top, gathered wood for the fire, milled the wheat for bread, fed the pigs, brought water from the well, picked the walnuts, gathered the geese and cleaned our bodies like you've shown us ... Yes, Father, I'm a happy child and thank you once again for having brought me into the world, with the help of the Holy Spirit, of course.

So pass the days of a shepherd boy in Portugal, far away from the turbulences shaking the rest of the world. What about Chile? We never knew. Why should we worry about what happens beyond the river? If the rain doesn't fall on our land that doesn't mean that it falls on other households ...

Tell me Lucía, how can she be so white and not stain her feet with mud when she walks? What do you mean you see her on a cloud? You're not listening, you're very little, don't do anything foolish that will anger the lady, perhaps that lady is lost and you're so dumb that you haven't marked the path well for her. And she wears jewels like those from the city? A generous diamond hanging from her hand, you say, large precious stones.

And she's the one who tells you she's the mother of God? Poor lady, what great misfortune will she have suffered to think such a thing … I'll bring a rope in case we need to trap her. Stop crying, I won't hurt her. Tomorrow, I told you, and be sure, since if she's the mother of God she'll probably want to talk with the priest or the bishop. I, a child like I am, can't tell the mother of the baby Jesus anything. Ah … She's the one who wants to give us messages, well tell her that we don't know how to write … or better that she repeats it and you, since you've got a good head on your shoulders, you remember it, because I no sooner finish counting the sheep than I've forgotten how many there were … you can't demand much from a little Portuguese shepherd boy.

Good night, loving parents, we are very grateful for the dinner you have given us and we will try to repay you with love and work … my sister, the poor thing no longer does anything but repeat the same thing, she told my deaf father that the Virgin personally sent her blessing … it seems that he didn't hear well because he replied that he, too, sent her many greetings and wondered if she'd gotten the oxen yet … and my sister sobbed between the sheets.

Stop crying, I want to rest, tomorrow I'll go with you, calm down … There the three of us were, the littlest one out of sorts doing nothing but asking when we'd get there and what were we going to ask for … I made her shut up. You're vile; we're waiting for God's Mother, not Saint Nick.

Well, that's what was going on when my little sisters clasped their hands like this and fell to their knees, and when I turned around, there she was, white like my sister said, on a little cloud with a bracelet all her own that reached to the ground.

I was dazzled, but I saw how her little blue eyes shined ... and then without moving ... she told us ... that the world was beside itself, that contortionists, I mean communists, would arrive in other lands. That they were very bad people and if we didn't pray every day with that bracelet she wore that she called the same name as our aunt who kneads bread ... Rosario ... we're going to see more suffering ... and that all of us should expect worse days, that people didn't have souls, and that prayer was the only salvation. That's what she told us we should communicate to the world ... and that we should come back because she had a second message for us. I'm sure that she realized our memory's bad, that's why she didn't tell us everything at once.

It seems that the Holy Mother left us with light in our eyes, because this time, yes ... not only our parents believed us, but the entire village and they told it all to those from other towns. The day before she came again they were already walking with all the crosses, praying, and the Ave Marias wouldn't let us sleep ... Lucía, but why are you still crying? ... Ah, from happiness. Child, with you there's no end to your tears ... Well, the second time, our parents bathed and combed us ... our skin turned so white, they even sprinkled us with perfumes. There we were, several hours in front of the bush and the little one already wanted to leave, how embarrassing! As if the Lady isn't going to appear with all these people waiting, Lucía ... that was when, on the same cloud as the last time, she reappeared ... people shouted and others called for silence ... this time she was angry, she said she was tired of humanity, that they didn't pay her any attention, but that man, dominated by the demon that had already taken possession of many souls, would create evil instruments so powerful that cities would cease to exist in a second, that there wouldn't be time to say good-bye to parents or brothers, that others would suffer terrible torments, millions would be left

without limbs, wandering the countryside, the fire would
burn fields and towns but man wouldn't realize the evil
that invaded, and instead of making peace, would produce
more torments ... Then she told us that she would return
a third time ... I was already a little tired of climbing up
and down the mountain, but well, it isn't every day that the
Mother of God comes asking you for favors ...

The third time there were more people there than for San
Juan's celebration ... the hilltops were so crowded that you
couldn't tell what was a bush or a head, or a lamb's body
from an overcoat ...

Lucía didn't talk to me because everyone was touching
her and the poor little thing, who couldn't stand it, did the
same old thing ... Stop crying, they'll leave us alone soon
... so that, that time, escorted by the guards ... followed by
the bishops ... we climbed the mountain. While we were
climbing she was already there waiting, I don't know if
we made a mistake about the time or if she was early ...
everyone else only saw a light in the sky, but we saw her
from head to toe. "Is it her, is it her?" The priests asked,
hiding themselves behind their capes.

This time she remained silent for a long time ...
"Children," she said, "what I tell you now is for you and
the saints of my church." And she spoke ... and I was
struck dumb ... and my feet trembled. Now Lucía really
did cry ... "what's she saying, what's she saying," everyone
asked. "Quiet, they can't hear" ... "Silence," people
shouted ... and the universe stopped there ... the earth
stopped turning, the animals stopped moving, and no bird
cut through the skies ... for the first time she opened her
arms and cried for us ... saddened that way she told us
... I can't tell you because you're near ... But, happy me,
the mother took me to heaven the following year, happy
not to have children or grandchildren or others who are
going to suffer ... that which you are suffering today ...
the prophecy begins this year. You won't be able to tell
from one day to the next, since it will be incubating ... you

will even accustom yourselves to the misfortunes that will
start to surround you ... And, of course, because man is
such an egotist, nothing will bother you until your home,
your children, or you yourself will be touched, and by the
time you will want to react it will be, well, because you are
already possessed and there is nothing you can do ... I see
it already in the color of your skin, I feel it in your smiles,
you won't talk to your neighbors, you'll walk alongside
millions and you won't see anything happening to anyone,
this is the beginning ... What the Holy Mother announced
. . . I can't tell you, I'm no longer here ... maybe today
you believe the poor little Portuguese shepherd more than
the very Virgin from Fátima, my town. Start getting rid of
everything because nothing you have will help you, only
when you are naked can you begin to feel full ... Return
to the earth and the water; go back to the beginning if you
don't want such a frightening end to come.

I'll leave you now; I must go tell this to others.

THE FORGOTTEN: I did pure evil; we even carried out black
masses with San Joaquin's goats. Killed a bunch of dogs
and drank their blood. We made a circle, invoked the worst
possible angel, which was good for me, it's when you no
longer have anything that you start believing in stupidities.
Who cares about cell phone roaming fees? When you're
born on the other side of the river, it's another story.
Besides, crazy people do what they like and who's going to
stop them. I knifed an old lady and came out the loser, the
other maniacs can grab you because they wear a uniform,
they can pull out your teeth, cut off your dick – put rats
up your ass – and then they'll burn you with paraffin or
throw you in the ocean in jars filled with cement, and these
madmen are now senators. How many did they throw out?
And how are they doing now? An expensive little car – a
condominium on the coast – they even own the beaches
– the bastards – and someone born without possibilities –
because I'd have liked to have come from the other side ...
being able to throw punches and pull out fingernails – for
that you don't need to study. It's cool – and on top of that

they pay you and you walk around like a king – a friend's
father did it ... now he's got a huge, cool house, the guy
doesn't have to work ... So who are you supposed to
believe – the madmen or TV? ... To the madman, you're
an ass if you do nothing but keep calm – but I've got them
all on a list ... a good ATM and I'm on the other side ...
three bullets in the paunch of the fat slobs – I'll steal your
jewels – rape your girl – drink your booze ... the joint's
luxurious my friend in comparison – a luxury hotel. Know
where I live? How could you know? ... You're familiar
with all the cities of Europe but you don't know where you
live – let's see ... How do you get to Santa Ana? ... To the
alley of the dead? Palmilla Cuatro? Renca Oriente? Do
you know how to get there? If Santa María de la Renca's
there as well? ... I assure you I live in the best parts of
town ... I'll sell you twenty grams and be set for a month
– if they're giving it out ... I'm saving up right now – I've
got to fill the piggy bank and the lovely 38 automatic pistol
with silencer – what more do you want – calm down, man
... If the assholes haven't been worried about me, what
do I have to worry about? ... spoiling the lady's hairdo –
frightening the little bastard ... I don't see any kids ... if I
put my finger on the trigger, it's more for the pleasure of
seeing the fear on their faces that makes me angry, than
to shoot them. I got rid of the knife – everything gets
dirty – they keep screaming – acoustic contamination.
And what are they going to do to me that they haven't
done before? ... Know where I'm going now? Look – I'm
carrying a backpack ... To Lo Vásquez – crazy, man – to
Lo Vásquez, walking – on nothing more than these little
feet – one two one two ... She never fails me and I never
fail her ... Round-trip this year–clean – without even
one – pure charity ... That's how I roll ... I've promised
her that if the attack goes off clean I'll drag myself the last
two kilometers on my belly. I owe it to her ... Might as
well throw me to the devil – on this side, between men,
the promises are different ... Chicks are chicks even when
they're hanging above the altar and you have to treat them

like chicks. I'm not going to tell her everything – she'll just worry later ... Yeah, I'm right, this shithole is worse than Sodom and Gomorrah – crazy people worrying about nothing but material things – the glitter – the little shoe – the little shirt. If the question wasn't for this side – if I'm the sanest of them all – I'll take care of what I've got inside ... When this is all over who are they going to reward? Me, of course, you maniac. No one understands, I'm cleaning everything up ... little by little, putting a tiny grain of sand next to another you make a beach. Yes, I'm clairvoyant I do it by telepathy. Before I enter a house, I see it all: the servant cutting her nails in the bathroom – the woman sitting on her bed plucking out hairs with tweezers – the chick on the phone – I make a quick survey – I see what they got in the drawer – yes – I'm a seer, man, I collect all the facts, then I tell myself who I'm going to scare first.

And I see it all ahead of time; I know the old lady's going to scream, the servant's going to cry and the nerd go mute ... that's how I operate ... when the police dicks come I see where they enter – I am inexpugnable – they tell me I'm invisible. It's a gift – crazy man – a gift they gave me – if you're going to amount to anything, it's got to be worth something. Now I see you're watching me. The gentleman over there's going to grab his chin ... look ... the madman over there – evil awaits you – they're robbing your car right now – they'll make you spend the night at the police station ... You, ah ... you're going to have to eat the cazuelita you left behind at lunch. And this is because I don't want to ruin the year ... I'm watching that one until the wake ... if there's one thing certain it's that every one of us will get a farewell mass ... but I know what's going to happen to me already ... it's clear that I am a reincarnation ... go on–laugh – I swear pharaoh's friend – I swear Nubian – you're not going to believe this – I lived in ... Now they've sent me here ... As it is written: you will see him and not recognize him ...

THE PROPHET: Smoke started going up my nose, it was frightening ... then they put a crucifix on my mouth and

I was smothered even more. That's when I said to myself "I'll suffocate before they burn me" ... Idiots, if it wasn't for asphyxia they'd have the whole story *(Breath.)* everything went cloudy ... I failed to see the humor, especially since I no longer looked at those insulting me. "Spit on me, you idiots, let's see if you can put out the fire!" I shouted at them ... But since everything was on my side, a breeze came and I could make out the bishops and slaves that were crowding together ... The rhythm of the drums gave it all a pretty solemn character ... I relaxed for a bit until the tickling began at my feet ... At first it was pleasant ... Suddenly *whoosh* a flame sprang up and it was like standing on top of a brazier ... That's when I started to scream. "I recant ... I recant" ... A little late ... I just managed to ask for reincarnation as someone simpler, normal. This business of challenging earthlings ... I've lived them all ...

THE OFFICER: The revolver's silhouette shone on top of my table, how many times had I rested it against other people's heads? How many times have I felt the resistance of a hard skull against its barrel? One movement and that person disappeared ... No more than that, a game ... Now I'm waiting to rest it against my temple ... This time it's only good for a trip to the destination that so many warned me about. Their confessions are on these pages, not the absurd ones about where those they hid, lived, nor beneath whose bed they hid the explosives ... or all the lies, because under threat of death human beings become all seeing, they don't confess because they know anything ... As my superior González explained so well, the principle of torture is to bring them to the point where the mind turns telepathic ... To save the body ... It didn't always happen, some of them died before reaching this perfect state for us, we who worked for the intelligence services ... That's why we had to liquidate them, they were no longer fit ... Besides, they would have remembered everything. They would have discovered where we'd hidden them since they would have been able to visualize the exterior ... reconstructing from the feeling of their bare foot on the cement and from

there constructing the building from the sounds, knowing
how tall it is ... where the next wall is ... their sense of
smell developed as soon as they felt the exhaust from
the passing busses ... their hearing from the laughter of
schoolchildren ... They'd recognize the distorted voices of
we who interrogated them ... That's why, once they'd had
the treatment, they couldn't see the light again, we had to
make them disappear. I started it all just for the uniform ...
I saw how women were attracted to the strength it reflected
... I was shy, not particularly dashing as you can see, I
didn't have money or was physically anything that would
make me stand out on the street, I was lonely as well ...
and here there was companionship ... together every
day, doing the same useless things every day ... but we
shared our laughter and healthy competition ... it was all
attractive to those of us who didn't want to be unknown ...
for me the army was a refuge ... I felt like those below me
admired me the same way that I admired those above me.
They envied the stars on my shoulder; they envied me for
eating with the officers ... They envied me because I was
their superior, but envy is the foundation for admiration ...
They were going to close the center and we had to get rid
of two women and a man who were left in the cells ... they
weren't worth much anymore ... but their absence would
maintain the terror for those outside these walls ...

The first one was a typical mulatta, short, thin, with black
eyes that still challenged. Perhaps it was the only way to
go calmly ... She was covered with marks from the electric
shocks and knowing as we opened the door that today
was different the sergeant whispered in my ear, "Do we
take care of her quickly, lieutenant, or should we enjoy
ourselves a bit?" ... And he tied her feet with wire, threw
her head back, light fell on her hook and the whole cell lit
up and she said ... "On your children and your land will
fall as many misfortunes as you abhor right now, you will
never feel love again, hate will destroy your homes, your
children will spit on their parents' tombs, and women will
be disgusted by your skin . . The land will dry up and you

will beg for bread ... Those who saw and kept silent will
see how their work bears no fruit and how their minds
can't perceive the earth's landscapes ... Because he who
raises the knife against his brother ... these people who
allow their children to be sacrificed and continue taking
pleasure from sex, will engender nothing but armies
for evil ... Drugs will destroy your cities and lies and
hypocrisy will fall again over your governments ... The
judges who signed these invisible sentences rocking in their
chairs ... will feel paralysis invade their limbs, they will feel
the disdain of everyone and will have to recuse themselves
in their poor homes ... Your names will be erased to
appease the fire's torments ... The angels will refuse to be
your guardians and you will live unsheltered" ... She didn't
wail or look away, but her words resound in my mind,
I'll only be able to silence her murmuring by pulling the
trigger. Not on my temple but on the demons inhabiting
my mind and who I have the right to destroy ...

THE PROPHET: But don't worry. There's a time for everything,
nothing ends suddenly and when it's ending we don't
realize it ... As a friend of mine who preached in the
valleys of Babylonia once said: There is a time for every
event under heaven ... A time to be born and a time to
die, a time to kill and a time to heal, a time to cry and a
time to laugh, a time to throw stones and a time to gather
stones together, a time to search and a time to lose, a time
to speak and a time to refrain from speaking, a time to
love and a time to hate, a time to keep and a time to throw
away. So he said, as we descried the hanging gardens.
I thought it was fantastic; I didn't have to urge him on.
Enough, but we made something ... to him everything
had it's time and place ... Josué, I said in the fifth year, I
agree with you but nothing happens even so, and to him
everything had its time and place ... he was more macro,
he spoke for the Universe ... but concretely, one is the
spectator of all the times that others live ... Or not ... I
don't know ... I fulfill the destiny that the gods have given
me ... Receive their signals through their prophecies and

transmit them to those on this ambiguous planet ... I don't expect to be heard, I haven't been in the last few centuries, and I'll be heard even less today ... Now I wait and imagine where I'll spend 3009 ... I'm sorry that none of you will be there with me. At least I've learned something: do what you say you will and the foreseen will come to pass ... Please, the signs, don't ignore them, it costs too much to send them for them to be wasted ... It's the end of the play I've been tapped to perform. Oh, I forgot to tell you what my last reincarnation is, it's this, to be an actor.

MIDDAY LUNCHES OR PETIT DEJEUNER DU MIDI

Presenting

ESTEBAN before the End

SENORITA CLARA on the Threshold

THE GUARDIAN in the Beginning

The Salmon

WOMAN

EPHEBE

SHE

LOCATION

In an infinite space.

Big, narrow fish tanks surround the actors.
A salmon in each of them.

ONE

ESTEBAN: I've already starred in my own work. No space left, except for my moving lips and the down that sprouts on them.

I need a camera. A gigantic screen on which to see them. I'd like to turn on the television and not find the same characters every day, every year, the ones who seem to be eternal, not eternally young, but yes, eternal. There they were when I played with colored blocks. There they were laughing, applauding, when they banged on the door and carried off my grandmother. There they were when the president no longer wore a uniform and there they are today, while the world plays on grass courts.

I already know it. I'll go first and you will follow me there, aging with the television lines, smiling so much, electronic buffoons. What a pity royalty hasn't met you.

But I'm human, and while I maintain my condemned condition I'll construct my revenge.

Don't worry, I won't show up at your houses, I'll leave your children alone, I'll just feed off your souls ...

I want to turn on a television and see my lips.

THE GUARDIAN: Esteban, turn down the delirium, the patients are sleeping.

ESTEBAN: How many days are left ... to see the gallows and feel the weight of the chains ... ?

THE GUARDIAN: Write in silence, the mayor promised to publish it, later ... he's even thought of a title ... "Diary of A Condemned Man".

ESTEBAN: I love the mayor, I love his management, I love his imagination. I should have gone into the guards. I was young when the dictatorship happened and at that time you couldn't be a detective or a carabinero, even less a guard, at the most a rock star, but I don't sing ... The period in which one can choose is too brief, I want to be a guard or be part of a piece of theatre, one of those in which the roles change as it goes along and you end up in here with me guarding you.

THE GUARDIAN: Yesterday I was a priest and slapped your cheek for your confirmation; today I'm a guard. You know what, calm yourself for a little while.

ESTEBAN: We're in this fiction in which nobody knows what role to play, fulfill, desire, schizophrenia.

THE GUARDIAN: Look, we know perfectly well who we are, it's just too complicated to say it.

ESTEBAN: Why doesn't everyone talk like this all the time, instead of repeating themselves so much? You've got to squeeze the lemon ... This way we won't get anywhere ... We have to do something ... Yes, we can't just wait around any longer. They don't know what to invent anymore ... There's no governability ... We're going from bad to worse, what do you say? ... They're all a bunch of scoundrels ... They have their interests, yes, sir ... You see them coming ... You know what they're into ... We're all guilty in one form or another ...

THE GUARDIAN: I brought you an electric toy, the time will pass faster.

ESTEBAN: Or more slowly, you know how it is with time.

THE GUARDIAN: Give me an opportunity and I'll take advantage of it ...

ESTEBAN: He's not going to publish me; the mayor likes poetry and the novel's called *Gabriela Mistral, Lesbian of Montegrande.*

THE GUARDIAN: Change the name and the people and they'll publish it ...

ESTEBAN: Never, because despite my swollen fingers, despite my lungs full of worms, despite this story so reiterated, despite seeming like I'm from another century or from one that no longer is, I am loyal to something even though I've been a traitor to so many things. What's left is a clean corner, clear, as the burnished parquet in the middle of an oily bodega, and this is my loyalty to my novel. *Gabriela Mistral Denigrated in Montegrande.*

THE GUARDIAN: You'll see three glitters across the bars tonight, that's the first sign ... Then you'll feel a siren ...

ESTEBAN: It was today, there was a reason you looked at me like an angel, I've said good-bye so often ... I thought that one day they'd arrive with the mayor smiling and pretending to take me to an interrogation, with the psychologist, something simple. So I'd warn them about the fourth premonition, giving them another secret for another day of breath, as if I'm the guardian of the secrets of Fátima. They say the Pope turned as white as his robes when he heard them ...

And no, nothing is ever the way you think, there's no way to prepare ... I also saw you arrive with a cup of coffee, a cigarette, you smiling and both of us knowing that sleep would come after one sip, so we avoided saying good-bye ... But no, it's going to be like in the movies, they'll march me down the corridors listening to the noise of the bowls on the bars ... I'll hear the good-bye shouts, the brave ones ... And the chaplain ... murmuring in my ear, reminding me that I'm going to meet my maker all alone. Why hold on? Between eternal heaven and cement walls there's no place to lose yourself.

Let me be all of the condemned.

TWO

The Death of Socrates

THE GUARDIAN: You want to die for logic and atoms ... take the hemlock.

ESTEBAN: I, Socrates, accept without rancor this sentence that you, free men, have applied. My Athens, white with wisdom, can no longer contain within its breast the lucidity of one of its citizens. I can hint at and palpate your envy, but how not to know it, if the moment I raised my voice in the agora of Ios I felt, in your frightened looks, the first sips of this poison.

Athens, your columns will continue to support the palaces of power, justice and science, but your marble will end up in splinters.

You're not giving me anything more than a ticket to other realms; my body's atoms will look for the material that will accept them. Remember that we are nothing more than reflections of our minds.

I am only Socrates because you have seen me.

I will be a name later on because you will speak of me.

The idea is what makes us, the gods send us their ideas and we construct them.

How sad they must be to have such poor masons.

Let her touch my mantle, so she stops her lament.

WOMAN: I want to go with you since it will be centuries before you exist.

ESTEBAN: Show us your tears since they are testament to our alliance between man and woman, so no one else sees them, not my daughters, or these scared adolescents.

EPHEBE: Who is more afraid, that one on the edge of darkness or me on the edge of light? That one with wrinkled skin or me with crystalline skin? You have cloaks to cover you; we have skirts that let you see our strong legs. Come on, Socrates, who gives more … Ask him, there he is, Falvio the Italian who you bathed so many times, who you seduced in a logic class. Who enjoyed it more? You or him? They say that he accepted the first time out of curiosity, the second out of boredom, and the third only for coins …

WOMAN: Be quiet, respect death, respect the silence … that will begin to invade us … Let me see myself reflected in these moving pupils for the last time. Let me feel his tepid hand, these soft hairs where I rested my flesh on cold nights, let me feel his breath

… (Socrates takes the hemlock).

THREE

(SEÑORITA CLARA carrying a rag and a bucket picks up the jar of hemlock.)

SRA CLARA: Forgive the intrusion, but the coffee spilled, I came to clean, but today it seems to me that sweeping is erasing. Understand me? ... like this is his mess and tomorrow you'll no longer be here, but the same bits of dust will ... There are times one's labor is uncomfortable, as I've been telling you. Move over there, I'm going to mop ... I'm not going to be the one telling you where to move. I realize it's a delicate moment and you want to go wherever you want ... Now someone arrives and butts in ... I was going to bring you a present for the time we spend together. But look how silly I am; what use would it be if you can't take it away.

THE GUARDIAN: It's all right, Clarita, no one's going to withhold your pay if you don't clean.

SRA CLARA: Excuse me, what I'm referring to has nothing to do with money ... As good looking a man as you are, as if you had to suffer a disgrace to end up attractive, you'll have noticed that those who were ugly, when they left for the pavilion, looked so beautiful. My doing, I became fond of them ... Here we are with the little madness.

THE GUARDIAN: I don't know, I can't begin to explain it, but he read my lips. It's been nine years ...

SRA CLARA: No need to leave him alone, I'll take care of him for a little while. Go on, go clear your head.

ESTEBAN: Clara, clean up this stain.

SRA CLARA: I was going to do it, Don Esteban, but I didn't want to bother you during your moments of privacy ...

ESTEBAN: I feel like instructing you ... Transferring everything they made me learn to you, so it will serve someone ... I was always a socialist, I feel like sharing, egalitarian impulses. Wouldn't you have liked to ride an elephant through the jungles of Ceylon?

SRA CLARA: No, Don Esteban, I'd die of fright before mounting one. Besides, we all have a purpose, imagine that I didn't exist, who would you be speaking to right now? … It's all the same if we share everything but on the other hand, either you're going to say that they never deceived you, or they never made you false promises, and that you didn't prepare for them to be fulfilled and were then disappointed … You should have been deceived as well, and the laughter, don't we all smile the same way when someone plays a prank on us? Or some little thing makes us feel good? And the worries, don't we all have worries? Me with my drug addicted son and the other one, the girl. Or they cut off the phone, because I have a phone too. Don't we all know the same news? Why should we talk about illusions? I'll take advantage of this time to tell you one, since you'll take the secret to the tomb … I'm sorry, Don Esteban, I didn't mean to be … You know, it's just an expression they use.

ESTEBAN: True, I could hear the most devilish, the most delicious, the most criminal secrets … I'm the only one who can make them secure. Secrets last until the moment they aren't worth anything any more.

SRA CLARA: Or until everyone knows them.

ESTEBAN: I guarantee that I will no longer exist, although I could ask for a pencil and betray you, tell me …

SRA CLARA: Why waste these minutes listening to foolishness, with your permission. *(Sits at his side.)* Imagine we're sitting on the beach and the boats are passing in the distance …

ESTEBAN: The water's icy.

FOUR

ESTEBAN: I realized today, looking at you, that this corridor is a wagon transporting me to another station. I realized today that nothing has been strange, that I can talk to you without my voice trembling and I can feel my body soaked with cold without my jaw chattering … Today, this precise instant when my feet feel the cold cement, when humidity nests in the corners, now I'm isolated. When I no longer have to achieve anything, I realize that all these years, ever since the howl in the clinic, since the first host between my lips, since I knew excited sweat, that it's all been nothing more than preparation for assuming this instant. That what I live today, is no more than a summary of a long preparation. Now I understand the aches so large that I had to palpate. For this I had to enjoy pleasures so fine, so that today Esteban Saint Jean can wait calmly. And look at his past as the sum of steps that have brought him to a place, not the place that his illusions believed in, but the place that life had reserved for him.

SRA CLARA: You're not going to tell me that you're born only so that thirty years later what's happening to you today is what's going to happen ... Since, it doesn't seem to me, I can't agree that you always take the wrong road. And me, perhaps I came into the world in order to be here today at this moment animating you before ... Oh, my god, if it's true, I'm frightened. That's what I've come for, to console you ... You know, it's better to think about the stars, then you'll be one of them.

THE GUARDIAN: The mayor wants to know if he can come see you personally. I'll stay with you. It may seem stupid, but I envy you in a way ... Susana wants it all to end so that you won't keep talking to her ... She's surprised because I haven't turned on the TV ... She's puzzled because I don't make love to her. It's difficult to start caressing her when you see what's happening here ... I can't get excited, it doesn't come naturally. She says she understands, that you can't buy a puppy until the old dog dies ...

Aren't you going to write?

ESTEBAN: It's written already, I just have to make some corrections and finish it. One shouldn't be frightened of deadlines, we always have to get used to time limits ... Pay the rent at the end of the month ... Take exams at the end of the semester. Vacation is over February 28. Parties end when dawn breaks, children leave because they grow up ...

THE GUARDIAN: There's no one outside, nobody knows, just the commandant, the mayor, me, and, well, you.

ESTEBAN: I felt the noise of the helicopter when it landed, I felt the silence when they entered, and I feel the fear that we have now that it's left. We shouldn't be conversing, you've seen it in many films, at the most you should go beat up the sleeping guards, and take me out in a rowboat through the fort's subterranean tunnels. We'd get away amidst the whisper of bullets and at dawn, on the other bank, hiding in rushes while we listen to the shouts of those who are looking for us, we would separate ... That's the only way we could continue to talk.

THE GUARDIAN: Sure, if I suddenly went off my rocker. If there's suddenly another coup in Santiago and another helicopter arrives with other orders and neither me nor the mayor, nor the commandant is here anymore ...

Why can't it be beautiful to go to heaven? Why can't I be reincarnated as a little seal like those on Coquimba point, tranquil, stretched out on a rock. And if it's all nothing more than this ... We'll keep talking and make everything stop ...

Listen, are you going to visit me in my dreams?

ESTEBAN: We can only see things from the end one time.

THE GUARDIAN: What do you mean? Once, when there were reels and the movie ended and began again. You know yourself, if it wasn't for the credits it made no difference if you watched from the middle or from the beginning. It's possible the end's already happened, and we just haven't realized it.

ESTEBAN: It's true that we arrived in the middle of a film and nobody promised us that we were going to stay until the end ... this top called earth has millions of revolutions left. One appears like an extra in a second, the film goes on, they've already filmed you, there's no reason to go on, your contract's over. I meant you can only see things once as you close your account.

THE GUARDIAN: I don't make up boring speeches like you. I mean, I've got another way of thinking about such things. For example, I should be crying right now, it would be logical for the two of us to be holding hands, consoling each other, as we should. But here I am, as if I was standing in the middle of a bus terminal, waiting for an arrival or a departure, lost. I've even forgotten to cut my nails.

ESTEBAN: This is what it means to see things from the end. Your nails won't grow long any more; you won't have to shower tomorrow.

THE GUARDIAN: Pardon me, this is getting tiresome ... Better if you read me what you've written, later, when I page through it again, I'll hear your voice.

ESTEBAN: Let's see, which part ... Navigation ...

FIVE

ON THE BOAT

(SRA CLARA appears smoking, playing the role of the poetess GABRIELA MISTRAL. ESTEBAN is the ship's officer, he approaches, lights her another cigarette.)

OFFICER: The lights of Callao, and what's shining like snow-covered peaks are the crags of the guano islands ... You smoke a lot.

GABRIELA: From New York to here is an eternity, from the Tropic of Cancer to the Tropic of Capricorn, from North to South we went through all the seasons and it made me nervous.

OFFICER: The Via Lactea has begun to shine on us and that's the Southern Cross ... I really had no intention of enumerating what you're seeing, but ever since we set sail I've been watching you ... I'm being indiscrete. An officer of the Reina del Mar shouldn't bother passengers.

GABRIELA: I've been watching you as well. You're Chilean, from Santiago, a merchant marine. Your accent, while it gives me pleasure to remember it, repulses me from my disturbed depths.

OFFICER: You should write it down. Not you, me ... Nobody's going to believe me when I tell them these words that you're saying to me ... The whole steamship knows who you are ... This has to be one of my most brilliant nights, brilliant isn't the right word ...

GABRIELA: A dream-like night. Fantasy is one of our most beautiful feelings.

OFFICER: Full of dreams and pride, let me reiterate. I'm so proud that, if it were up to me, I'd never let the lights of Callao get any closer.

GABRIELA: It's humid and hot, the odor of the Pacific penetrates you, on Long Island the ocean's already lost its odor, it's nothing more than a plain of water. Here it's still untamed ...

OFFICER: I write too: "My God, how can you see the little children's feet blue from the cold and not cover them?" Well, for the most part ... "Our Father why have you forgotten me? You remembered about fruit in February" ... You'll feel them digging at your side and that the other's strange ...

GABRIELA: You're mistaken ... I'm an old woman, one the doctors haven't given much time in this world. I'm returning to these ports because I promised God I would, to vanquish rancor and pride. Please, no signs of admiration nor even less of adulation, since, even if I accept them from a stranger, I've never consented to hearing them resonate on the lips of a ...

OFFICER: Chilean, I know. Look, it's just us; tomorrow you'll no longer be you. I've heard on the radio that there are rowboats, barges; schooners rocking in wait in Arica bay, waiting for you, the coast is full. They're painting the Alameda in Santiago. No one's asleep in the entire country waiting for you. And I've got an opportunity. There's a tear slipping down your left cheek, it's going to reach the corner of your mouth, here comes another ... Please, don't cry.

(They embrace.) I promise that no one will know you're here, the ship will change course and in three more days we'll watch the dawn break in the Orient.

THE GUARDIAN: Dawn in the Orient, what will that be like? A pretty love story, the only problem is that she's an old lady who can't anymore and the officer could be her son. How would it end?

OFFICER: They call it open ended ... whatever you imagine.

THE GUARDIAN: I think that if the ship changes course the Captain will catch you, and, when you disembark ... she'll be received with honors and they'll take you off in chains ... If the mayor gives the word, just as soon as this has all been resolved, they're going to publish it just the same ...

SIX

The Trial

ESTEBAN: All that I lacked was a sentence, a trial. Where they would have recorded my defense ... Writings for schoolchildren to study later on, where my allegations would be transformed into symbols of a dignified humanity ... A trial with a packed house, cursing and cheering. A trial with a wooden railing where I'd rest one hand while waving the other in the air ... The deaf gavel banging against the bench ... While I raise my voice above those who accuse me. A trial like Joan of Arc's, Giordano Bruno's, Eichmann's, Sacco and Vanzetti's, Louis XVI's, or a serial killer's.

But this, kidnapped in the middle of the day, without anyone knowing about my last cry, without knowing the eyes of those who accuse me, where it's all the same whether I die a coward or brave. How can it be that they haven't listened to me for even five minutes? It doesn't matter since they've already fixed the moment for my execution. At least let there be witnesses who can paint the picture of me standing before the firing squad. But I don't know my sentence either, will I be beheaded, poisoned, drugged and then buried alive? Or disintegrated in some chemically powerful powder?

No one will paint my picture. My death has already happened, from the moment I heard the noise of the helicopter. It'll happen without a photo, without a shout of "Long Live Shitty Chile", or "Army Assassins". This can't happen to me ... If that's the way it is then I've lost ... but that's not right, since I feel I've won.

THE GUARDIAN: But they've given you a trial, you just don't remember, I've got it here, recorded, and when you've got the opportunity ...

ESTEBAN: Yes, that's the way it was, pardon me. I got confused. I got confused about the year, the place, the country, the history ... Because I want to deceive myself.

SEVEN

The Other Day

SRA CLARA: Good morning, Mario, did you sleep well? And is Susana feeling better?

THE GUARDIAN: Sra Clara, it's not dawn yet, and you cleaned just a few minutes ago ...

SRA CLARA: Shhh ... I couldn't sleep and knew that they were going to wake me and he wouldn't be here ... Besides, we have to make him believe that he slept well and it's already another day ... Good morning, Don Esteban ... but look at the mess you've made for me here.

ESTEBAN: When I went in the car, I hoped that it was going to crash and everything would end right there. Then in the airplane I wished we'd crash, so that everything would be the product of an accident, not a mistake or something premeditated ... But accidents have to be accidental and not when you need them.

THE GUARDIAN: And what about the other passengers? Look at how egotistical you are, perhaps it suits you to end it all there, but the others …

ESTEBAN: You're looking at me with rage now; the tender guilty feeling has disappeared …

THE GUARDIAN: Nothing guilty about it, thinking that's all. When have you seen me tender? Now that we're on this there's something I can't believe. Tell me, did you really eat them all, or just the ones you tore to pieces? They say you made ankle casseroles.

I've also had to do terrible things while in the service. We shoved them into metal urns, narrow ones, but not lying down, standing up. We heaped them together.

I can't tell you; it was like a murder of crows, with the shouts and the putrid smell. Since they were already maimed we weren't going to take them out, we weren't going to clean them up. So we gave them a potato puree filled with rat poison, waited for them to finish rolling about and then threw them in the square of the silent.

It was an act of duty, but it would never have occurred to us to eat them.

I'm really asking, only out of curiosity, tell us what it tasted like? Like marinated rabbit, or grilled turtle … ?

ESTEBAN: We always made soup out of the heads; the sauce goes with the head, a boiler so they loosen up, five minutes in boiling water, sufficient … You eat the brains with a spoon; it tastes like something between testicles and sheep's brain.

THE GUARDIAN: But were they all faggots, those you ate, I mean to say, the ones you cooked. Or were there normal people as well? Because if they were strange, well, their fate nothing more, as my sergeant said before we faced the condemned. These bastards could have saved themselves. We gave them the opportunity, but no, they preferred to go for evil … and that's on them, you couldn't do anything …

But this mania, let's say, it was like an addiction, after the stock was finished ... There was nothing left to dispense, you understand ... you filled it again.

ESTEBAN: I never looked for them, they always arrived, they were born to find themselves with me. I didn't take them by force. Sometimes I'd go out to buy the newspaper for breakfast in the morning and there, at the kiosk, a smile and we'd be having coffee, conversing, caressing. I'd give them a sleeping pill and they'd fall asleep in my arms.

THE GUARDIAN: So, poh, whoever. No, I imagined that you corralled them with an electric fence and cut them up alive, and they ran around missing a hand while you, zuaz, attacked again and cut off a leg and that's the way it continued, you understand me. But if they're asleep, they never realize. Then it's the same with the pieces, belly with rice, spiced kidney with purée, grilled rib, chest tapa, a good thigh ... Looking at it that way, it's really nothing much.

ESTEBAN: It all goes back to a problem in my childhood, they raised me that way, my father would leave and not be back for months. I'd press myself to the window waiting for him, every time he left I'd cry for him to take me with him, I'd run after his car for kilometers, following the tracks in the tar, feeling the way his smell dissipated, believing I'd catch up to him at the next traffic light ... I'd return home feeling abandoned, without a hand to hit me on the head, without an arm to embrace me. It was simple, if everything is so easy ... Once they entered my house, I couldn't let them leave, because that would revive this torture from my childhood, and the only way to get them to stay forever was to put them to sleep. I didn't eat them, like they say, I joined them with my body, so they'd never leave, so I'd never have to press myself against the window again.

SRA CLARA: Even I might have done the same if they'd left me like that, from one day to the next. He put some bills on the table and left, I begged him to stay, that if he wanted to continue his adventure I gave him permission, one understands how men are. I begged him on my knees not to leave me in an empty house. It never occurred to me, I should have eaten him.

THE GUARDIAN: Señora Clara, don't you see it's the novel he's writing.

SRA CLARA: Yes, but it felt so real, how can you even think, do you believe I'd be here waiting if it were true ...

ESTEBAN: I'll change the title, Midday Lunches, or perhaps Passionate Meals would be better ... The bell rang, they're coming.

EIGHT

Confessions

SRA CLARA: Who would come at this hour, keep calm, I'm going to brush you. Me, when I get nervous, I like to be brushed ... *(While she brushes him she puts some hairs in her apron.)*

THE GUARDIAN: Sometimes one asks oneself why you do what you do? Like in this case, let's say, I could have you blindfolded, even gag you so you don't bother us with any questions. Susana tells me it's because of what happened to my brother. He was younger, we played ball every afternoon, I'd shoot it far away. I didn't want to go look for it, so I told him to do it. I threatened to hit him, and he had to go, and that's when the truck plastered him. I wanted to kill the driver, but he, lying there all bloody, called me over and said to me ... "It's your fault, you asshole" and he went.

SRA CLARA: Ay, we're like little birds, flitting from one place to another and then, uff, off to the next world. Listen, you've got a lot of dandruff ... take some soapbark with lemon ... Excuse me, Don Esteban, I didn't mean to ...

ESTEBAN: When you brush me it seems like you're counting my hairs and every brushstroke is a memory that surges, but now that the comb's tangled, the memories have stopped. I dream of what might have been, of everything I didn't become.

SRA CLARA: The same thing happens to everyone, at some point we all want to be something else. Not a movie star, nor a radio announcer, even less a soap opera actor, not to mention a famous singer ... I'd like to have been something like Evita, but more of the people you understand. Like this woman who fights for her people, for the indigenous. Or like the other little old lady, with her white handkerchief on her head, who began to walk around the plaza asking them to give up her children ... Every Thursday at the same time for twenty years. Like that, a figure like them. But as time goes by you become insensible ... Foolishness, keep writing, so that you finish your novel, we're listening.

NINE

In the Garden

ESTEBAN: No, Clarita, I won't write anymore ... The story that's left is the beginning ... It's her and a garden ...

(SHE in the garden.)

SHE: You've got your grandfather's eyes, my nose, and these hands are so small ... I want to be able to hug you ... I was tender and spoiled, but well, one day they'll tell you ... you'll see light and it will be silent and this garden that I planted ... you'll play with the worms and you'll eat the dirt between the plants ... that's where you'll find me ... they'll call to you from every side and you'll want to go to them all. Please, step across the threshold with the signal in the doorway. I haven't said your name but I still don't know what it should be, I don't dare anticipate. It would be a costly mistake and I don't want to pay any more. I'll name everything for you so that when you arrive you'll see ... if they tell you other sentences, other verbs that my voice has not enunciated, don't learn them and that way they won't exist ... A last commission, that I hope won't make you mad; choose a planet where I can look at you ...

SRA CLARA: I feel like ... and what's next ...

ESTEBAN: I don't know, it's the beginning.

THE GUARDIAN: When I get home, I'm going to write it …

TEN

The Final Song

ESTEBAN: Sing me a lullaby, I'll fall asleep and you'll keep singing. With the song in the background, put the pistol to my skull … Don't stop, keep singing, something sweet. But don't make me dig my own grave like the others and then oblige me to align myself with its borders. I don't want to feel like I've dug enough, that my body will fit in the earth now. Time will prolong itself, converting every second into twenty-four hours of terror, two seconds into … Keep me from this.

(They sing – He tries to sleep.)

DONA CLARA: Let's see, what should it be, the one about the little chickens?

THE GUARDIAN: Why not a bolero? A love song, it's more appropriate.

DONA CLARA: Which one would you like them to sing you, let's see …

THE GUARDIAN: Let's just start; we'll see what comes … slowly, yes, so the mayor doesn't hear us.

(They sing.)

ESTEBAN: No, it's too false. Besides, you don't have a weapon to do away with me, I'll be left asleep so as to be awoken by the suave voice of someone who will take me not to the gallows, since English traditions aren't known here, nor to the guillotine, since the skill needed to construct that machine, it's pillars of oak, the metallic laminate, is very refined. Why talk about the electric chair, or the gas chamber? They're too visible. Besides they'd have to be approved by the public health system. Everything is so illegal that it generates it's own law, creating the finest of legalities.

It won't be a lethal injection either, lying on the cot, wrapped in a green petroleum apron. It will be like it's always done around here, by betrayal. Perhaps the priest himself, when I incline my head, he'll stick the dagger in. Or it will be the mayor who tells me, go ahead, and stuns me with a hammer blow. If not that, his favorite game ... He'll leave me tied up at the bottom of a tank of Texaco petroleum, with cement up to my neck and there they'll wait until it sets. Until the concrete closes up my pores and impedes the movement of my thorax. And if all these agonies seem horrific, terrifying our imagination with the suffering of these great torments, it's not like that. It's more the fear that causes your existence than the reality of your personal experience.

My body will defend me; it will pump up my adrenalin so that I'll be ecstatic. I'll feel like I'm submerged in the lukewarm water of a thermal bath. I'll already be in the next world; my mind will have gone before my body dies. Then, although I'll be lying there, amputated, my eyes cut away, I won't be there. Clara, go to sleep and wait for the dawn and everything that they'll say to you, everything they'll tell you about the suffering ... It's only what we feel when we don't suffer it. It's a trick, a taboo so that we behave. A taboo so big that we only see it before the end.

THE GUARDIAN: The mayor's coming down, it must be a transfer order.

SRA CLARA: And the salmon, Don Esteban, what should we do with the salmon?

THE END

SEBASTOPOL (DESERT TIMES)

Characters

CRISTINA/MARY JO
From the Future

SIDNEY
The Young Chemist

HUMBER
The Impresario

MARY HELLEN
British

FRANCIS
The Manager

LUIS
From the Present

LUIS
Miner

MANUEL
Miner

ESTANISLAO
Miner

MARIANO
Miner

THE PRESS-GANGER

SARAH

A Beginning

LUIS – CRISTINA

(1997. LUIS and CRISTINA run through the abandoned desert mine in Sebastopol. It's getting dark.)

LUIS: This is what they call an abandoned desert, nothing's left and everything's still there. Life's so fresh; death's so fresh, a good phrase.

CRISTINA: It makes me sad, anxious, I don't know, but I'm having a great time all the same.

LUIS: A kiss in Sebastopol ... I love you.

CRISTINA: It gave me goose bumps.

LUIS: A good sign ...

CRISTINA: You can see the snow from here, so much frozen water, it's like a joke.

LUIS: It's the desert's envy, let's go ... We should get back; they'll be waiting for us at the bus.

CRISTINA: They'll be bored already, let's go, – first one back's a . . .

(CRISTINA leaves, falls into a mineshaft.)

LUIS: Cristina, can you hear me? Are you there? ... Answer ...

CRISTINA: It's cold, Luis, it's dark, get me out of here.

LUIS: Please don't stop talking to me, do you hear? Rub your hands together ... Cristina, please.

2

In the Port of Iquique

SIDNEY – FRANCIS – LUIS – THE PRESS-GANGER

(On the dock the workers brought from the south are washed and disinfected. FRANCIS counts them and receives them. SIDNEY stares at the bay.)

FRANCIS: 18, 19, 20.

THE PRESS-GANGER: I brought you twenty robust ones ready for the shovel, all single. It gets more difficult each time ... They're starting to talk in the south ... You, come here, tell the man.

LUIS: They say there aren't any grape arbors to lie under, no streams to plunge your hands in, that there's more than one valley in drought, there aren't any cows to herd, no trees in which to discover nests ... But, mami, when I return I'll buy you land and we'll have kid goats for cheese and lots of fig trees for sweets ... They say the white sodium nitrate burns your eyes, that there's no time to think, that the exhaustion means that all you do is sleep and that you never sleep enough, that you keep working even in your dreams, that men burn themselves as if they were in hell, and their skin is torn off by the steam. But they also say you make good friends, you play at night and tell stories about the horizon and the frontier ...

THE PRESS-GANGER: Okay, that's enough.

LUIS: ... that you meet people from China and blond girls who take you to immense lakes with their looks, they say that from here great mansions are built that the stars keep company ... Mami, the house will have halls where we'll put benches and sit grandmother down ...

THE PRESS-GANGER: Hey didn't you hear me? ... As you can see, we'll have to raise our commission for each head.

(SIDNEY remembers his farewell with SARAH standing alone on the dock.)

SIDNEY: Don't cry, Sarah, there's no need; I know that you love me and I'm carrying you with me.

SARAH: Sidney, I'm imagining silly things, that some savage beast will eat you, or you'll be blinded by one of those strange tropical fevers.

SIDNEY: It's a place in the desert, a working class city, full of industry; it's not the jungle.

SARAH: You're just saying that to calm me down, Sidney. How sweet you are ... *(Shows him her breasts.)* ... It's my farewell gift, no man has ever touched them ... *(Sidney desperately kisses her breasts.)*

FRANCIS: It's a beautiful bay ... Francisco Maclure, machine chief for Sebastopol Station. And you must be Sidney Coleridge, our chemist from Sussex.

SIDNEY: It's a pleasure to meet you. This is truly impressive. The whole trip's been like one of Darwin's adventures. ... I never thought that steam ships, electricity, trains ... would have arrived so far away.

FRANCIS: You'll be even more surprised, you'll find everything here, but you'll lack everything as well. It's an ideal place for reflection, to play ... we've got polo, cricket, tennis, whatever you want ... Good beer, and plenty of vaginas, not as white as the English girls, but they perform the same function ... You'll love it, that is if you have a taste for the exotic and the inexplicable. You'll never want to leave ... This is wonderful, Sidney, we're going to be great friends.

SIDNEY: "Francis was a friendly guy, with a profound disgust for the locals. He loved sports. When he shook my hand I had a presentiment that something terrible linked us together."

SIDNEY: It's a pleasure, Francis. On the steamship there were only toothless mechanics, gold bugs on their way to California, and an aristocratic family from Santiago that did nothing but go on and on about the lack of servants and fresh vegetables ... insufferable. It's really a pleasure.

3

In Sebastopol Station.

MARY JO – MARY HELLEN.

MARY JO: You know my name's not Mary Jo! I was taking a bus tour; we were on the way to Esmeralda Station. From there we were going to Iquique ... I'm at the English nuns school ... I need to get back to Santiago ... please ... it's ...

MARY HELLEN: For the love of god, my dear, go on, tell me what's bothering you now? Every time your fancies strike you start with your stories: you're from Indochina and you fell in a boat, now this one about tours ... Mary Jo, mirages happen in the desert. Out there you can imagine whatever you like, but don't keep filling my house with stories. I told Humber: That little book about Alice in Wonderland wasn't appropriate for children, and what did he do? Read it to you every night. ... Bathe yourself, cover yourself in perfume, the young chemist from Sussex arrives today ...

MARY JO: Mary Hellen, I assure you that my name is Cristina Fernández and I live near Nuñoa Plaza.

MARY HELLEN: Look, I asked the captain from the south, the one who's always lived in Santiago, and there isn't any Nuñoa Plaza. Please, Mary Jo, do me a favor and behave normally, merci ...

MARY JO: Let's go to Santiago together, mom.

MARY HELLEN: I'm not your mother. I'm your cousin, sister, your godmother, anything but your mother. Or do you think we have the same profile? Never! To top it all off, you're the daughter of your abstemious father ... Oh noo, the siren again ...

4

The Reception.

HUMBER – SIDNEY.

HUMBER: Manchester is a children's game ... Here we build the cities of the future ... We're organizing them; we're creating a new man, a worker, strong, one who is only in contact with his family, his friends, and his work. We're the true conquistadores; we're populating places where nobody would have even spent the night before. The only temptation here is nothing and we offer everything. Look at these bottles. Beer from München. There's a tennis court, and football, we'll teach you football ... A dance hall ... And why not swimming pools? It's always fine weather, isn't it marvelous? Sarah will love it. Yes, this is a challenge for a man. This is what God would want ... We're feeding Europe. One day they'll thank us, Sidney.

SIDNEY: Fantastic, sir, it's an honor for me to participate in ...

HUMBER: Don't be silly. Sebastopol is proud to have you among us. There's no place on earth where you could live what you're going to live here.

SIDNEY: The pleasure is mine, sir. And, as you charged me in your letter, I've brought several studies about accelerating the liquefaction of nitrate and bringing it to greater purity.

HUMBER: Good, good. Young man, we'll put everything into practice. The ships await and the cargos are slow ...

SIDNEY: Strange latitudes. I'd heard about them from friends who'd been in Suez. But I never imagined ...

HUMBER: Forget about everything you've heard. Atacama will fill your head with fantasies not even the best French authors could believe. ... Look at this black sky; have you ever seen so many stars at night? There they are, for us, illuminating us, calming and guiding us, above all, Sidney, guiding us through this century that's just beginning.

SIDNEY: It will be a great century, sir, technologically; new uses for electric energy are being discovered every minute. It will displace steam, and electric acoustics, sir; your voice will be able to travel for miles ...

HUMBER: I don't understand a lot of this. I apply it. I construct. Let it all arrive and let it be for the good of all. Isn't that right, Sidney?

SIDNEY: And what's it like further south in this country?

HUMBER: Chile? What a strange name for a territory. New Britain would have sounded better. It's a dock, a freight platform. There isn't any country; they fought with other savages over these lands. The Chileans are smarter and they won, period. But the rest we've done ourselves. Trains ... ports ... roads. We take the water from the sea and we distill it. Isn't it wonderful, Sidney?

5

LUIS' First Day.

MANUEL – LUIS – ESTANISLAO – MARIANO.

(White from the dust.)

MANUEL: The grinders spit dust.

LUIS: It's worse than swallowing a sack of flour. How do I get it off me ...

MANUEL: Try this. ... Welcome to Sebastopol, tomorrow you'll already be a miner.

LUIS: Thank you. Luis Sanfuentes. I'm going to work hard so I don't go back empty-handed.

MANUEL: Manuel Gómez, from Curicó ... here we work and converse, don't bother remembering anything: pastures, brooks, the women waiting ... here you'll become old and from here you'll never leave.

ESTANISLAO: Estanislao Rojas Rojas, they found me out of work in Salamanca. When the siren sounds we're going to swim in the stream. We'll catch some good trout and dinner will be ready.

MARIANO: Mariano Ramírez, from Chillán. Here we play *brisca* and look at the moon.

LUIS: They say you can take a train through the nitrate fields, race mules, learn songs in other languages.

MANUEL: The only thing we're familiar with here is the hills. That one over there is a friend of mine, single like I am, with love troubles. But sometimes I wake up happy and suddenly it looks like a woman lying down and I, from a distance, caress her.

ESTANISLAO: If she's such a good friend of yours, why don't you ask her out? … Me, tonight I'm going down to Iquique. I haven't been down there in more than a month.

LUIS: The horizon is empty.

MARIANO: It looks empty, but it's full of the spirits of those who are gone and those who don't want to leave. Those who've gone crazy and go howling through the rocks.

LUIS: They're celebrating in the administration. … How pretty she is …

MANUEL: It's not worth looking over there. It'll just make you angry, they're having a party.

6

MARY HELLEN's Birthday.

HUMBER – MARY HELLEN – SIDNEY – MARY JO – FRANCIS.

MARY HELLEN: Sidney, you don't know how happy we are to have you with us.

SIDNEY: You're too kind, mam.

MARY JO: I feel like you'll understand me.

MARY HELLEN: Behave yourself, Mary Jo, he's a terribly nice young man.

HUMBER: We're building a country, Sidney, if we have enough of our own coins.

FRANICS: Up until now only tokens.

MARY HELLEN: I designed them. I told Humber that they needed to be metallic, but he made them out of this strange material.

HUMBER: Rubber, my dear, it's cheaper.

MARY JO: The cake's ready. I made it from a recipe I saw on TV.

SIDNEY: TV?

MARY JO: Yes, a little box like a radio ... but with people that you see ...

HUMBER: Fascinating, Mary Jo.

SIDNEY: My congratulations, mam, I wasn't aware that it was your birthday, but permit me. *(He kisses her hand.)*

MARY HELLEN: Humber, didn't you promise to change the name of the station for my birthday and call it Mary Hellen?

FRANCIS: It would have to be in Spanish, María Helena.

MARY HELLEN: If that's the case we'll keep calling it Sebastopol.

MARY JO: Father, when will you take me to the mineshaft where you found me? Or let me go to Santiago? ... Sidney will accompany me.

MARY HELLEN: Mary Jo, my dear ... let it go or we'll have to commit you and the sanitariums are terrible ... I just read about them in a novel ...

HUMBER: Well, 'Happy birthday to you, Happy birthday dear Hellen'...

FRANCIS: What's all the fuss about?

MANUEL: The fuse exploded on Cirilo, he's bleeding to death.

FRANCIS: What do you want us to do? Exhaust the mules? They'll never make it to Iquique ... Time for him to accept and go content ... Tell him not to take his eyes off the sky; it's a splendid night. The angels will happily descend to look for him.

HUMBER: Come on, man, don't cause a scandal ... The station will pay for an urn. Oregon pine and bronze handles. It's what those who die for progress deserve ... Mary Hellen, it's time to listen to Bach. Put the Victrola in the window so that these wretches can calm down.

7

A Night at the Mine.

MARIANO – ESTANISLAO – MANUEL – LUIS.

MANUEL: They're six of us and only three mattresses. You get old Arnoldo's ...

LUIS: It stinks...

MANUEL: The old man gets drunk and pees. You'll have to leave it outside to air...

LUIS: I'd rather sleep on the ground...

MANUEL: Calm down. Cigarette?

ESTANISLAO: *(ESTANISLAO enters with a box full of chickens.)* I sold my gold tooth in Iquique and bought some chicks: Rosita, Pinteada, and Micaela. We're going to have eggs and then we'll make some great stews.

LUIS: We'll make them grow with sodium nitrate.

MANUEL: Did you go see the Red Star of Tarapacá play?

ESTANISLAO: They could barely handle the Victoria Ramblers ... A little wine from Curaco?

LUIS: I like the desert. We're going to have a good time.

ESTANISLAO: I bought two women, for the whole night. One of them put the question to me here; the other worried me there ... And the union sent you this. Hide it, we don't want any trouble...

MANUEL: Don Luis is a prisoner again!

LUIS: The Worker ... The Voice of the People.

ESTANISLAO: You know how to read?

LUIS: And add, divide, subtract, write.

ESTANISLAO: Let's drink to that … To the educated worker!

8

About Friendship.

SIDNEY – FRANCIS

(In the Sebastopol baths.)

FRANCIS: You're too white, Sidney. The Indian women are going to be after you for that. We're going to be great friends.

SIDNEY: "I don't doubt that we'll spend a lot of time together, and that there will be instants we'll think we're unique. Nor do I doubt that we'll swear eternal brotherhood and that it will cheer us up for me to see you smile at the end of the day and for you to hear my stories. Nor do I doubt that at dangerous, or even sad moments, we won't have another shoulder or hand than the other's with which to feel the warmth of absent humanity. I predict that like you I become complacent. You'll pick up my clumsiness and I'll take on your deformed sensibility … But, Francis, let's not deceive ourselves. Even when you have to sustain me in my agony, we'll never be friends. Just two people taking advantage of the existence of the other in order to survive the moment. I don't doubt, Francis, that if I visit you in Santiago or you me in Southampton, that we'll be friendly with each other and respond like the gentlemen we are, with hospitality … But I've already given my friendship to someone who isn't here and that relationship isn't precisely what I want to establish with you … Everything fine now and then travelling companions like before." Of course we'll be excellent friends.

FRANCIS: So much so that we'll have to find a couple of twins or both marry Mary Jo.

9

First Meeting.

MARY JO – LUIS – MANUEL

LUIS: Manuel, there she comes.

MANUEL: They're afraid of us. If she comes close she'll take off.

LUIS: She won't be afraid of me … Miss Mary Jo, do you need any paraffin?

MARY JO: You know my name?

LUIS: Of course, you're the most beautiful thing about Sebastopol.

MARY JO: No, I'm not.

LUIS: You're always looking at the horizon, as if you're hoping for something.

MARY JO: I look at the mountains, the snow; it's the last thing I saw.

LUIS: Yes, mirages on the desert…

MARY JO: And you, what's your name?

LUIS: Luis.

MARY JO: Luis?

LUIS: Please don't cry. I don't know what to do…

MANUEL: Let's go. She's pretty and the only one who understands us, but she's sick …

10

Badminton Game.

SIDNEY – FRANCIS

SIDNEY: Francis, why do they scream so much?

FRANCIS: Don't break my concentration. They burn themselves with the steam, then they run out and scream.

SIDNEY: A few railings would be enough …

FRANCIS: You've been spending a lot of time with Mary Jo. Forgotten Sarah?

SIDNEY: Impossible.

FRANCIS: In solitude even the demented are attractive.

SIDNEY: I won't hit you, Francis, out of respect for our friendship ... Keep playing.

FRANCIS: The English don't know how to lose ...

11

Burnt Hands.

FRANCIS – LUIS – SIDNEY

FRANCIS: What good is a man with burnt hands? It looks like you did it on purpose ...

LUIS: The levers were boiling hot, and the steam ...

FRANCIS: Where were your gloves?

LUIS: I don't have any, sir.

FRANCIS: Ask for some then ... Now go count sacks...

SIDNEY: Come, this will make it feel better ... (*Takes out cologne, dabs it on a handkerchief and gives it to him.*)

FRANCIS: You've been taken in by the story of Florence Nightingale and the Red Cross.

12

The Call to Attention.

HUMBER – FRANCIS – SIDNEY – MARY JO – MARY HELLEN

MARY JO: Sidney, I suffered as well at the beginning. Then I told myself: this is only an instant, nothing is eternal. Like nightmares, they disappear. For now, you're part of them.

FRANCIS: Mary Jo, don't bother the young chemist. You'll terrorize him with your bombs that will come and destroy everything. Cheers.

HUMBER: It looks like Sebastopol agrees with you very well, Sidney.

SIDNEY: Nevertheless, it never ceases to surprise me, sir. That's precisely why I wanted ...

HUMBER: Sidney, I've heard some strange things about you ...

SIDNEY: You're referring to my treatment of the Sebastopol workers, sir...

HUMBER: Exactly, you have de-authorized certain practices that allow this station to function in an exemplary manner.

SIDNEY: I wasn't brought up, sir, to accept punishments that are on the margin of labor relations.

HUMBER: Young Sidney, look out the window. What do you see? ... Empty plains, millions of dry stones, the worst place on the planet, where neither the most detestable pus nor the meanest insect dares live. These men have only recently been introduced to civilization, Sidney. And I have the obligation to educate them, teach them. It is a harsh apprenticeship, Sidney, but they thank me for it. They are men in embryo and when they become men we'll treat them like men. But for now I'll ask you not to interfere in their formation. I'll thank you for that.

MARY HELLEN: Humber, "Humpty Dumpty sat on a wall. Humpty Dumpty had a great fall. All the King's horses and all the King's men couldn't put Humpty together again"...

FRANCIS: Charming, Mary Hellen ... Charming.

MARY JO: We're in a world they invented and we live only so that we don't die. Then there's silence. A cognac?

13

Sunset.

MANUEL – LUIS – MARY JO – SIDNEY – MARY HELLEN – ESTANISLAO.

SIDNEY: My god, it's really impressive.

MARY JO: It's the most entertaining part of the day.

LUIS: That's the reason they say "my sun".

ESTANISLAO: (*Opening the cover on the chicks.*) It's time to stop pecking and sleep.

MANUEL: So should it be always.

ESTANISLAO: Colorful and fresh.

SIDNEY: It reminds me of Turner's paintings. Sarah loves them.

14

The Harangue.

MANUEL – LUIS – ESTANISLAO.

(MANUEL drags a chair into place, climbs up on it and harangues.)

MANUEL: The day will come when the workers in the desert, the children of this earth, will be the owners of the riches this land has given us. If we have to live here, where the gold is white, the sediment from prehistoric seas left behind so a man could live in abundance, and so that his children could grow up with dignity. Foreign capital is robbing our riches in collusion with the oligarchs in Santiago. Those who have sold their country for some crumbs and some run down mansions. The working classes are the true patriots. We're the ones who fought the war, who stain this desert with our blood. Our hands laid the railroad ties, it's our skin that's dried and wrinkled, our children who weaken in the fog of the desert and die by the train tracks waiting for medicine. We're the ones who brought this desert to life. Our desert, from which springs the fresh green fields in the North and the South. Thanks to our labor people feed themselves. Europe eats and wheat fields grow higher than a meter. And how are we repaid? With exploitation and misery. Comrades blinded by steam. Amputated by the crushing machines. The hour has come for them to listen to us. For us to begin to organize with the other stations, the bakers, the stevedores. Together we'll make them value the rights of the workers on this land. (*They sing The International.*)

15

Listening to the Workers.

SIDNEY – MARY HELLEN – HUMBER – FRANCIS – MARY JO.

MARY HELLEN: Isn't it fabulous? It must be the record that's sold the most since that girl in '17. Isn't it marvelous, Humber? The way the same words and notes shouted by socialists in the parks of London now resound with the same flavor here on these horizons. It fascinates me. I remember Europe listening to them.

FRANCIS: There's also that Argentine, with the name of a bird. He doesn't do too badly with sales. Of course, I agree with you that he sings an incomprehensible dialect...

MARY HELLEN: Rady was in Mexico and brought some fascinating recordings. A mixture of operetta with zarzuela and histrionic screams.

HUMBER: These people will do very well with music ... But they don't understand anything about trade unionism. ... Have you noticed that their meetings all look like carnivals? They remind me of the Holy Week processions in Madrid.

MARY HELLEN: How depressing. Don't even talk about it. When I was a little girl we saw one of those in Seville and let me tell you, not even the worst Lovecraft story can provoke such nightmares ... In order to get us to eat Nanny would threaten to send us to Spain...

SIDNEY: The wind's blowing ...

MARY HELLEN: Sidney, dear. ... Open the window. I need to feel the freest wind in the world.

FRANCIS: There is the basis of liberty, it only exists in nothingness ...

HUMBER: Obviously. From the moment we become two we are restricted, and when we are millions, nothing is left of liberty. Not even the L.

MARY HELLEN: Humber, you've always been so good at politics. You should have stayed in London. You'd be in the House of Commons by now ... It's a nice dream, but it's just a dream. Cheers, Humber.

16

The Barrel.

MANUEL – LUIS.

MANUEL: Did they tell you down south that you'd have to empty the gringos' shit?

LUIS: Why is it so heavy ... ?

MANUEL: Because they eat and drink so much. Just think: Mary Jo's shit is in there...

LUIS: I feel like opening it. It would be the only contact I'll have with her.

MANUEL: How will you know what's hers? They're all mixed together.

LUIS: Lovers recognize each other.

17

Another Sunny Afternoon.

MARY HELLEN – SIDNEY – FRANCIS – HUMBER.

MARY HELLEN: Another sunny afternoon. Doesn't it seem completely out of place? ... It's no good for anything ... Not even for a picnic. Not for wearing summer clothes, not for taking tea on the terrace, not for making the flowers bloom, not for lighting up the cathedrals, it's completely awkward. ... I tell you, Humber, at least let's see a cloudy day. I've begun to think that rain never existed, that it's nothing but a figment of my imagination.

SIDNEY: The opposite happened to me in Sussex. I began to believe that the sun had been extinguished...

FRANCIS: Poor people. But at least you'll never have to walk with muddy feet. Don't you find, Humber, that there's nothing more terrible than having to put up with all of these soaked people's looks. With their oozing clothes. The brutes get a splash of victory and it leaks. In reality, rain is depressing.

HUMBER: They should be grateful the nitrate fields aren't at the pole. If they were they'd have the right to organize themselves. Man will always find a reason to be unhappy. Have you ever seen a giraffe make a fuss because it hasn't eaten, or because it's wet, or because it lacks clothing ...

MARY HELLEN: There's too much progress, Humber, it does nothing but make people neurotic and envious...

HUMBER: You think a lot, Mary Hellen, and it makes you, if you'll permit me, talk more than is necessary. At times it's a bit distracting...

MARY HELLEN: You're a true gentleman to tell me to be quiet. It so happens that you are my loving husband and have the obligation to listen to me so I'll continue. By the way, I feel the noise of the train. There might be news from Norwich, or some missive for Sidney. ... Well, I'll go talk to my flowers.

18

The Robbery.

MANUEL – LUIS – ESTANISLAO – MARIANO – SIDNEY – HUMBER.

MANUEL: *(Playing Brisca.)* Come on, place your bets, and take another token.

ESTANISLAO: I double ...

MARIANO: Me too...

LUIS: How's this? ... It's a bottle of iodine.

MANUEL: *(Breaking the bottle.)* They'll cut your ear off for this in Sebastopol. It's just Luis' imagination.

FRANCIS: If it isn't a bottle from my office, "Iodine From the Nitrate East Company of Sebastopol."

(*Takes out a knife, goes to cut off his ear. A scream resounds in the desert.*)

SIDNEY: Sir, the conveyor belt. Pardon me, they're …

HUMBER: Ears, a collection, Sidney. A gift from the Bangalu when I was in Ghana.

SIDNEY: I find them repugnant.

HUMBER: Don't be silly. The more ears you have of your enemies, the less harm they'll do you …

MANUEL: Be careful. They see everything here. For starting a union they tied Ermenigindo to a telegraph pole and left him there until he died of hunger and cold.

ESTANISLAO: Don't cross yourself! This one will say that you're drugged. Can't you see that religion is the opiate of the masses?

MARIANO: There's a comet. They come from other planets where they are watching us.

LUIS: From that hill you can see the lights of La Noria, you can see how in a ship sailing they're eating in one window, someone's undressing in another. I close the curtain, put a hand on her face and feel the moisture on her lips. It's an old woman, a little boy, it's my saliva and it's so cold up there that I can't feel my own body, or the heat of my blood. I get up and when I open my eyes everything is green, a flowering fig tree. I empty my purse and they look at me unbelieving and I tell them: "Mami, there's enough here to buy the land."

MARIANO: And the house, plus a plow. And I present her, "She's my wife," I say, and they take off the veil but everyone's dressed in black and I ask, "Why are you in mourning?" And they respond: "Twenty years have passed."

MANUEL: And over the administration office waves the red flag.

LUIS: Night, Manuel, is the only thing that's left for us all.

ESTANISLAO: Until a sign appears that says: Don Humber's Stars ... Ya, I'm annoyed. I'll bet all the chickens for three grocery tokens and one water token.

MANUEL: You lost. Go slaughter the chickens and we'll build a fire ...

ESTANISLAO: Rosita, Pinteada, Micaela, don't look at me like that. Everything comes to an end one way or another. Nobody told you we'd be together forever. Of course, you'll have to go like this, suddenly, without having really lived, not even laid any eggs, or knowing what it's like to be confined for twenty days and then be happy with chicks scratching at your feet. You're the only ones who listen to me in the afternoons and know my secret: that I'm never going to leave Sebastopol because I came here to hide from myself. Because the only thing I have in this world is the dry desert and you. You can never separate yourself from what you love the most. At least I've learned that. Don't cry now, let's go and hurt ourselves...

19

Picnic in Atacama.

MARY HELLEN – MARY JO – HUMBER – SIDNEY – FRANCIS – LUIS.

MARY HELLEN: Humber, are you sure there aren't any dynamite charges here?

HUMBER: Don't be ridiculous, Mary Hellen. Lay things out, I'm dying of hunger.

SIDNEY: This is all splendid.

MARY HELLEN: Scones?

FRANCIS: Delicious.

MARY JO: Sidney, lemon pie. The only thing I learned in technical manuals.

HUMBER: Francis, the parasol.

MARY JO: That's a strong wind across the plains. It sounds like words. Let's see if we can hear each one.

MARY HELLEN: It's like someone calling Maaary Heeeellen ... Maaary Heeeellen ... Someone's calling me. It must be Aunt Virginia. I can see her running with a plate full of cookies. Maaary Heeeellen. Can you hear it?

FRANCIS: Much too romantic, Mary Hellen ... It's more like the shouts from San Enrique ... Revoluuution ... Revoluuution...

SIDNEY: That seems a bit catastrophic to me...

FRANCIS: Well then it's saying, Saraaah ... Saraaah ...

HUMBER: It's the sea. The sound of the sea. There must have been swells in the Pacific.

MARY JO: And you, Sidney?

SIDNEY: It's wind, only wind ... Declaring itself and finding us in its path ...

HUMBER: Enough of this nonsense. Put on the Victrola and let's dance...

20

The Rain.

MARY HELLEN – SIDNEY – HUMBER – MARY JO

MARY HELLEN: Oh goodness. Mary Jo, I don't know if you're infecting me but I seem to have felt a drop ...

SIDNEY: No, so did I.

HUMBER: Rain?

MARY JO: Make a wish. (*It begins to drizzle in the desert. The workers stop working. Everyone looks at the sky and makes a wish...*)

The Wish.

LUIS: A grilled roast.

MARY HELLEN: London, London …

MANUEL: That the miners unite.

MARY JO: Please, I want to go back.

HUMBER: Ten cents more on the pound.

SIDNEY: Sarah, remember me.

FRANCIS: Everyone under the umbrella.

ESTANISLAO: Honey fritters.

22

About Love.

LUIS – MANUEL.

Night, cold.

LUIS: Imagine it. She comes and I tell her that I long for the same thing. But I don't dare.

MANUEL: It's a dream, kid, nothing more.

LUIS: No, Manuel. She looked at me and moved her lips without speaking. "I love you," she said, "I love you."

MANUEL: That would be rich, blondie. I'd give it to her all night long.

LUIS: Careful, she's mine.

MANUEL: She's whoever gets there first.

23

FRANCIS – SIDNEY.

FRANCIS: What color are Sarah's eyes?

SIDNEY: Infinite green, like the fields of Scotland.

FRANCIS: I need to think about someone. How fortunate you are, Sidney.

24

MARY HELLEN – MARY JO.

MARY HELLEN: It's too uncomfortable and I feel the necessity of communicating it to you. It all began with a little tickling in ... then I looked under my arms, in my hair ... but it seems they only nest there ... One knows that there are different kinds of fauna in distant territories ... They're like miniscule little spiders, tiny, inoffensive in appearance, but a terrible anguish has taken possession of me. Maybe they cause some sort of plague or provoke madness or perhaps death ... Oh, my God, don't tell me I'm the only one. I'll have to tell Humber ... Mary Jo, you're my only friend, help me.

MARY JO: You've got lice, Mary Hellen. Don't worry; you're not going to die.

25

FRANCIS Punishes, SIDNEY Stops Him.

FRANCIS – MARIANO – SIDNEY.

FRANCIS: *(FRANCIS whips MARIANO.)* So, you like to read? Answer me, imbecile! ...

MARIANO: It's not against the law, no ...

FRANCIS: Law, law, what do you know about the laws, shitty nigger? Tell me who gave it to you. Answer me, you wretch ... Or do you want me to kill you?

SIDNEY: Are you mad? (*He takes the whip from Francis.*) What are you doing?

FRANCIS: Don't stick your nose in again or I'll hang you by the neck ...

SIDNEY: Francis, he's a worker!

FRANCIS: It's for his own good, don't you understand? We're transforming these savages into men ... But they're not there yet, Sidney. And don't you ever discredit me in front of a worker again.

SIDNEY: It's only a newspaper. In Brighton there are ...

FRANCIS: Forget about Brighton! Forget about the London School of Economics! Look around you. Do you see any mansions, any universities, any Ministries of Justice? Sidney, we're creating everything anew here and it will be better this time ... This isn't a school for sissies, and if you don't like it, go back where you came from...

SIDNEY: You've got a lot of problems, Francis ... Here...

26

HUMBER's Fury.

HUMBER – MARY HELLEN.

HUMBER: They've put out a newspaper! Did you see, Mary Hellen? They're editing a newspaper!

MARY HELLEN: I can't imagine what the society pages will look like...

HUMBER: This isn't the time to hear one of your incomprehensible jokes...

MARY HELLEN: It's sarcasm, not a joke ... Humber.

HUMBER: Now that we've built everything for them they want to take control of everything we've achieved. How would you like to see yourself pulling a cart, Mary Hellen?

MARY HELLEN: It would be an experience. How touching ... "the present is organized on the basis of egotism, which is the negation of love. There can be no love where there is exploitation and tyranny." Look, Humber, they're asking for compassion ... Let's organize them some parties...

HUMBER: Their ideas excite you, don't they, Mary Hellen? ... Do you hate me so much that the only thing you want

is to see me destroyed? ... You'll go down with me, my
dear. Without me Sebastopol doesn't exist ... It'll go up in
smoke. A stick of dynamite under every rock I've raised
and another in the mouth of every one of these miserable
wretches...

MARY HELLEN: We need a vacation, Humber. Feel ourselves
back in civilization. Here our ideas get all twisted ...
Excuse me; I'm going to water the roses ... Ah, Humber,
when will we get a telephone? ...

MARY JO and LUIS Look For the Mineshaft.

MARY JO – LUIS

MARY JO: Where did you say the fairies come from?

LUIS: I didn't say. It's what others have told me. ... When you
get lost in the desert they bring you water and guide you.

MARY JO: Come on, Luis. Maybe the fairies brought me here.
We have to find them.

LUIS: There are thousands of mineshafts, Mary Jo, thousands.
They've asked me to direct at the Philharmonic. I'll write
a play.

MARY JO: As long as it's not about cowboys and sauces and
people eating grapes. I know that you like them, but it's
gotten boring already.

LUIS: No, it will be about the future that awaits us. When we'll
all be happy and equal...

MARY JO: Communist.

LUIS: If you say so. Wouldn't you like to act in costume? You'd
make a good future.

MARY JO: I'd do it quite well for you. But don't let anyone know.

The Assassination of the Servant.

SIDNEY – MARY JO – HUMBER – MARY HELLEN – FRANCIS – THE SERVANT.

SIDNEY: How agreeable to know that you're a part of the Sebastopol countryside.

MARY JO: If I'm part of these walls, look at me always, help me.

SIDNEY: I'd do it even if you didn't ask, but in what way? …

MARY JO: Don't worry, I'll tell you. English music is going to be so good.

SIDNEY: Let's not waste time with that.

MARY HELLEN: Dear Francis, one never loses time here, time loses you…

HUMBER: British women are surprising. Mary Hellen, you're brilliant.

MARY HELLEN: Humber, remember that we can't stand each other. You're being much too affectionate. (*THE SERVANT spills tea on HUMBER's pants. HUMBER grabs the pot and smashes it against his head.*)

HUMBER: You nigger bastard! … (*Beating him.*)

FRANCIS: It seems you hit him a bit hard.

SIDNEY: He has no pulse.

HUMBER: Don't be silly. Tricks. They invent all kinds of things, no … Get him out of here; the wretch did it on purpose … My pants, Mary Hellen, you saw what he did to my pants. (*Kicks him where he lies on the ground.*)

MARY HELLEN: Atrocious, Humber. Calm down. That noise again, those grinding machines, insufferable.

HUMBER: There's a job for you, Sidney. Get rid of the noise these machines make.

SIDNEY: I'm a chemist, sir…

MARY HELLEN: All the more reason … Music.

SIDNEY's Dream of Sarah.

SIDNEY: Sarah, I know this letter will not reach you. At least I got out of the war. I'm afraid for you, rather I'm afraid for me ... I can't tell you that I've arrived in a country ... it's more like a territory. You can't imagine, Sarah, there aren't any trees ... and that means so much. There isn't any shade. There aren't any branches, the leaves don't fall, no worms climb up the trunk, no birds perch, no nests are built, the branches don't turn coffee-colored, they aren't covered in snow, you can't lean against a trunk ... Sarah, I can see you beneath a tree ... and it's so beautiful.

MARY JO's Secret.

MARY JO – SIDNEY.

MARY JO: Sidney, shh, come here.

SIDNEY: What are you doing out at this time of night?

MARY JO: Come to the Philharmonic at nine, you'll see me act, at nine...

At the Theatre.

LUIS – 1ST WORKER, MANUEL – 2ND WORKER, ESTANISLAO – 3RD WORKER, MARY JO – THE FUTURE, CHORUS (ALL).

LUIS: The theatre group Art and Revolution presents "Workers Misery: Chilean Miner or Chilean Slave", by Alejandro Escobar Y Carvallo, plus the socialist thinking of Don Luis Emilio Recabaren ... In the union hall, Sebastopol Station.

(Three Workers and THE FUTURE.)

1ST WORKER: Like large laborious beehives
they erect enormous stations resembling mysterious prisons.
There work dirty people
Fighting hand to hand with the hard crust
Sweat bathes the sunburned forehead
And the virile musculature trembles.

2ND WORKER: The pale women of the desert
grow old from anemia and chlorosis
And she who doesn't engorge herself with greed
Is gulped down by tuberculosis.

3RD WORKER: The foreigner with arrogant gaze
is the tyrant of the trampled desert.
He is the cause of the Chilean living like
A miserable slave in his own beloved land.

THE FUTURE: Let there be no more laments and litanies
in these stations. Let's fight for the happy society of the
future, where exploitation, hunger, and tyranny will all
have ceased. Happy because art, culture, and all means
of communication will flourish. Workers, unite beneath
the sun of socialism that will transform egoism into love,
destroying savage capitalism.

CHORUS: Let the people recover their power and break the
chains that oppress them. Rise up, people, follow your
destiny like Christ at the summit of Mt. Calvary. Have
the courage to submit today to make Chile egalitarian
tomorrow!

The Orgasm.

MARY JO – SIDNEY.

SIDNEY: That was fantastic, Mary Jo, my most sincere
congratulations. I'm left, nevertheless, worried about the
possibility that they'll find out …

MARY JO: Sidney, you're so like the friends I had in Santiago.
It's like you're from another time, that's why I need to ask
you for something.

SIDNEY: Mary Jo, you too are the person here most like my
friends in Sussex.

MARY JO: And that gives you confidence?

SIDNEY: Yes, it makes me feel good.

MARY JO: Then take off my blouse.

SIDNEY: You don't feel well?

MARY JO: And then take off my skirt and let your warm hand run wherever you like, Sidney ... If you don't do it I feel like I'll grow old, and this flesh will never be able to give itself without shame ... Please do it.

SIDNEY: I ... want to, a lot ... and yes.

MARY JO: I'll start ... close your eyes.

(She undresses.)

MARY JO: See, naked it's like we were wherever we wanted to be. There is no place, there is no time ... It's like our eyes are the same pupils from centuries ago. It's the same orgasm that people will have a thousand years from now. Isn't it comforting to see things that way, Sidney? ... And not lament about losing something or feel like days are passing without anything that moves us...

SIDNEY: That was marvelous, Mary Jo.

MARY JO: Don't call me Mary Jo, my name's Cristina.

SIDNEY: "In reality, it was one of those experiences that without a doubt I will remember until I'm old and that I will tell my most intimate friends. It will be a secret that the woman I marry will never know ... I saw her eyes sparkle and my flesh trembled as if it were the first time ... Mary Jo, you could be the woman of my life, the one destiny offered me along the way, but who, on finding her, like now, I destroyed ... But I don't believe it, and only believe that this impulse of hers confirms her demented state. But at the same time I know she's the one protecting me and I will just have to reject her ... I can't distinguish between my reason and my feelings. I can't know ... if it's a euphoric state possessing me, or her madness infecting me. I'll know when it's already too late... But today, Sidney Coleridge ... with the pain of knowing that I'm losing the most precious ... "

SIDNEY: Mary Jo, I hope this won't happen again, because it's left me with a sensation of restlessness, while simultaneously feeling that I'm violating the kindness with which your parents have received me.

MARY JO: I know what you're really thinking ... I wouldn't dare become involved with someone demented either. But you've given me enough strength to continue waiting until I wake up ... Goodbye, I understand you.

MARY HELLEN's Horrible Dream.

HUMBER's Indisposition.

(MARY HELLEN dreams (and we see) two workers enter her room through the window. They maltreat her and rape her.)

MARY HELLEN: Ah, it's you. What a frightening nightmare, Humber ... A shipwreck, in the middle of the Atlantic, we lost everything ... Ay, I hope it's not an omen...

HUMBER: Shall I get you some tea?

MARY HELLEN: Always so kind. No, I've pulled myself together...

HUMBER: Dreams of shipwrecks, Mary Hellen? ... You'll find it amusing, but I was crying. ... From my desk I looked at the station ... I've done great things, Mary Hellen ... I looked at the splendor of the lamps reaching the horizon like stars ... I saw them happy, conversing ... the men unloading tons ... the sacks lined up like the Wall of China ... it never fails to enchant me ... We'll put electricity in every house ... the streets will be lit ... The White Nail arrives tomorrow with five trucks, the best, Mary Hellen, with more than five tons of cargo ... We'll begin building the school; we'll have education and a library in Sebastopol. This is my ship, and I am its captain.

MARY HELLEN: Of course, Humber.

HUMBER: Nevertheless, today I saw it sinking ... foundering ... eaten away by the sand ... the sails dropping, Mary Hellen ... and that's a torpedo ... I'm scared to read the paper, afraid I'll see some headline announcing saltpeter's been discovered in the Sahara or the American desert. ...

You can imagine what will happen to us… We'll close up and go … Never! I'll go down with it. (*Cries.*)

MARY HELLEN: Don't torment yourself with fantasies … But, Humber. Will we never return to London?

HUMBER: On vacation, Mary Hellen, only on vacation.

MARY HELLEN: (*Laughter.*)

The Future.

MARY JO – LUIS.

MARY JO: You won't have much more time here Luis … they will close the station.

LUIS: Well, I'll go to another.

MARY JO: They're going to close them all… They'll take the wood from the windows … The train tracks. They'll leave the locomotives sleeping in their machine shops … There won't be any more stations.

LUIS: That can't be. Where will all the people go?

MARY JO: They'll put them all in a truck and they'll leave them there, in front of the train…

LUIS: Will I at least be able to save something?

MARY JO: I don't know, Luis, but you'll continue to worry about the workers, fighting against the industrialists, believing that the worker will build a better city.

LUIS: Yes, I'll do that. Like in Russia, where there aren't bosses and those of us who work own everything … and where no one is fired, there isn't any misery, everyone can go to the doctor for free, and my children will be able to study.

MARY JO: And you will succeed. There will be miners as mayors, communist senators, even a worker's president.

LUIS: Seriously, Mary Jo, so much happiness brings me pain. It's a dream … I'll tell Manuel, he's done so much for this. And then?

MARY JO: What difference does it make, Luis? By then you'll be like everyone else, buried...

LUIS: Of course it matters! You give your life in order to put an end to exploitation ... It's like the father of our country; he gave his life to create a country ... even though he wasn't even able to die within it ... That's why...

The Rose Garden.

MARY HELLEN – SIDNEY – FRANCIS.

MARY HELLEN: You have to be cautious in these places, Sidney. Hydrangeas, this little one, camellias, irises, flowers all year round.

SIDNEY: I can't imagine your garden in Norwich.

MARY HELLEN: There were only bushes, Sidney, it wasn't necessary ... Have you visited the cemetery?

SIDNEY: Yes, extraordinary. A garden of metal flowers.

MARY HELLEN: Precisely, Sidney. Promise me that if I die in Atacama that by no means will you let them cover me with these oxidized metal crowns. I want flowers on my tomb, Sidney, real flowers, understand? You'll do that, won't you?

SIDNEY: If it comes to pass, I promise.

MARY HELLEN: That calms me down. Sarah hasn't written?

SIDNEY: Not really.

MARY HELLEN: What a pity. Mary Jo, despite her poetic states, is a beautiful woman. Don't you think?

SIDNEY: Yes, she's enchanting.

FRANCIS: Am I interrupting?

MARY HELLEN: Not at all, Francis, but you know *(Indicating one of her roses.)* Carol is allergic to you, I'm sorry.

FRANCIS: Forget it. The reds are preparing a strike. Agua Santa station warned us ... Humber wants to talk to you.

The Strike.

HUMBER – SIDNEY – FRANCIS – MARY JO – MANUEL.

HUMBER: I'm sorry, young man, but it looks like we'll have a mutiny on board.

FRANCIS: The last thing we heard from Agua Santa is that the afternoon shift didn't appear and that there are men from La Coruña on the outskirts of town.

SIDNEY: But is that legal?

HUMBER: Legal? Who understands that word, legal? They'll eat us alive. At the least they'll poke out your eyes and sack the administration. They'll assault the general stores ... and poor Mary Hellen and Mary Jo will have to get to know various black and foul smelling organs ... it's the bad luck of being women ...

SIDNEY: Are you sure, sir?

HUMBER: Definitely.

FRANCIS: Keep singing whatever you want, but leave the administration immediately ...

MANUEL: The workers of Sebastopol have eight demands; make sure the administrator hears them.

FRANCIS: You signed a contract and accepted ... well then, what do you want?

MANUEL: They're just and for the good functioning of the station ...
An end to the tokens system.
The right to gather and petition.
The establishment of a primary school for each station.
An end to charging for drinking water.
An end to opening mail.
Job security, railings for the crushing machines, and compensation for accidents that happen on the job.
An end to the company store, free commerce.
An end to korporeal punishment.

FRANCIS: Corporeal punishment with a "k", "company store" with lowercase letters ... everything else good. But this station is a place for work and production, we're not going to turn it into a playground ... withdraw.

MANUEL: Sir, if you won't consider our requests, we'll have to call a strike.

FRANCIS: Call whatever you want.

HUMBER: But what do these imbeciles want? We give them shelter, food, teach them how to work. To revolutionaries you can only respond with a single word: No.

SIDNEY's Retreat.

MARY HELLEN – SIDNEY – MARY JO – FRANCIS.

MARY HELLEN: I really envy Sarah. I hope it will be a fantastic wedding.

SIDNEY: It's been a pleasure to meet you and I'm very grateful for your hospitality. You've been very kind to take care of me.

MARY JO: You'll miss me, Sidney. Here, may you have the biggest flowers in Sussex. (*Hands him saltpeter.*)

FRANCIS: We'll wait for you. When you get back the cricket pitch will be ready and we'll arrange something for Sarah. ... Punctual, like the English trains you've told me about, bye-bye.

SIDNEY: (*From the train.*) Thanks, Francis. Mary Jo, we'll see each other soon. "I know perfectly well that I'll never see you again, Francis, nor these hills, nor the houses lined up in Sebastopol. Nevertheless, I can't help feeling enormous sadness. I'm incapable of assuming neither your great beauty nor your greatest misfortunes. Sebastopol, you'll be nothing more than a name in my memory. The name of the first and last place from which I fled. Now all I want to see is the sea and the coast of Dover. Good-bye, Mary Jo, we'll see each other in another life. Perhaps then Sidney Coleridge will dare tell you what he is incapable of expressing today... "

Rebellion.

MANUEL – LUIS.

MANUEL: Go to San Gregorio. Tell them that crushers, rippers, and stevedores have all united. This will be the biggest strike the north has ever seen. They'll have to listen to us now.

LUIS: Sebastopol finally rises. They're not going to believe it…

MANUEL: Luis, follow the telegraph poles, don't lose them.

LUIS: Manuel, I'm so happy. Up with the soviets!

The Night Before.

HUMBER – MARY JO.

HUMBER: Cover yourself, little girl, you should be sleeping.

MARY JO: Perhaps I'm sleeping now. Father, where did you find me?

HUMBER: There's no point in asking about the past. You can't go back. All you can do is prepare for tomorrow and hope that it will be better than today. If not, nothing makes sense.

MARY JO: Sebastopol is quiet.

HUMBER: A disturbing silence that won't let me sleep. It would be better in the Scottish mines, at least they speak English …

MARY JO: You'll go back and then you'll want so much to be here again … But there won't be anything left. The only thing they won't carry off will be the crosses in the cemetery …

HUMBER: Let's go in. Nights like this disturb the mind…

The Strike Ends.

FRANCIS – HUMBER – MARY HELLEN – MARY JO

FRANCIS: *(Receiving a telegram.)* Humber, good news. The army has put down the subversives in San Gregorio and now controls the situation in the whole region. ... The revolt is over.

HUMBER: Jolly good. This army of the Chileans is a true army. It understands where the best interests of the country lie. Take out the glasses ... We'll have to tell them in London to congratulate this prime minister in Santiago. They'll be elated.

MARY HELLEN: I must admit, I was worried. Cheers.

HUMBER: Let the sirens ring! We'll fire a number so they know how Sebastopol reacts.

FRANCIS: The first one to go will be the one with who you look for fairies and put on plays. We're not stupid, Mary Jo.

(MARY JO's crisis.)

HUMBER: Hold her, she's delirious.

The Farewell.

MARY JO/CRISTINA – LUIS – ESTANISLAO.

ESTANISLAO: *(Carrying his chicken cage and the union banner. He runs, pursued by the administration's horses, falls, the birds peck at his body.)*

LUIS: They shot them point blank, Cristina, they were singing. I don't want to be Chilean, Mary Jo.

MARY JO: Go on, take this ... please run ... hide yourself ... go back to Ovalle ...

(The sound of horses is heard.)

LUIS: Mary Jo, I love you very much ...

MARY JO: Forward, Luis, always forward, I'm going with you.

LUIS: No, Mary Jo, stay, stay ...

(The galloping approaches, bullets whistle, two workers fall, a rope wraps around MARY JO, a bullet hits LUIS.)

Epilogue.

LUIS and CRISTINA.

(1997. At the edge of the mine shaft LUIS revives CRISTINA. The rope from the previous scene is what hauled her out ... LUIS gives her artificial respiration.)

LUIS: Shh ... You came back. Breathe, I love you so much ... You can't leave me like this ...

CRISTINA: The snow on the mountains.

LUIS: Yes, you remember ... It's a desert mirage.

CRISTINA: Luis!

THE END

DOWNSTREAM (RÍO TORMENTOSO)

Characters

EUGENIA
47-55 years old, Waldo's mother

MARCIA
24 years old, Willy Asenjo's daughter

LORENA
21 years old, and Chip, her stuffed animal

WALDO
25 years old, the River's friend

WILLY
55 years old, Marcia's father

CRISTIÁN
23 years old, a photography student

DRUG DEALER
35 years old

THE WOMAN WHO OWNS THE KIOSK
44 years old, Roley's mother

OTHERS:
THE BOY FROM THE RIVER – THE NOUVEAU
RICHE WOMAN – THE YOUNG MAN – THE
PIMP – WILLY'S WOMAN – THE THIEF – THE
YOUNG MAN-DISCO – THE EVANGELICALS –
THE DETECTIVE – DRUG DEALER II – FATHER
– GIRL

SCENIC ANTECEDENTS:

The play takes place in a three-storey building.

Scenographically, this is represented as a plastic abstraction of a building, six rectangles superimposed with a stairway running through the center. (Each rectangle is an apartment, with its magnetic furniture, lighting, and other elements in bas-relief.)

Distribution by floor:

The apartment on the first floor stage right is covered with a metallic curtain that never opens. Everything that happens there is done in silence, but follows the action on the rest of the stage. For example: people get up in the morning, make love, eat meals, etc.

On the first floor stage left: one finds a small store or kiosk, THE WOMAN WHO OWNS THE KIOSK's place.

On the second floor stage right: WILLY and his daughter MARCIA's apartment. It's pink, decorated with military banners and trophies, and a Chilean altarpiece.

Second floor stage left: EUGENIA and her son's apartment. It's Nile green. Decorated in wicker, artisanal weavings, and pots of geraniums.

Third floor stage right: CRISTIÁN's apartment. The young photographer, his apartment is gray. The walls are covered with photographs and posters.

Third floor stage left: Lorena's apartment. It's blue, antique parasols and fans with stuffed animals.

Moments in the stage action are shared by all of the inhabitants. That is to say, by the building as a whole – these moments will be determined by the staging. The organic life of the building is constant and parallels the actions called for by the text.

The location of the building is that of a city block on the outskirts, near a river.

The building is situated towards the back of the stage and is covered by a scrim during the first few scenes.

Downstage, both left and right, are oil drums and tires that represent the riverbank.

The lighting follows the stage action, marking the narrative progression, moving the spectator's gaze from plane to plane.

First Sequence

SCENE I

Night – WALDO on the riverbank.

WALDO: Everything's quiet, river. It's time to smoke a cigarette and converse. Great music, great vibe. Over there they're snoring, you're like me, calm without noise. I'll let you know something ahead of time, a full moon's coming and you'll reflect it. There you'll be, all dolled up and ready to party, you don't have a mirror to see yourself with, but believe me, it's when I see you best . . .

(On the banks of the river ... a scream is heard – THE WOMAN WHO OWNS THE KIOSK with packages, a silhouette in the back.)

THE WOMAN WHO OWNS THE KIOSK: I bet they're there, I'm sure of it, hidden like lizards, I know they're listening to me ... Tell Carlos I'm going to catch him one of these days ... he can't keep hiding. Nelly already told me everything, be a man, come home and take responsibility for your wretch of a son ... We're all miserable because we're women alone. Didn't you have a mother? I curse you, all of you sitting on the rocks and darkening the riverbanks, all of you, you won't amount to more than this cursed river, always carrying waste and your lives won't be more than the mud you breathe, the same filth you contemplate ...

WALDO: Go watch TV ... At least we're not stuck like that. Isn't that right, river?

(THE WOMAN WHO OWNS THE KIOSK sings: "Que grande viene el río, que grande se va a la Mar.")

SCENE II

A motorcycle arrives upstage, a young man bringing LORENA home.

LORENA: Uyy, here at last!

THE YOUNG MAN: It took long enough.

LORENA: *(As he tries to seduce her.)* Come on, not here, take it easy …

THE YOUNG MAN: Ok, see you.

LORENA: You know, Leo, I really like you, ciao. *(He leaves.)* Waldo, are you there? … Waldy.

(WALDO lights a match on the riverbank. LORENA runs to him and sits at his side.)

LORENA: I had such a good time, Waldo. Such a handsome boy, and his eyes … I've arranged to call him; I hope something comes of it … Uy, it's freezing here.

WALDO: It's humid, not freezing …

LORENA: The night was so short, it's morning already. What are you thinking about?

WALDO: About … How's the little monkey? …

LORENA: He's not a monkey, he's my friend Chip. The stars are disappearing already. We're so small, imagine when the aliens land, what do you think they'll be like?

WALDO: They won't come. We have such bad energy that if we ever come into contact with them we'll destroy them.

LORENA: Liar! I'd love for a flying saucer to come and take me away, they must be wonderful.

(A moment of silence.)

LORENA: Remember the blackout? It was my first time, with tongue and all.

WALDO: It was Roly you wanted to do it with, we had you all primed …

LORENA: I can still feel the noises here.

SCENE III

The Night of the Protest

The noises called up by LORENA begin to invade the space, which transforms itself into a night of protest. Candles are lit, the noise of pots and pans being beaten gets louder, the sounds of helicopters and bullets inundate the night ... LORENA kisses a young man in silhouette. Upstage several young people run from the police and shots are heard. One of them falls, wounded. His friends pick him up and carry him off announcing:

CHORUS: They killed Roly! They killed Roly!

LORENA: And I thought Roly was kissing me, when it was you.

WALDO: He was late.

SCENE IV

THE WOMAN WHO OWNS THE KIOSK, Roly's mother.

THE WOMAN WHO: It's past midnight, Roly. You turn twenty-one today, fifteen on earth and seven in heaven. ... I won't bring toys to the cemetery anymore, but I bought you this musical card, so you can hear it. ... They didn't even send a letter. If only I'd have fixed the pickup truck, or used my savings to pay for a garage so that they wouldn't have destroyed your little head. ... I should have been there ... they would have listened to me. "Señor, don't shoot, señor. We'll pay you for fixing it, it's nothing personal." We're always throwing rocks here, whether it's to drive away the dogs at night, whether it's playing hit the bull's eye with the oil drums, of course, they say these pickup trucks are expensive and afterwards they're left damaged. That's life, some win, some lose. My son lost, that captain got a promotion. ... Roly, they killed my Roly!

LORENA: Sleep, Lorena, the river will carry you. Now I understand what it means to take care of sleep.

(MARCIA arrives plastered.)

MARCIA: I love him more than hell itself. What do I feel? Let's see, am I ugly? That's it, bitch, you're ugly. Or maybe I don't know how to kiss? That other one is ugly, she has cellulitis, and all those bastards line up for her. ... Do I smell bad? No, it must be my personality. I get fed up. I need to be cool, tranquil, relaxed, talk less. ... Make yourself two lists: on one everything good, on the other everything bad. Do something! I love him more than hell itself and the bastard gives me nothing ...

(CRISTIÁN talks to a sex chat line on the public telephone.)

CRISTIÁN: I'm Cristián, you? Yes, it's late. Me? 1 meter 75 tall, thin, 24, and you? ... I don't know, I've never measured myself. Top or bottom? If you wanna go that way ... depends with who ... OK ... I don't have one, only the public phone. OK, give it to me. Yes, I'll call you, ciao ...

SCENE V

THE BOY FROM THE RIVER – WALDO.

A boy appears in a school uniform, short pants, school bag full of mud and water.

BOY: What time is it? Where am I?

WALDO: Hey, what happened to you? This is not time to go swimming. Besides the beach here's no good.

BOY: I'd promised to do it and I did, but it looks like I slipped on the rocks.

WALDO: How many bridges did you pass?

BOY: I didn't count them, but where I began there were only rocks and willows, then I crossed gardens, buildings, highways and then I ran aground here.

WALDO: Are you in one piece? Let me look.

BOY: I thought it would taste like chocolate milk.

WALDO: Christ, are you stupid?

BOY: I wanted them to find me, the police. I wanted them to carry me off in the ambulance so my mother would worry about me, but it got dark and only you appeared.

WALDO: You're weird! Don't you have any consideration? I'd never make my mother suffer like that; she's already had it up to here. I want her happy, smiling, I want to buy her a house, take her traveling. You can do what you want to everyone else, they aren't worth shit, but not to your mother.

BOY: I want them to realize what they're missing; I want them to believe that I'm dead. I want to see her regretful, lying over the casket, and all my schoolmates, especially the ones who stole my pencils, having to carry me. And the church full of parents and tutors ... I can't go back now.

WALDO: I'm beginning to like you.

BOY: I don't have any friends. We met and you talked to me and I said to myself: whoever finds me is destined to do so; he'll be my true friend. Hi, I'm Raúl. How are you, my friend?

WALDO: Waldo, friend.

BOY: What's she doing here?

WALDO: She's dreaming. I'm stuck here in my place. People don't fish this river, they don't see the snow it brings or the sea it's going to be. Besides, I've known it since I was a kid. Here's where I first masturbated, that's where I got knifed, it's all crazy, all ...

BOY: It looks like I have to go back. I feel my mother's wails. Waldo, friend forever ... When you see a lot, you see the future and the future looks at you ...

WALDO: You just got heavy.

BOY: No, the future's right in front of you. This river, these stones, there where it turns, look at it. A hundred years from now whoever sits where you are Waldo will see the same thing, but you'll have already seen it.

SCENE VI

In the Building.

Shadow play behind the scrim from WILLY's apartment.

WILLY: You'd think I was just anybody. I had responsibilities, they gave me important operations. I carried out that undercover operation – what did they call it – Eagle Four, without a trace, two stars on the board ... That didn't come out in the papers. How do you think I bought you the washing machine? Stole it? Never, on my merits, my own merits. " *Yo tenía un compañero otro igual yo no tendré,*" etc.

WOMAN: Come to bed, Willy. I'm tired.

WILLY: The night ... You don't know how to enjoy the night ...

Second Sequence

SCENE I

Dawn.

LORENA: What a beautiful dream.

WALDO: You fell asleep.

LORENA: Chip was partying it up.

WALDO: Let's go.

SCENE II

Scene: The Wall.

Choreography of waking up. The scrim rises. Alarms sound in the building's apartments. The inhabitants get dressed, brush their teeth, THE WOMAN WHO OWNS THE KIOSK arrives, a woman and the inhabitant of the mysterious apartment leave …

LORENA: Waldo, do you know what I imagine each time
I hear the alarm clocks? I see everyone as if they were
in the video for "The Wall." Get it? "We don't need no
education" …

(The whole building does the choreography for "The Wall" by Pink Floyd. Then everything returns to normal.)

SCENE III

In EUGENIA's Apartment.

EUGENIA: *(Singing with a feather duster.)* "*Se va enredando,
enredando, como el muro la hiedra*" … (Violeta Parra). You
have to clean, Manuel! So that everything's in its place.
That way, if they come, they'll see that we are honest
people – "they treat you the way they see you." Did you
come from the river? They've been down there early,

snooping around, they say they pulled out a boy, in a uniform and everything ... I would have taken care of him ...

WALDO: Mama, wouldn't you like to have a friend? Instead of spending the whole day alone ...

EUGENIA: And if your father returns?

WALDO: Mama, he's not going to return.

EUGENIA: Who told you that nonsense? They're brainwashing you. How can you even think such a thing? They'd have notified me, by mail, from the court, by means of a legal medical document, by ...

WALDO: Mama, no one will ever notify you.

(EUGENIA goes out to sweep in front of the building.)

EUGENIA: "*Se va enredando, enredando, como en el muro la hiedra*" Manuel, do you remember when you took me to the Municipal and there he was singing "*Suena la sirena son cinco minutos y dónde está ... con él ... con él*" (Victor Jara). And the tears fell from my eyes and you said to me: "the compañera's turned cry baby on me." But no, that wasn't it. It was a premonition. "*Suena la sirena son cinco minutos ...* " And where are you Manuel ... Manuel! You saw that I wasn't a cry baby.

THE WOMAN WHO: Señora Eugenia, remember that you owe me for a quarter kilo of sugar, half a bottle of oil, and half a kilo of rice ... Oh, and Waldo asked for two sticks of gum, it's all written down.

SCENE IV

In LORENA's Apartment.

LORENA: Marcia, I met a great guy, he gave me his number and everything.

MARCIA: I did it with Dano!

LORENA: You did it!

MARCIA: Yes, girl.

LORENA: And what did you feel?

MARCIA: I don't know, I was too plastered.

LORENA: Maybe he was just small.

MARCIA: Dano? Shh, Lory, he split my lips open at the clit. I nearly died, girl, I nearly died.

LORENA: But then …

MARCIA: It was wonderful; I seem to have fallen in love. I see him all day long, I want him now, I want to kiss him all over, understand? I want to feel his smell … I fell in love.

LORENA: I don't understand you, Marcia. How can you be so crazy? You fall in love every time you go out. For me there'll only be one.

MARCIA: Look, Lorena, what I'm looking for is someone who'll treat me like a queen, understand? And if someone comes along who'll treat me better, I'll drop him. I want to have a great time for the rest of my life.

LORENA: Ay, Marcia, how can you be like that? I'm going to find someone who writes me poems that say: "Lorena, my flower, I will never let you wither, I will nurture you with the water of my love."

MARCIA: If you find him, let me know, I'll take him from you. I'd cut my wrists for Waldo, but the nut's so stuck.

LORENA: Marcia, hush, you're upsetting me. Don't you have anything to eat? I'm so hungry …

SCENE V

WILLY with the DRUG DEALER.

In WILLY's apartment. They play dominoes.

DRUG DEALER: Yes, Willyto. Things are hard …

WILLY: Not at all, you've just got to apply the same treatment to these delinquents as to the others. You saw the results. Nobody ever thinks about running around shouting and painting slogans now. It was harsh, but effective. I bet three.

DRUG DEALER: You were the good element, Willy.

WILLY: I always think of this one young brat, the one I had to send with Lalo. The woman gave herself to me, out of pure love. I wanted to save her but she was marked. I've never fucked better, I can't tell you the panic I felt upon finding myself in front of the mother, with the photo stuck right there. I won't give her to anyone.

DRUG DEALER: That's love, Willy. Pass.

WILLY: And you, with that faggot, the one you decided to get familiar with using the family-sized coke bottle, and then the neck broke? How the bastard howled. Christ, were we bastards! I bet five.

DRUG DEALER: Times past, Willy. Now you've got to work hard at business. Sales are down. And, you know, Willy, it's not all about making money. Part of it is about helping out brothers with problems. You, lawyers, rents are expensive … And here where you live you could do good business.

WILLY: You've come far, good instincts, a good nose, no problem. A little drink?

SCENE VI

Musical choreography, general movement throughout the building. The DRUG DEALER leaves, CRISTIÁN arrives, LORENA goes to make a phone call at the same time as THE WOMAN WHO OWNS THE KIOSK. EUGENIA comes out to sweep.

CRISTIÁN: Where are you going so fast?

LORENA: I'll tell you in a minute.

(Worrying, LORENA waits for THE WOMAN WHO OWNS THE KIOSK to finish her phone call.)

THE WOMAN WHO: How is everyone there? We're all well here, Juanito's good, grandmother still has her aches and pains … yes, well, the third age … and already in day care … how time flies … And how's Nelly? … that's great, I'm so happy … Yes, you have to be careful when you go out, of course, only carry the money you need. Yes, the worst is the documents, plus filling out all those forms ... yes ... and the time you lose ... And after all that you don't get it.

(While EUGENIA cleans THE NOUVEAU RICHE WOMAN arrives with packages. This scene parallels that between THE WOMAN WHO OWNS THE KIOSK and LORENA.)

EUGENIA: *(Singing.) "Juntemos todos las manos los negros sus manos negras, los blancos sus blancos manos"* *(Quilapayún)* ...

NOUVEAU RICHE WOMAN: New hairdo, things are going so well for Lucho, thank God. We just bought an apartment in Maipú; it's beautiful, with an intercom, a stupendous washing machine, completely equipped.

EUGENIA: Different from these blocks.

NOUVEAU RICHE WOMAN: Yes, a great difference. And how's everything here?

EUGENIA: Good, it seems.

NOUVEAU RICHE WOMAN: Everything's just the same, the line for the phone, the garbage, how amusing.

EUGENIA: Are you here to see your sister?

NOUVEAU RICHE WOMAN: Yes, I brought her an electric toaster. They're giving them away in the shops. Ciao, and, listen, that car, the red one, it's mine. Beautiful, isn't it? Go take a look at it ...

THE WOMAN WHO: Yes, I put the other one there, of course ... they got along so badly ... yes, well, children are harmed the most. The bell is ringing, Laura, hello to everyone, tomorrow ... yes ... yes ... Ay, we got cut off.

LORENA: Hello, could I please speak to Leonardo? Hi Leo, it's me, Lorena, hello, you know something? I woke up feeling so good because I dreamed about you and that made me want to see you. It was like we were at the beach ... Ah, a friend just arrived, well, could we ... You call me, let me know what time. ... At seven ... *(He hangs up.)* ... Kisses.

LORENA: *(Climbing the stairs, counting.)* He loves me, he loves me not, he loves me, he loves me not ...

SCENE VII

NOUVEAU RICHE WOMAN: My radio, they stole my radio! Resentful little ...

(In CRISTIÁN's apartment.)

WALDO: Here, take it, it's a gift.

CRISTIÁN: Why'd you get it?

WALDO: I was interested in the cassette, listen to it ...

Third Sequence

SCENES OF SATURDAY AFTERNOON

Brief sequences of music and action in each apartment: 1) THE WOMAN WHO OWNS THE KIOSK arranges herself in front of the mirror, bolero 2) MARCIA dances modeling in her apartment, samba 3) In CRISTIÁN's apartment he shows WALDO how they dance in the discotheques, Madonna 4) A Romantic Ballad plays in LORENA's apartment, she's lying across her bed.

As this survey concludes General Music plays throughout the building as each of them repeats a gesture: 1) THE WOMAN WHO OWNS THE KIOSK arranges her breasts and tugs at her skirt 2) EUGENIA cleans, then shakes out her dust cloth 3) MARCIA pulls on socks and does her hair 4) CRISTIÁN adjusts his pants 5) LORENA brushes her hair 6) In the mysterious apartment they dry themselves off with a towel and apply deodorant.

SCENE I

MARCIA: *(Calling to WALDO who is going towards the river from her apartment.)* Hi, Waldo! Remember we're going out … Don't forget!

WALDO: I'll be there …

DRUG DEALER: The chick likes you. Well, what do you say? You'll make good money, or would you prefer to work your ass off from seven in the morning until eight at night?

WALDO: If you say so.

DRUG DEALER: I don't say so, the facts say so. "The facts, baby. The facts."

WALDO: How much?

DRUG DEALER: What you'd earn in a month in one day. This is serious. "Big business." You understand English?

WALDO: A little bit.

DRUG DEALER: Look, Waldito, we're all friends here, coin talks, but if you play us false things change. We put too much confidence in one guy. All of a sudden he took off with a kilo. On top of that he became a snitch. Know what happened to him?

(Lights up on the mysterious apartment. A young man comes running and is grabbed.)

DRUG DEALER II: On the ground, you piece of shit.

(They shoot him in the forehead.)

DRUG DEALER: Here, just to get started ... You won't be sorry, "see you."

SCENE II

Photography Session.

CRISTIÁN's apartment. LORENA and MARCIA arrive.

CRISTIÁN: Hurry, look, a picture like that is where it's at.

LORENA: No, I can't, I'm embarrassed.

MARCIA: Ayy, what a picture, I love it. Take it, wrap yourself up ...

CRISTIÁN: That's it, a "look", hot and romantic.

MARCIA: One tit, nothing more ... *(She exposes one of her breasts, then LORENA does the same.)*

LORENA: Ayy, I'm so nervous, cover your eyes, Chip ... come on, hurry up ...

CRISTIÁN: That's it, with passion, now from the other side, such sensual chicks, now with your mouths open ...

MARCIA: We're artists, bitch!

LORENA: Listen, Cristián, don't you show these to anyone ...

(In the kiosk conversing with the DRUG DEALER.)

THE WOMAN WHO: It's gotten to the point where I can't even watch television. I get scared, so many maimed people, so much shock, so much disgraceful behavior. ... that's where we'll end up one day ...

SCENE III

WILLY's Apartment.

WILLY: How touchy you both are coming from that guy's apartment, the one who's running out of ears for his earrings.

MARCIA: Cristián? He's healthier than yogurt.

WILLY: That little bastard is weird.

MARCIA: Weird? How?

WILLY: That's what civilians lack, initiative. What do you want? Do I have to draw you a little picture or should I just give you orders? Stay here, quiet in the apartment.

MARCIA: But, papa, we're going out with some ... engineers. Tell him, Lorena.

LORENA: Yes ... from ... from ... the University.

MARCIA: Besides, I'll be with Lore ...

WILLY: All right, but make sure you stay in line.

SCENE IV

On the river banks.

WALDO: River, I don't know, but when I see you flowing down, slowly passing by, without a sound, as if you don't want them to see you, as if you want them to forget you're here. Christ, river, we're the same, I'm going to sit at your side, like two friends, you'll feel me next to you but I won't ask you anything. This is the best:

(CRISTIÁN takes his picture.)

WALDO: You're glued to that camera.

CRISTIÁN: And you to the river.

WALDO: Taking photos is a way to have everything, but only on paper, nothing more.

CRISTIÁN: I'd never thought of it like that. I used to come sit here too, to think about what to make of myself.

WALDO: Man, too much.

CRISTIÁN: I'd just learned how to look in people's eyes. I thought they'd realized, that they'd chase me. The worst was with my dad; I didn't want them to suffer.

WALDO: You took a lot on yourself.

CRISTIÁN: I thought that it would be better for me to be dead, you know? So there wouldn't be any scandal.

WALDO: You love what you love. You're neither queer nor macho; you're just a young man, nothing more.

CRISTIÁN: A young man? Well ...

SCENE V

The scrim that covers the set is lowered. MARCIA and LORENA arrive. Smoking a joint.

MARCIA: Here we are.

CRISTIÁN: No kidding?

MARCIA: What a great smell.

LORENA: Ay, I'm so nervous.

WALDO: Walk away.

CRISTIÁN: Uh-oh, Chip's getting pale.

MARCIA: I'm so stoned.

LORENA: I feel like straw floating on air.

CRISTIÁN: We're on the interplanetary ship, entering the magnetic zone.

WALDO: It's Tunik, the lost planet.

MARCIA: Let's return to base, let's return to base, "please" ...

LORENA: I'm receiving alpha signals. Pip ... pip ... Let's have a good time ... I don't know why, but I feel like ... Maria in *The Sound of Music!*

(The Sound of Music music, LORENA hits each of them with her teddy bear and they all get up stoned and sing 1) CRISTIÁN: "Do a deer" ... 2) MARCIA: "Re, a drop of " ... 3) WALDO: "Mi, a name" ... 4) LORENA: "Fa, a long," ... They dance the song from the banks of the River until they get upstage.)

SCENE VI

In the Discotheque.

They advance in a line from upstage, as if they were modeling in the street. When they reach the lip of the stage the music and lights change, indicating they are now in the discotheque. THE YOUNG MAN and THE YOUNG MAN-DISCO appear alongside them.

MARCIA: People are looking ...

LORENA: Let them look.

MARCIA: I'm going after Waldo tonight.

LORENA: Didn't you say you were in love with Dano?

MARCIA: That was yesterday, Lorena, don't get yourself stuck. Go on, hit on that one ...

(LORENA goes towards THE YOUNG MAN-DISCO. CRISTIÁN seduces THE YOUNG MAN.)

MARCIA: You've gotten so serious as you've gotten older, Waldo.

WALDO: I'm just coked up ...

MARCIA: Give me some then ... *(They snort.)*

(LORENA dances with THE YOUNG MAN-DISCO. MARCIA and WALDO move away. CRISTIÁN retires with the YOUNG MAN.)

YOUNG MAN-DISCO: I've got an incurable illness: progressive cirrhosis.

LORENA: I'm also condemned to death without a cure. I've got a tumor in my brain that grows everyday, it's insufferable.

YOUNG MAN-DISCO: Do you believe in reincarnation?

LORENA: Yes.

YOUNG MAN-DISCO: I too will be born again. I'm sorry, I can't hide it any longer, I love you.

LORENA: Why talk about love now?

YOUNG MAN-DISCO: Because love is life, and that's what we need.

(THE YOUNG MAN-DISCO disappears. LORENA realizes she's alone, leaves. The scrim rises exposing the building.)

Fourth Sequence

SCENE I

Saturday Night in the Building.

Parallel Loves.

WALDO-MARCIA.

MARCIA: I've gone crazy … Here's safe.

WALDO: Let's go to the river.

MARCIA: What for? Right here … Come on, put this on *(Passes him a condom. They remain in the building's stairwell.)*

CRISTIÁN – YOUNG MAN.

(In CRISTIÁN's apartment.)

YOUNG MAN: Your pictures are good. Artists are so sensitive. Do you want me to model for you?

CRISTIÁN: You're the one who offered.

YOUNG MAN: Well then, let me take off my shirt … .

(CRISTIÁN takes photos.)

YOUNG MAN: Christ, you're nice. *(Embraces him, they begin to caress each other sexually …)*

WILLY – WILLY'S WOMAN.

WOMAN: No, not that again! You're going to tie me up.

WILLY: What do you want me to do, look for someone out on the street? All couples have their …

WOMAN: Just not so tight.

WILLY: Shut up, you bitch. Now you'll see, you snitch. We'll give you what you like.

WOMAN: Willy, they'll hear us next door!

WILLY: That's what you like. Bitches.

(Throughout the building WALDO and MARCIA, CRISTIÁN and the YOUNG MAN, WILLY and the WOMAN all begin to make love at the same time. LORENA gets excited and masturbates. EUGENIA gets up to see what's happening at the sound of a collective orgasm.)

YOUNG MAN: You know what? I lost control. I don't want to have anything to do with this.

CRISTIÁN: We were having a good time.

YOUNG MAN: Not at all. You know what? If we run into each other out there stay away from me, OK? ... If I've seen you, I don't remember you. Get it?

CRISTIÁN: You wanted it.

YOUNG MAN: I don't understand, I don't recognize myself ... Know what? I'm taking these. *(He takes the roll of film from the camera ... runs down the stairs. CRISTIÁN spits at him on the street from his apartment.)*

LORENA: Dear Diary: I had such a good time with Cris, Waldo and Marcia. We got so stoned! The worst thing was when I was dancing, I was so carried away, his name was Pato and he told me: "wait for me, I'm going to the bathroom" and I waited right there for like an hour and then I saw him really into some other chick. Can you believe it, Diary! Ok, that's all, Chip.

Fifth Sequence

SCENE I

Sunday – Morning.

The young people are sleeping. EUGENIA gets up to the sound of leftist music. WILLY gets up as well, but in his apartment the radio plays the tonada "Chile, Chile lindo, lindo como un sol". EUGENIA sweeps in front of the building.

EUGENIA: *"De pie cantad que vamos a triunfar"* (*"El pueblo unido"* de Quilapayún.)

> *(Shifting gears.)* Manuel, it was like dancing, you were so happy, you said to me, let's do it again. I only had to look at you and I got all choked up. You took me by the hand so firmly and we shouted, laughing and we made the whole Alameda jump. You picked me up and everything was moving: "Whoever doesn't jump is on the right!" And that's when I realized, Manuel and I, we're going to get married. "Because it's not just about getting a new president this time, it's going to be" ...

> *(WILLY violently grabs her broom.)*

WILLY: Listen! You can stop singing; you're not so refined.

EUGENIA: No, I wasn't singing ... It was the radio, I'll turn it off. The kind of music they play these days, I like boleros.

WILLY: Calm down, baby, no more explanations. Show some respect, OK?

SCENE II

Cleaning the Building.

LORENA and CRISTIÁN with some rags.

CRISTIÁN: You know what? Today we're going to help her.

LORENA: Chip brought a little rag.

EUGENIA: Start with the windows I can't reach and in the corners where the spider webs form. But don't clean that door *(Indicating WILLY's door.)* let the earth cover it.

(THE EVANGELICALS enter singing while the others clean the building. At the head of the column are two evangelicals with guitars, a woman with a tambourine, and behind them WILLY and the DRUG DEALER.)

SONG: *"Alabado sea el creador, que nos guía y nos conduce por la senda del perdón."* *(repeat)*

DRUG DEALER: You're right, Willy. Christ loves us.

(The Building Dances. LORENA – CRISTIÁN – EUGENIA – and THE WOMAN WHO OWNS THE KIOSK all dance. MARCIA and WALDO watch from their apartments.)

LORENA: You're always singing. Look, learn this one.

SONG: (Rumba-Merengue) *"Mi negro bonito, mueve, múevelo despacito. Vamos, vamos a la playa Chica y baila con mi Corazon."*

EUGENIA: That's a pretty song, Lorena.

LORENA: Ayy, look at the time. He said he'd call now.

CRISTIÁN: Good luck, Lore.

WOMAN WHO: Don't forget about the three Belmont you owe me.

SCENE III

MARCIA – WALDO.

MARCIA: Waldo, what are you doing?

WALDO: Calm down. What's wrong?

MARCIA: Nothing, it's like I've got the plague, nothing ever works out for me. I believe everyone and it's always lies and here we go again. I gave myself to you and you don't pay me any attention, you don't even realize that I'm happy because I'm with you.

WALDO: Yes, I love you, Marcia. But I feel blurry; I watch everything that goes by, like the river. Get it? Flowing, always flowing ...

MARCIA: Well then, hook up with the River. Ciao, you're on your own.

(LORENA on the telephone.)

LORENA: Hello, is Leonardo there? ... Lorena ... Ah, well, have him call me when he's not busy.

SCENE IV

MARCIA – CRISTIÁN.

MARCIA: I'm so bummed. Throw the coins for me, tell me my fortune.

CRISTIÁN: But you have to do what they say.

MARCIA: You think I'm stupid?

CRISTIÁN: Not at all.

MARCIA: I understand you very well. I can't stand chicks, so if I were a man I'd be like you. My dad finds you unbearable, but I think it's because he's frustrated. Maybe he even wants you, you're all so mixed up ...

(CRISTIÁN reads the I Ching.)

CRISTIÁN: Crossing streams, step by step you will find the path from the swamp. Careful that the sound of the water doesn't chase the bird away, walk the path of the seas.

MARCIA: Ayy, that's just what's happening to me ... thanks.

LORENA: *(Counting off the steps on the staircase.)* He loves me, he loves me not. Do you think I'm fat?

CRISTIÁN: Lorena, you're divine, all the same, you could lose a few pounds.

MARCIA: She's padded. Look, I'm saying this as a friend; you need to take aerobics with me. Feel me here, go on, pure fiber.

LORENA: You think?

MARCIA: These days if you don't enter the competition you're lost.

LORENA: Oh, you're overdoing it … Ay, our song … "*Amigas, Amigas, que linda esa palabra suena hoy …* " ("*Amiga*" *de M. Bosé*).

(The three of them sit on CRISTIÁN's bed singing and choreographing the song.)

SCENE V

People come to buy cocaine from WALDO. He goes to the riverbank. WILLY enters.

WILLY: You can't sleep either.

WALDO: I sleep when I close my eyes.

WILLY: I got used to the nights. You had to stay alert, work. Now I feel them calling me, telling me we're going out on a mission, that I need to be ready. I'm left with my reflexes, like the dogs.

WALDO: Dogs don't make other dogs disappear.

WILLY: You were just a kid, you don't understand.

WALDO: Keep your distance, please.

WILLY: You were a hero, they put stars on the board, and now I have to hide. Was the pilot who dropped the atom bomb guilty? He wasn't anything more than an instrument, and the German soldiers, they're the fathers of all the Germans that exist today, and how do they carry themselves? Chests in the air … Sometimes I think it would have been better to be a prisoner, explain it all on TV.

WALDO: Do it on public television, very educational. Chapter One: how to rip off fingernails, … leave me alone.

WILLY: You don't understand a thing. Wait until you're in a war, the Argentines will cut off your ears …

WALDO: Ay, river, drown this land … *(Snorts cocaine.)*

Sixth Sequence

SCENE I

Doing Aerobics.

LORENA – MARCIA.

MARCIA: You have to lie to guys.

LORENA: What do you say?

MARCIA: That I live in Nuñoa ... that my dad's an engineer, I'm going to start at an Institute, whatever ...

LORENA: Marcia, that's cheating, how can you?

MARCIA: Do you think they tell you the truth?

LORENA: Yes ... or, no?

MARCIA: *(Applauding.)* Great class, it's great that you came.

(They exit.)

SCENE II

DRUG DEALER counting the bills he gives to WALDO.

DRUG DEALER: What did I tell you, huh? You've got a big smile on that dirty face of yours ...

WALDO: It's quite a lot ...

DRUG DEALER: We support the good elements. *(Gives him a package of cocaine and a pistol.)* This is for when they get heavy and tell you they'll pay you tomorrow. Get it?

WALDO: And if they pull one on me?

DRUG DEALER: Leave them with a couple of bullets. *(Hands him two bullets.)* But at their feet, nothing more, "Understand?" Or you're on your own.

SCENE III

Morning.

EUGENIA is cleaning and singing in her apartment. THE WOMAN WHO OWNS THE KIOSK enters.

EUGENIA: You look good today, Patty.

THE WOMAN WHO: Yes, that's what everybody tells me: You're still young, so graceful. Why don't you look for some company? And it's not like I haven't had any offers. But you've also got to see the other side, how easy it is to be single. No one asking you where you've been and not having to tell anyone what you've been doing. Suddenly I say to myself, of course, to go to the movies, but to go out you need some company, someone at your side.. But I also tell myself, if you can eat rice without salt, you can do without the other thing. Although, between us, Eugi, that's never been my problem. What a good man your Manuel was, what nonsense, no? So, I'll put you down for those noodles.

SCENE IV

Building Scene.

Presents.

WALDO downstage, shopping.

WALDO: Yes, the teddy bear, the biggest one, the calculator as well. And this, is it a good brand? Does it have a warranty? … You can send them. Yes, cash …

(Each person in their apartment opening their presents.)

LORENA: *(A Gigantic Teddy Bear.)*

MARCIA: *(An aerobics outfit.)*

CRISTIÁN: *(An automatic camera.)*

EUGENIA: *(A pot.)*

THE WOMAN WHO: *(A calculator.)*

(WALDO on the banks of the River.)

WALDO: River, I brought you a present, so you have some company ... *(A paper boat.)*

SCENE V

Spaghetti dinner

(Happy musical choreography throughout the building, all the characters come down, showing each other their presents. First, EUGENIA with her pot, everyone else follows. They serve themselves in THE WOMAN WHO OWNS THE KIOSK's kiosk. LORENA, MARCIA, CRISTIÁN eating spaghetti downstage. EUGENIA eats with THE WOMAN WHO OWNS THE KIOSK. WILLY eats a sandwich by himself in his apartment.)

LORENA: Have you seen Chip's little brother? Ayy, just the smell is driving me crazy ...

CRISTIÁN: Hungry, huh?

MARCIA: Lore, your diet, no more than five, count them now.

(WALDO enters.)

EUGENIA: My dear boy, I needed it a lot.

THE WOMAN WHO: Ay, Waldito, I'll never forget the kindness you've shown me.

MARCIA: Waldo, it's so cool, incredible ...

LORENA: You're so wonderful; Waldo, and you spent your whole salary ...

WALDO: Take it easy, it's no big deal, let's eat ...

EUGENIA: They're just like you taught me, Manuel, "al dente", with a little bit of Knorr's, enough water, yes, and a little bit of salt ...

(They eat in silence. Music, thought.)

CRISTIÁN: You outdid yourself with the camera. I asked my dad for one but he didn't pay me any attention. You've never told me anything about yours.

WALDO: My dad? I see it like it was in the movies. They take him away in a truck, put him up against a wall and he, erect, raises his fist and shouts, "we'll win" … and there he falls, but as if it were another country. I have trouble imagining it, here, against a cement wall, between rolls of toilet paper and mosquitoes biting your neck, I don't know, I told you I see as if it were in the movies …

CRISTIÁN: That's powerful, …

LORENA: Boys, I'm so happy, I feel like Tinkerbell. *(Music of Tinkerbell's flight. LORENA starts dancing, the others laugh.)*

MARCIA: Wow … Ay, Lorena, it was a joke.

SCENE VI

MARCIA's Apartment.

WILLY: I warned you not to get mixed up with that one, or do you want to give me degenerate grandchildren …

MARCIA: That's got nothing to do with it.

WILLY: Nothing to do with it. Do you know how they straighten out a tree? *(Hits MARCIA.)*

(The DRUG DEALER enters.)

WILLY: She's a good girl, a bit obsessed with a loser … but you'll see. My dear, come here, I want you to meet a young man.

DRUG DEALER: How are you? It's a pleasure.

MARCIA: Very well.

WILLY: He's a friend's son. Excuse me.

(EUGENIA spies on WALDO as he cuts up paper to make packets to distribute grams of cocaine.)

EUGENIA: You're nervous, Waldo. What are all these little pieces of paper for?

WALDO: Nothing, mom. It's for the guy upstairs, click click … Art … art.

DRUG DEALER: I've badly wanted to meet you. I've seen your pictures, and your father has told me a lot about you …

MARCIA: Pure lies.

DRUG DEALER: No, I think it's all true. I'm very perceptive, I feel what people are like inside. I tend to spend a lot of time alone, very few people entertain me, attract me, let's say, and when I find myself in front of someone like you, how should I put it? If you'll permit me. ... when I tell you that I'm not wrong, I know that we could be good friends.

MARCIA: I'm very sociable.

DRUG DEALER: Let me tell it to you straight, I was immediately attracted to you, and I'd like to demonstrate that to you, without any commitment ... I'm a simple man. Do you like to go to the movies?

MARCIA: Who doesn't?

DRUG DEALER: How's tomorrow? I'll come pick you up.

MARCIA: No, better if we meet each other, at the entrance to the Rex.

DRUG DEALER: At the Rex at 7 p.m. on the dot.

SCENE VII

Staircase and MARCIA's Apartment

LORENA sees MARCIA with the DRUG DEALER.

LORENA: You know you're my friend, that's why I'm telling you ... he's bad news; I don't want to talk shit ...

MARCIA: You fat thing, you're telling me what to do? Go back to your own place ... do you think I want to find myself parked like you playing with stuffed animals? Are you crazy or what?

LORENA: You do it in bathrooms with guys at parties and you're doing the same thing with Waldo.

MARCIA: Enjoy it, flabby. Tomorrow you die and what will you have tried? Enjoy it while you've got it, besides, there's never ... What do you know!

LORENA: You think I'm stupid, but I'm afraid I've lost you.

MARCIA: Listen; you know what your problem is? You're jealous. You like chicks.

(LORENA launches herself on top of MARCIA, they fight.)

MARCIA: Let go of me, you're crazy … get out of here, don't talk to me again . . . Boring blimp.

(LORENA runs up the stairs, MARCIA follows her.)

MARCIA: Lori, let's not fight. Damnit, you know how much I love you …

(Music. "Amigas" by Miguel Bosé.)

SCENE VIII

The Assault on THE NOUVEAU RICHE WOMAN.

WILLY: Señora, I'll help you, if you'll allow me …

NOUVEAU RICHE WOMAN: *(Scared.)* Ayy, don't worry, it's light as a feather, some clothes, nothing more, for Laura, Don Willy, you're always such a gentleman.

WILLY: Good manners, señora, good manners.

NOUVEAU RICHE WOMAN: My taxi will be here in a minute. This way nothing can happen to my car. Bye-bye.

(The assailant drags her by her handbag, rips it from her and takes refuge in LORENA's apartment.)

SCENE IX

CRISTIÁN with THE PIMP.

In the second floor hall.

THE PIMP: I know what you like, but first, give me something for my mind.

CRISTIÁN: I don't have anything.

THE PIMP: You had me come all the way here for …

CRISTIÁN: I don't know, you followed me.

THE PIMP: Are you new to this or what? Come up with something, go buy a little bottle.

CRISTIÁN: You know I don't have one.

THE PIMP: Shhh, now you tell me. Hand me the camera, then.

(THE PIMP runs off with the automatic camera. CRISTIÁN takes out a slingshot ... hits him offstage. WALDO and CRISTIÁN run after him, they return with the camera.)

SCENE X

ASSAILANT: Calm down, tubby, this is for you. *(Gives her a necklace.)* This is for me. *(Takes the purse.)* Shh ... goodbye.

SCENE XI

At the Entrance to the Building.

MARCIA: What a great movie.

DRUG DEALER: You liked it? It was a bit violent.

MARCIA: I like it rough, if it weren't I'd become a nun ...

SCENE XII

LORENA: Dear Diary: I was scared, but then I felt like I was protecting Robin Hood or Zorro. He was so handsome ...

SCENE XIII

THE WOMAN WHO OWNS THE KIOSK and WILLY.

THE WOMAN WHO: How happy you must be, Don Willy! No?

WILLY: Yes, not everything can be bitter, señora Patty.

THE WOMAN WHO: It seems like it was just yesterday that Marcia was dipping Oreos in milk.

WILLY: She was a handful, but now she's going to have to learn.

THE WOMAN WHO: Her fiancé's handsome, well built, you can tell he's a worker. How lucky for Marcia! Above all now, when people are like they are.

WILLY: That's what I tell myself.

THE WOMAN WHO: I can see her all in white, going into the church and then my view gets cloudy. *(Crying.)* Forgive me.

WILLY: Well, that's the cycle of existence, señora Patty.

THE WOMAN WHO: Yes, it's clear in your mind, Don Willy, but the heart is something else. I should cross her off then?

WILLY: Affirmative.

SCENE XIV

MARCIA's Farewell.

LORENA: Chip and I are sad.

MARCIA: Don't worry, silly, I'll be back.

LORENA: It won't be the same.

MARCIA: Friends through good and bad. What do you want me to do? Hang around here begging Waldo to notice me, or keep going out with Dano who barely has enough for candied peanuts?

LORENA: Does he love you?

MARCIA: He keeps me like a queen, buys me everything, is super respectful, treats me like a lady.

CRISTIÁN: Some photos for you to put up in your place.

WALDO: Listen, all the best, a little stone … the river sent it for you.

MARCIA: Yaaa, you're going to me cry …

(They're going to embrace but the DRUG DEALER appears. He takes MARCIA's suitcase and she gives her final goodbye.)

MARCIA: Ciao, you bastards.

Seventh Sequence

SCENE I

Depressed Building.

In EUGENIA's Apartment.

EUGENIA: Waldo, why won't you look at me? … You don't clean your plates anymore … so many possibilities come to mind.

WALDO: Calm down, I know you well; you're going to lose it.

EUGENIA: No, I wasn't going to sing. You're going to go, I know it, that's the way it has to be, but it's not that … you're scuttling around like the mice, scared, going out secretly. Perhaps Manuel …

WALDO: Leave Manuel alone for once, ok?

EUGENIA: Is this you?

WALDO: It's me, me, who else? Know what? You make me exhausted, crazy, get it? Crazy … Understand? Well, you're going to understand … I'm fucked.

EUGENIA: Ears, these ears aren't mine, these words aren't yours … someone's changing things.

WALDO: Things change by themselves; all you have to do is understand them. Ciao …

EUGENIA: I don't have a belt, Waldo, my voice isn't threatening, I wear skirts. You've got a pistol in your room. Why, Waldo?

WALDO: They're watching me. I'll tell you once: do your own thing, nothing more, OK?

(EUGENIA tries to stop him when he leaves, WALDO pushes her – EUGENIA sings: "Yo pisaré las calles nuevamente … " (Pablo Milanes)

WALDO's Rage Machineguns the Building.

(WALDO runs to the front of the stage, lets out a scream, the sound of a machinegun, all the inhabitants fall down dead.)

SCENE II

DRUG DEALER: Take off my shoes.

MARCIA: I'm not your maid.

DRUG DEALER: You didn't hear me *(Pointing at her.)* ... get my shoes ... you know what I like.

MARCIA: Not me.

DRUG DEALER: Don't make me repeat myself, it wears me out ... you do it on purpose. *(Violently hits her.)* You little bitch, that's what happens when you drive me crazy, see, your nipples are hard.

(Music revives the characters.)

SCENE III

The Rape of LORENA,

YOUNG MAN: Hey, you, girl ...

LORENA: I'm in a hurry ...

YOUNG MAN: Hold up, I just want to ask you something, nothing more, are you scared?

LORENA: No, it's just that ...

YOUNG MAN: Have you seen that nut, I don't remember his name; he wears a black cap, like this, with a silver band ...

LORENA: Waldo, he went to the river.

YOUNG MAN: Hard to get there. Listen, where you going? Let's take a walk.

LORENA: He's handsome, but he wants to trick me, don't put up with it, Lorena ... Let's talk for a bit.

YOUNG MAN: Puh, what are you doing? ...

LORENA: Yes, but keep it down ...

YOUNG MAN: You have beautiful eyes …

LORENA: You think so?

YOUNG MAN: I've never done it with a fat one before.

LORENA: I better go …

YOUNG MAN: Feel it, you feel it? Big and hard, why don't we take a look? We're going to have a lot of fun.

LORENA: Hey, let me go. *(She becomes paralyzed.)*

(He hits her with a rock, rapes her. Flashback – raped by her father.)

FATHER: Lorenita, are you sleeping? *(Father in LORENA's apartment.)*

LORENA: No, papi.

FATHER: Calm down, you'll wake them up, my dear.

LORENA: I don't want to do it again, papi, it hurts me, no papi, no!

YOUNG MAN: I'm not your father, you nut. Shh, take advantage of this … this is much better than doing it with those potheads you run around with …

(LORENA is left lying on the ground. She cries.)

Young Man – Waldo

(On the riverbank – Night.)

YOUNG MAN: There you are, Waldo, here's two.

WALDO: This goes for twelve.

YOUNG MAN: You've gone up, shh.

WALDO: You're sweating.

YOUNG MAN: Forget it, my chick always makes me crazy … I left her there in the jeep, she's going to want more, come on.

LORENA – CRISTIÁN

LORENA: Cristián, Cristián …

CRISTIÁN: What happened, Lori?

LORENA: Grab him, get him, he, he …

CRISTIÁN: No, it can't be, I swear that from now on I'll take care of you, girl ... I'll kill him ... I'll kill him ...

LORENA: I'm going to make all the stones in this river shine; perhaps it will be a magic spell ... and when a fairy appears and says to me: "Lorena, make a wish, I'll say, little fairy ... " *(She cries.)*

SCENE IV

WALDO's Robbed.

The three of them in bed. In the mysterious apartment.

GIRL: I don't want anymore. I'm spent.

WALDO: Leave her alone, man, I told you already, if you want I'll do it for you, but calm down, can't you see she wants to sleep ...

YOUNG MAN: I'm going someplace better. Didn't I tell you it was going to be fearsome?

GIRL: Yes, but that was yesterday ... Don't leave your number and don't dare call me. OK.

YOUNG MAN: Filthy ... ! *(Grabs WALDO's jacket and leaves.)*

WALDO: My jacket!

SCENE V

In EUGENIA's Apartment.

EUGENIA: "*Que dirá el santo Padre que vive en Roma ...* "
Manuel, they're going to build a park there in the garbage dump, on the riverbanks, remember what you always said: "You could fix this neighborhood with a park." ... There will be native trees like in Collipulli: Myrtles, Araucarias, Hawthorns, Laurels, Cinnamon, a Chilean park.

(LORENA talking on the public telephone.)

LORENA: Hello, Marcia. How are you? It's been so long, why don't we get together? Why do you always hang up? ... You can't stop talking on the phone!

Eighth Sequence

SCENE I

WALDO and the Threat.

DRUG DEALER: You know what happened to that guy.

WALDO: So kill me, who cares? What's the difference? It's for the best. They say things happen for a reason, it'll be a change. It's just what you're used to, get it? I'm used to these hands, to my voice, to eating, I'll have to get used to something else, that's all. Kill me; I'll tell you something, I'm more afraid of pain than death.

DRUG DEALER: So brave, you want to be a man, first make those grams appear, then we'll do you the favor!

WALDO: I don't have them.

DRUG DEALER: Didn't you hear me? Make them appear tomorrow, you hear? You've got beautiful eyes, some advice: take care of them.

SCENE II

In EUGENIA's Apartment.

EUGENIA: Manuel, where shall we go on vacation this year? Yes, after the volunteer work. Quintero's gotten very ugly, what do you think about going north? Sheep's cheese, figs, maybe Waldo would like the beach. Another cup of coffee? ...

SCENE III

WILLY's Apartment – DRUG DEALER.

(DRUG DEALER II waits in the hall.)

WILLY: You know how it is, Jaime, don't let your hand tremble. This is business, that's all, this bastard: a lost cause.

DRUG DEALER: That's clear, I respect seniority, that's all, Willy.

SCENE IV

MARCIA Arrives with Her Foot in a Cast.

CRISTIÁN: What happened to you, Marcia?

MARCIA: Nothing, I'm in a big hurry. Warn Waldo that Jaime's looking for him. Lori, it's very serious, ciao and don't call me …

(LORENA goes towards the building, CRISTIÁN runs offstage. WALDO enters quickly, gets to the entrance to the building when THE WOMAN WHO OWNS THE KIOSK calls to him.)

THE WOMAN WHO: Waldo, psstt, Waldito, they're looking for you, they're there, between the branches, sometimes they stand beneath the overpass, you know, I don't want anything to happen to you, hide yourself for a while.

WALDO: Where do you want me to go? I was born here, not in China.

(The DRUG DEALER and DRUG DEALER II follow LORENA up the stairs. WALDO hides in the Kiosk.)

SCENE VI

Interrogations.

LORENA – DRUG DEALER – DRUG DEALER II.

LORENA's apartment.

DRUG DEALER: We've got you, tubby, give it up, now.

LORENA: I don't know what you're talking about.

DRUG DEALER: Where's your little friend, you know what I mean.

LORENA: Don't touch Chip.

DRUG DEALER II: That must be where it's hidden, let's open him up.

LORENA: Hit me but don't do anything to Chip.

DRUG DEALER: You've got till three. ... One, Two, Three.
(They tear the stuffed animal apart.)

Persecution.

> *(Scene of music and violence. They run through the building, searching each apartment. WILLY gives instructions on his cell phone. They frighten EUGENIA. WALDO runs towards the river. Pistols unholstered, shouts, gestures, they get to the kiosk, they attack THE WOMAN WHO OWNS THE KIOSK, CRISTIÁN arrives, two of them grab him, they drag him along, aim at him.)*

DRUG DEALER – CRISTIÁN

DRUG DEALER: Quickly, now. Where's Waldo hiding?

CRISTIÁN: In his house.

DRUG DEALER: Look, man, do you know what we do to rice burners like you?

CRISTIÁN: I don't understand.

DRUG DEALER: You're the neighborhood faggot!

CRISTIÁN: No, I'm just a young man.

> *(They beat him. The drug dealers exit, running.)*

Ninth Sequence

SCENE I

WALDO's Assassination.

A moment of silence. WALDO runs along the riverbank, then he stops.

WALDO: I've got to take a new tack, new directions, other branches. You know what I mean, river, it costs you the same to make your way as it does to stake your claim, your territory, and get them to leave you alone, calm, you've beaten them all ... we'll see each other again ... "Downstream."

(DRUG DEALER and DRUG DEALER II enter behind him.)

DRUG DEALER: Waldo Salinas!

(WALDO falls, the shots alarm EUGENIA, CRISTIÁN and LORENA run towards the third floor hall.)

SCENE II

CRISTIÁN: They didn't catch him, Lori, he got away, Waldo's safe.

LORENA: Yes, he's safe.

SCENE III

They arrive to tell of WALDO's death.

EUGENIA: Don't tell me, where's that trickster hiding, come in, some coffee, you've brought me a letter, something official ... I knew you'd come ...

DETECTIVE: Does Waldo Salinas live here?

EUGENIA: Waldo is really Eduardo, when he was a little boy he couldn't say Eduardo so he said Waldo.

DETECTIVE: You will have to go down and ...

EUGENIA: No, don't say anything, don't you dare say it, get out ... get out ... Eduardo will be back at ten.

DETECTIVE: Señora, let me explain.

EUGENIA: I've already told you, you're not listening to me, this is my house, I clean this building ... and everything is all right ... Get out ...

(The DETECTIVE leaves. EUGENIA takes WALDO's jacket and cries into it, then she goes to the bathroom, she combs her hair and, for the first time, takes off her apron, straightens a few things, picks up her broom and goes downstairs. At the same time WILLY prepares to go out ...)

SCENE IV

EUGENIA sweeps with rage in front of the building, WILLY sees her and is about to go, but returns.

WILLY: If you had any brains you wouldn't ... Cretin!

EUGENIA: Señor Asenjo, Señor Asenjo *(Takes a revolver from her dress and points it at him.)* You realized I turned off the radio, your eyes are crying like mine, it must be the humidity. The climate is changing, they said so yesterday, the earth is warming, your eyes perspire, now, your pores can't cope ... it's the water, they say, it's full of substances, that's why we're saltier each day ... *(She licks her hand.)* ... Señor Asenjo, there isn't any more fresh water, they can't do baptisms, it's in the rain, no more clear puddles. You used to be able to see snow here, remember, when you had work and could smile. *(WILLY tries to take the pistol from her, EUGENIA fires.)*

EUGENIA: I promised you, Manuel, no other man would ever put his hands on me ... Take me to him, now I know everything ... now I know it all ... I'm happy ... Am I happy?

(THE BOY FROM THE RIVER appears, goes towards WALDO.)

BOY: Friend Waldo, it's me, Raúl.

(LORENA in her apartment, with her diary and a pencil.)

LORENA: Dear Diary, I don't want to write today. *(She breaks the pencil.)*

(EUGENIA drops the pistol center stage. THE BOY FROM THE RIVER next to WALDO's body — CRISTIÁN flung across his bed — LORENA grasping the broken pencil …)

THE END

ECSTASY OR STEPS TO SAINTHOOD

Characters

ANDRÉS
Passion

ESTEBAN
Friend

GRANDMOTHER
Memory

MARÍA
Desire

VIVALDI
The Canary

ASSAILANT – LADY – PRIEST – ANGEL –
THE CAPTAIN – MANUEL – SHE – MAN – 1ST
TESTIMONIAL – 2ND TESTIMONIAL – DOCTOR
SANTOS – MOTHER – THE CLIENT

Sequence One—Teachings

SCENE I

At the Movies.

ANDRÉS – ESTEBAN.

Leaning against the wall at the back of the theatre, ESTEBAN chews a lozenge, snatches of "The Last Days of Pompeii", or something similar, can be heard from offstage.

ESTEBAN: Not this again, Andrés. We've already seen it.

ANDRÉS: You never finish seeing them, Esteban.

ESTEBAN: Did you see? … She turned around, she wants me, let's go sit down.

ANDRÉS: We're good here. When I see how they go to martyrdom, so sure of getting the holy palm leaf, so happy … My only desire is to have been there with them, look how their faces glow… .

ESTEBAN: Take something for your nerves, here's a mint… .

ANDRÉS: There are still Romans, Esteban, there still are… .
(ANDRÉS tears at his chest, lion claws mark his skin.)

SCENE II

From the window of their apartment on the sixth floor.

GRANDMOTHER – MARÍA – VIVALDI THE CANARY.

GRANDMOTHER, holding up VIVALDI's cage, scrutinizes the movements in the other apartments. The canary sings.

GRANDMOTHER: Yes, Vivaldi, yes, but what are we going to do? We don't have any other scenery than the people across the way. Come on, sing, sing to your little old lady … There she is, María, that anorexic one, who spends all day in her pajamas …

MARÍA: Could she be sick? I'm just asking ...

GRANDMOTHER: Sick from laziness, with the brute she has to maintain her. María, come here, look, there he is, that brat is playing with himself in the bathtub again.

MARÍA: Maybe he's scratching, he put out the light ...

GRANDMOTHER: Did you gather the branches ... You have to interlace them to make the crown, make sure the little piece of cloth isn't too stiff; it has to be a little bit wrinkled. Haven't you seen how it looks on the cross? There comes that hypocrite, he's arrived in a taxi for a week now...

MARÍA: He must be making more now ...

GRANDMOTHER: He'll have turned to robbery ... drugs ... who knows what. Let's see, a little bit wrinkled I told you; they've got to be real. Isn't that right, Vivaldi? Come on; let's go pray to Julia.

SCENE III

The Show.

ANDRÉS – MARÍA – ESTEBAN.

ANDRÉS, nude torso, makes up his wounds in front of the mirror.)

ANDRÉS: You know I didn't ask for this, it was Esteban's idea. Besides, what we earn from tickets will go to help the poor in the parish ... I know that I'll never be able to equal your passion, and that it would be vain to think that I could look like you, but enlighten me, if the wounds and the nails are false, at least my soul can feel this immense pain of suffering for love ...

MARÍA: The cloth is from an old sheet and I made the other with nothing but branches, I couldn't find any rosebushes in the plaza ... I wish I could go see it ...

ESTEBAN: Here, let me put on lots of lacquer so the curls don't slip ...

The Performance.

(He puts on the wig and the crown. Covers himself with the mantle, plays Christ arriving to Jerusalem on an ass. Music from "Jesus Christ Superstar", Hosanna. In the back, Christians with palm leaves celebrate him. ANDRÉS tears off his costume, interrupting the show.)

ANDRÉS: Esteban … Esteban … take the belt and whip me, I need to really feel it …

ESTEBAN: There's only one person who can take off my belt, come on, relax …

ANDRÉS: No, I can't disguise myself like this. You know, I've always been different, while others read *Little Lulu*, I liked the illustrated lives; instead of collecting photos of soccer players to fill albums with I gathered prints of the saints …

ESTEBAN: I feel different too, but I also want to be like everyone else: when I see someone on a motorcycle, I want his bike. When I go to a friend's house, I want his house. I even believe that others make love better than I do. When I'm with someone I want to be with the girl he's got … It's like everything I want to live is being lived by others …

ANDRÉS: Esteban, I know why I'm on this earth and what my existence means, but I have to pass earthly trials, which aren't these …

SCENE IV

GRANDMOTHER – MARÍA.

GRANDMOTHER: This shirt is ready to be thrown out. Nobody believed the little shepherd girl – she took her two little brothers to the grotto and told them the mother of God will appear over there …

MARÍA: Of course, no one believed her because she was poor …

GRANDMOTHER: She went and told her mother that an incredibly beautiful woman dressed in celestial blue asked her to have them build her a church there, but her mother, who was a peasant ... Look, there she is again, the lazy cow is still in bed. Enough, go to bed, it's late ...

(ANDRÉS. Night, wrapped in a sheet.)

ANDRÉS: I pull on the sheets, I grasp them firmly, I sweat, I don't want the souls in pain drawn from her to come throw off my sheets, I urinate and I can't get up because there are vipers nesting beneath my mattress, I can't look out the window because I see an old man banging on the glass, and I don't know who he is, I don't dare open my eyes even though I can't sleep, because there are silhouettes between the slats of the blinds.

(A memory. Rain, thunder. The GRANDMOTHER behind the window, ANDRÉS downstage.)

GRANDMOTHER: You're sleeping, child, it's raining and when the water falls it's because the saints are urinating.

ANDRÉS: Grandmother, you're awake ...

GRANDMOTHER: I don't like your parents' house, I want to go ... I want them to come look for me ...

ANDRÉS: Go to bed, Grandmother ...

GRANDMOTHER: I'm not going to sleep; I want death to catch me with my eyes open. It's time for the end of the world, time for the final judgment. Why continue? Sleep, child, sleep; don't listen to this crazy old lady ... Your mother's crying, she's being beaten again ...

ANDRÉS: Why does she let him? I want to go defend her.

GRANDMOTHER: Leave her alone; she's paying for her sin. The devil tempted them and she gave herself before marriage. Flesh, desire, and that's how you were born, outside of wedlock. This house is cursed; you can see it in your father's eyes. That's why I don't like to come; they're paying for their faults here. Tomorrow I'll begin a vow of poverty so that peace will come to this house, I won't eat anything other than hazelnuts and I'll only shower once a week, for three months that will be my offering to Saint

Lucy. You've got to offer something, I'll offer poverty.
Sleep, Andrés, sleep, dream with the angels...

(ANDRÉS' dream. An angel with metallic wings and phosphorescent eyes, carrying a bloody shroud. Canticles.)

ANGEL: She didn't stop singing the Lord's praises even when she was drawn and quartered by him.

ANDRÉS: Trees bend over and the clay springs from the earth ...

ANGEL: Close your eyes so the light doesn't blind you.

ANDRÉS: They tighten her crown and the saints and the angels receive her ... It's my mother, he killed her, he killed her.

ANGEL: Be happy, be happy, Andrés ...

MOTHER: They've kidnapped my child! They've kidnapped my child!

GRANDMOTHER: Your mother keeps having that nightmare. You've got to beat the whites well, put in lots of salt, and let your hands soak for half an hour, it's the only remedy for arthritis, Laura's gotten very good results ...

MOTHER: My child! My child!

GRANDMOTHER: Her religious vow lasted three years, from the day of the kidnapping she decided to dress up like Lourdes.

ANDRÉS: That's what it was for.

GRANDMOTHER: Yes, she suffered a lot, you should have seen how they filled the house, the number of journalists at the gate, it came out in all the papers, she was younger, yes. I was always suspicious of Manuel, you only had to look at the way he raised his eyebrows ...

(Through the window a memory dream.)

MOTHER: *(With a cake and candles, gives ANDRÉS a present.)*

ANDRÉS: *(Blowing out the candles.)* Lord, show me the path of humility and sacrifice. I won't eat any cake, mama, give it to the poor.

GRANDMOTHER: They'd put together a party and he planed wood.

(MANUEL planes.)

(MANUEL enters with a radio on his shoulder, listens to a soccer game, begins to plane, ANDRÉS enters with his mother's present.)

ANDRÉS: You've got strong legs.

MANUEL: Well, I play soccer.

ANDRÉS: Don't you get bored?

MANUEL: No, I use the time to think, Friday's coming and I'll go out for a beer, about what could happen tomorrow, I have to wash my soccer jersey, about finding someone for my bed … I think, I'm fine.

ANDRÉS: I think too, and I read, I try to be good like them. It amuses me to see how wood becomes clean again, how you shave away the grime, as if you were trying to make it pure again … I think about how I could plane my soul, make it shine like a diamond …

MANUEL: I find the black floors and then I go and leave them like new, that's what I like.

ANDRÉS: My skin could be wood; it would be enough for you to rub the plane on my chest or my face. Would you do it?

MANUEL: You've got a lot of imagination; you better go do your homework …

ANDRÉS: Your leg is like a lion's without down, look at my chest, Manuel, it's white … but unlike the floors, the wax of the years builds up below, the grime sticks to it, spit, vomit, drops of wine, come on, shave it …

MANUEL: You awaken bad instincts in me … I don't know, my head's boiling, I feel the same way I felt when I was fifteen and we trapped this little girl who wore a mini skirt, we took her to the field and the three of us burst her … I didn't want to, but the fever took over, I squeezed her wrists hard and I bit her lip … She shivered, but quietly …

ANDRÉS: Did she forgive you?

MANUEL: I was the only one she didn't denounce … Now I like to bite lips and squeeze wrists …

ANDRÉS: Hands turn blue and pain releases your saliva.

MANUEL: And then I get big and I hurt them...

ANDRÉS: It seems like you have to suffer to feel pleasure ...

MANUEL: Well, I'm going to go now ... I've got an hour's worth of travel ...

ANDRÉS: I'll go with you; I want to see your house, your furniture ...

GRANDMOTHER: They gave him three years, three.

ANDRÉS: He left me in my underwear, up against the wall, hands open, he squeezed my wrists, his eyes shone ... Then he began to shave my pubic hair.

GRANDMOTHER: The telephone rang and rang, I told your mother: "Manuel's taken him."

ANDRÉS: But when I was up against the wall and he began to nail me six pins in the shape of the cross, I could make out an illustration of the Last Supper on the wall, and while he bit my testicles I thought he was a pagan lion, and I discovered that my purpose in life was to be a martyr ... I'd already offered up my life when I sensed the sirens, the beating at the door and my mother's screams.

GRANDMOTHER: I went too, but I stayed in the car ...

ANDRÉS: I felt greatly deceived. That interruption frustrated my path to eternal glory.

GRANDMOTHER: Sleep, Andrés, and don't forget about your mother, may she rest in peace.

ANDRÉS: From that day on my only desire was to come face to face with some pagan who craved my martyrdom. I asked my friends to spray me with paraffin like they did with cats so that the fire would transform this carcass into carbon that only yearns to complete its mission.

Sequence Two—Kindnesses

SCENE I

In the Church.

THE PRIEST – ANDRÉS – LADY – ESTEBAN.

Church chandeliers lower and a stained glass window appears above the rectangle below, the PRIEST enters singing "My people, why have you offended me", then ANDRÉS enters and joins in the song.

PRIEST: You sing better every day, Andrés, it's a heavenly gift, the Lord spoke to us by means of the word, your vocal chords together with your heart are the most sacred parts of the body, without celestial choirs could we even imagine heaven? No, Andrés ... Song is what guided me to my vocation, and I said to myself I would become a priest. I believe that I reach divine ecstasy in those same cantatas ... *(He jerks ANDRÉS off.)*

ANDRÉS: Squeeze it harder.

PRIEST: Don't try to destroy these urges, just conquer them.

ANDRÉS: We've been carrying out this exorcism for more than six months and I still don't feel purified.

PRIEST: The claws of filth and ignominy are very strong, Andrés, come on, commit yourself ...

ANDRÉS: Here I am before you, waiting for you to appear one day as you have done with so many others ... Lord, consoling the afflicted and those who suffer will I begin the path to holiness ...

(A LADY carrying packages enters. ANDRÉS goes to console her.)

LADY: *(Picking up her handbag.)* I don't have any coins.

ANDRÉS: I wasn't going to ask you for any ...

LADY: Go on; go on, this church is quite large so if you're not here to beg, you want another sort of thing ...

ANDRÉS: I only want to console you.

LADY: Console me? What group are you from?

ANDRÉS: None, I'd like to share your pain and combine our prayers ...

LADY: I come here all the time, after going shopping my feet swell up and I can rest here and make a few requests, it's a habit of mine ... You must be pretty bored.

ANDRÉS: No.

LADY: Look, I don't pray, I converse with the Lord, sometimes with Saint Anne, or Saint Gemma, depending upon what it's about, I chat with them and entrust myself to them ...

ANDRÉS: And they answer you?

LADY: If they answer me they wouldn't do it here, they'd do it over there, above one of these altars.

ANDRÉS: I talk to them too, but I want an answer.

LADY: Answers appear by themselves. I asked Saint Francis to get Nelly settled so much, her time was passing, and I didn't know how I was going to take care of her, and within the year she got married, but the idiot husband is a woman-chaser and the girl comes crying to me, I want her to leave him, but you can't ask for that, it's anti-Christian, if it were up to me I'd ask for them to take him away if he's so wicked, but you can't ask for that either, it'll backfire on you. So I prayed that he'd fall in love with someone else and leave, but that he'd leave Nelly with a pension so she could take care of herself ... The hard part is that Nelly seems to be expecting, the idiot doesn't tell me anything and that complicates things, because you can't pray for the child to be taken by the angels, but if Lucho falls in love with someone else and leaves Nelly all alone with a child ... Then everything's all the more complicated. I was going to do three penances: give up coffee, stop knitting, something I like a lot, it calms my nerves, and, finally, the biggest sacrifice: no butter on my bread for three months.

I've got that all clear, but I don't know how to fix the situation ... What's making that sound?

ANDRÉS: Stones, *(He scatters them.)* I don't know, reading the exemplary lives of the saints ... Have you ever read them?

LADY: Outside of the music I'm not much of a fan of ...

ANDRÉS: That's where I learned that Saint Rose carried a log in order to better comprehend what our Lord suffered beneath the weight of the cross. I carry stones, to remember his presence; I increase the weight every day ... I'm going to do it for a week until I won't be able to move.

LADY: Here, you missed one ...

ESTEBAN: I can show you a trail where there are some gigantic stones ... laugh ... Look at these shoes, I'm walking happy, can you tell?

ANDRÉS: How easy it is for you.

ESTEBAN: The girl from the movies, remember? We talked at the exit, she's a poet, worried about the seas and the trees, we walked together ... we held hands and felt a strong heat ... we rolled in the hay and everything turned around, ah ... no neuroses ... I like her, I think ...

ANDRÉS: You've given me a sign.

ESTEBAN: Me?

ANDRÉS: Yes, love, my girlfriends always read the magazine *Susy: Secrets of the Heart.* The covers always showed a girl with tears streaming down her cheeks while behind her you saw her best friend kissing the man she loved. It's clear, in love there is suffering, I'm going to fall in love ...

SCENE II

MARÍA – ANDRÉS.

Song and dance, a musical comedy scene, while MARÍA cleans.

MARÍA: Don't look at me so much, it makes me nervous.

ANDRÉS: Your name attracts me, María.

MARÍA: It's Rosa María, but I like just María.

ANDRÉS: I bought you some cream for your hands, the dust ...

MARÍA: Thank you, this will be very useful, the chlorine's the thing that damages them the most ...

ANDRÉS: Would you like to go to the movies, have a drink?

MARÍA: That would be great, but what would your grandmother say?

ANDRÉS: That you work hard and this is very good, you help out around the house, you're full of kindness.

MARÍA: I'm going to finish up now ...

ANDRÉS: I want to take care of you, be a good girl, tell me what you need ...

MARÍA: I'm going to take off my apron and put on my shoes, I'm so happy, I never thought you noticed me ...

ANDRÉS: We could go to a park, to a party.

MARÍA: My fingernails are so ugly ...

ANDRÉS: Let me kiss your hands.

MARÍA: I'm laughing; you're making me nervous.

ANDRÉS: I'm going to touch your face, close your eyes.

MARÍA: You're tickling me; I'm going to put on a bit of perfume.

ANDRÉS: You are resplendent, you don't need anything ... You are so pure ...

MARÍA: Please, get up ...

ANDRÉS: You are unique.

MARÍA: They all say the same thing. Yaa, they can see us from over there..... .

SCENE III

All alone. The first temptation takes hold of his body. He begins to masturbate wildly.

ANDRÉS: No, I don't want to, stop my hand, please stop my hand ... Vile rasping ... *(Finishes.)* Inoffensive liquid that looks like mother's milk, but doesn't nurture anything other than the pleasure of a piece of flesh. The claws of evil ferment inside of me. I will conquer you; I won't let this body made for praising the Lord become fodder for his destruction.

SCENE IV

ANDRÉS – ESTEBAN.

In the gym, ESTEBAN takes a shower.

ESTEBAN: Pass me the towel, I want you to meet her, we'll all go out like we used to ...

ANDRÉS: I can't, Esteban, I have another mission and only so much time in which to do it, it's irrecoverable ...

ESTEBAN: I'd like to feel your passion, something that fills me with energy, that would make me detest sleep and get me out of bed, I don't know, I can't find that, maybe with her.

ANDRÉS: When you find it you'll find the beginning of an infinite thread.

ESTEBAN: I doubt it. I detest doubt, because I don't know if what I feel today will be what I feel tomorrow. What will happen after we kiss, after we see each other every day? I don't know, I doubt.

ANDRÉS: To doubt faith is to fall into the abyss of nothing, there's nothing to hold on to, nobody to stop your fall. Temptations are great and sacrifices so insignificant ... Let me go, I have to be with Him and think about those who suffer.

ESTEBAN: Andrés, look at me, I suffer.

ANDRÉS: I see you, I'll think about you and everyone. Let me go ...

(ANDRÉS in his room, reading the Bible, he sleeps.)

ANDRÉS: I know He is here inside this room, I sit still for hours waiting to see his reflection, waiting for the moment He appears and gives me orders, I know He's watching me, punishing my curiosity. It will be when I least expect it, perhaps sitting on a branch like a kid or turning my face towards the cross. It will be during an instant of carelessness precisely when I'm not expecting it. That's when He'll come to bless me and reveal himself to me. *(He sleeps.)*

SCENE V

ANDRÉS – MARÍA.

MARÍA: I brought your breakfast, you read so much.

ANDRÉS: I have to learn, María, learn how to love you. What's love have to be like in order to be pure white? I don't know how to do it.

MARÍA: Here's a little present, it's been such a long time since anyone said pretty things to me …

ANDRÉS: To be an example of love, a blessed pair, surrounded by angels. You are pure but I am stained, there are thoughts in my head unworthy of you.

MARÍA: You are the best that has ever touched me.

(MARÍA begins to stroke him.)

ANDRÉS: Avaunt, thief, you are temptation; you want to steal the only thing I have, my chastity, withdraw!

MARÍA: I don't understand, you invited me to the movies, you look at me with desire, I only wanted to do the same and this is the way you treat me …

ANDRÉS: Pardon me, I know that you didn't want to do it, you were only possessed, it wasn't you who I shouted at, but at that wretched angel who wants to destroy His kingdom.

MARÍA: Damn it, I always make a mess out of everything.

Sequence Three—Mortifications

SCENE I

Desire.

ANDRÉS rends his vestments.

ANDRÉS: I can't put my hands together without feeling this malign heat, I try to concentrate my sight on His image but obscene bodies appear calling me from their rooms, my back feels the heat of fingers running up and down and penetrating my buttocks, my lips are opened by tongues that bath my gums with liquids. My cock hardens, vulvas squeeze it and I can't prevent the bile from oozing. Let them come, let them satiate my body, absorb my testicles and nibble away my flesh. They want to stop me from praising You and make me ferment in my own original sin … I will subject this flesh contaminated with the cells of desire.

(ANDRÉS prepares his cell. He ties his hands to cords hanging from the walls, as a conductor he puts on metallic underwear.)

SCENE II

GRANDMOTHER – MARÍA.

GRANDMOTHER: Prip, prip, prip … Vivaldi, it can't be, this child is still in the bath. Let's show him something. Look, you degenerate, do you see these breasts, you don't want to see this, look at them and calm yourself down …

(MARÍA enters with bundles of spikes.)

GRANDMOTHER: Ay, this pain in my breasts won't stop.

MARÍA: Señora, everyone's looking out their windows, there must have been an accident.

GRANDMOTHER: Nothing, lazy people. Beat me more whites and take these sacks to Andrés, he's just like Julia, trying to get rid of his sins.

SCENE III

ANDRÉS – MARÍA.

MARÍA: Are you sure you don't want anything to eat … Did you like the mattress? I filled it with spikes.

ANDRÉS: I have to purify myself, María.

MARÍA: If you could only guess, the first time I went out with Julio I wouldn't have done my hair, or put on blue socks. How was I to know that he didn't like blue or buns? … Have some of this broth, here …

ANDRÉS: I can't María. Men soap themselves, rub on deodorant, smooth their skin with creams, and prepare their bodies for desire. I prepare mine to receive divine aura.

MARÍA: If you could only guess … How was I to know that I'd meet him, that we'd understand each other so well? When they took me to the Sisters of Perpetual Aid, at first I mopped the halls, and I saw them go by all in a line, so silent. I didn't dare, I could have been a nun and you a priest, and we would have met there in the convent, I would have told you my sins, you would have given me communion, then we would have prayed together. You would have squeezed my body to draw out temptation and I would have made your bed of thorns … If you could only predict.

SCENE IV

Hallucinations.

The Saints' Visit.

ANDRÉS delirious. He sees Saint Rose of Lima and Saint Martin of Porres who smile at him, then his mother enters.

SCENE V

With MOTHER.

MOTHER: Don't stay inside, Andrés, go out, go out and play ... *(She realizes that he sees the bruise on her forehead.)* It's nothing, a blow, a blow ... on the table ...

ANDRÉS: Wait for me, mama, I'll be there soon with a golden aura, and I will lift you up in my arms and present you to my Lord ... You'll be so proud, I see the tears in your eyes and your grimaces to avoid them, but your tears will be the dew of a wintry morning. You'll see, I'm close, I can feel it ...

SCENE VI

ANDRÉS – ESTEBAN.

ESTEBAN: You look content, thin, happy. On the other hand I'm wandering around bored of the newspapers, the printed letters, the pictures of smiling people with full cups. I'm bored of the smiles on the screens, of having to iron my pants, of so many brilliant cars and tin buses. I could begin to believe in you, become your disciple, have a passion.

ANDRÉS: I've got a fever and can't hear you too well, it seems the bells are ringing, Esteban, cover my sight and bind my fingers ...

ESTEBAN: She came every day, we made love well, she smiled and kissed me softly, she left me feeling light, happy, I could get up early and greet the light of day, now when she calls me she doesn't say a thing, we're both silent, she gets tired of listening to me, no longer smiles, I don't feel her kisses, it's lost.

ANDRÉS: We need them to persecute us again, so that we build catacombs where, in the midst of the humidity and the darkness, our faith revives, without knowing whether it's day or night, only listening to the martyrs while they are flayed in glorious agony … We need to be afraid of our faith, afraid of being recognized and sacrificed. Esteban, you have to be dismembered to see the divine light …

ESTEBAN: To be dismembered I'd need to see how others squeeze her breasts and she repeats the same phrases, surrenders the same sighs, at least I could calm down, I'd realize that it was nothing more than part of a prerecorded video. Andrés, if we have to construct catacombs it's not to give us fear, but to give us strength.

ANDRÉS: Esteban, I've realized that this isn't the path I should follow, the nails have infected me and if the vehemence of the flesh is so strong it's because He is pointing the way. He wants me to confront evil … I should conquer the demon flooding our earth; I should clean these floors and prepare for His coming.

ESTEBAN: Let me cut you down.

Sequence Four—Evil Acts

SCENE I

ANDRÉS: I will carry Archangel Gabriel's sword into the depths of evil, and I will battle the anti-Christ who is already here, I know now that I have found the mission you have selected for me, I will not fear, because I am your soldier and celestial armies support me, I will be ferocious ... I will find and open the pass to the Final Judgment. I will go into the street, I will confront wickedness, the vices that have taken over your kingdom, and I will be the first crusader of this new conquest. I will feel your glory flowing through me, I float, angels lay their hands on my forehead, and I'll be worthy of that golden aura you granted my predecessors ... The heavens open, the earth moves to sing praises, blessed be the universe, the stars, everything you have created bows down before you ... Praised be you. Gloria ... Gloria ... Gloria ...

SCENE II

Farewell.

MARÍA irons.

MARÍA: You're preparing to leave, you started eating, got up, as if you weren't here already.

ANDRÉS: Yes, it's true.

MARÍA: It was just the same when my dad left the house, he moved differently, as if he didn't want to touch things. Are you going to come back?

ANDRÉS: My body won't be here, María, but everyday at 8PM pray your rosary looking at the Virgin. I'll do the same and that way we'll be together ...

MARÍA: A secret between us.

ANDRÉS: A secret between the three of us.

MARÍA: Now I'm calmer, I took a picture in the plaza … here … I'm going to punish temptations too …

SCENE III

Night-Park.

A man passes, urinates, the ASSAILANT observes him. ANDRÉS enters.

ASSAILANT: Hey, got any matches?

ANDRÉS: A light?

(The ASSAILANT takes out a knife, puts it to his neck.)

ASSAILANT: That's it, calmly, give me your money and don't move.

ANDRÉS: I understand you, you're poor, maybe you had to sleep two or four to a mattress, you've had to listen to your mother's moans when she sinned, or feel the mattress rock when your brother masturbated and I'm sure that scared you, because you didn't know what they were doing. You got up in winter, in the damp, and pissed in an old pot, I know, I imagine it, I try to see your mother, obese from bread, always washing the same plate, but she's blessed because she resisted the temptation to sell her flesh, and accepted her humility like a gift, but you fell into greed for possessions and terrestrial pleasure …

ASSAILANT: Yes, I shared my bed but with my sister, and during cold nights I took advantage of her, she was younger, and I liked it, you're rich, they must have brought you breakfast on a tray with warm bread and melted cheese, you wore pretty pajamas and went out in the car when you were bored or to the movies, whatever you wanted. When I'm bored I play with my shoelace and that's where I am, stuck.

ANDRÉS: It's dark and in the darkness our feelings flourish, the night is for angels and the devil but during the day everyone pairs off, we forget about ourselves.

ASSAILANT: The day I forget about myself I'm lost, understand?

ANDRÉS: The knife is no longer ice, your hand relaxes, someone stops you and impedes you from cutting me ...

ASSAILANT: I haven't buried you because you talked to me and you got deep, I like the feel of your hair and your clean smell, but it's the same thing that makes me want to put you in the ground.

ANDRÉS: Before I would have begged you to cut off my head little by little, so that I felt the pain and the anguish and could agree to martyrdom that way, but I believe that an angel is guiding you and that this is a test, I forgive you, wound me.

ASSAILANT: Don't think I can't, I've buried this in women's teats and old men's kidneys, but I don't know what you're bringing.

ANDRÉS: The only thing that's mine you will never have, take my money, my watch, do you like my shirt? And then let me share with you, I want the most malign furies and hatreds to possess me, I need to confront them...

ASSAILANT: Let's see if you can do it, here, use it ... What are you waiting for?

ANDRÉS: I could take out your eyes, I'd be doing you a favor, you'd no longer desire metals, plastics, fibers, you'd be left looking inside yourself and there you'd find the light, but I still can't.

ASSAILANT: What did you take, give me some ...

ANDRÉS: Nothing.

ASSAILANT: And what are you doing here at this hour?

ANDRÉS: I have to reach the doors of darkness and come face to face with him; maybe you're one of his angels and will take me ...

MAN: Cold night, got a match ... Thanks, the park's boring today, nothing much happening.

ASSAILANT: Depends, what you do you want to happen?

MAN: Your friend's nice. Armando, pleased to meet you.

ASSAILANT: He likes good whiskey.

MAN: I've got a bottle at home, come on, I live over there ...

ASSAILANT: That's where we're from ... come on then ...

(ANDRÉS looks at his watch, takes out his rosary and follows them.)

SCENE IV

In the Apartment.

MAN: It's more pleasant with a little light. You're both so quiet.

ASSAILANT: No, just waiting for a drink.

ANDRÉS: The walls are damp, the rug's dusty.

ASSAILANT: This is a good apartment, things are going well for us, did you see the ring, and what do you think he's got in his wallet, huh?

MAN: Ice ... Johnny Walker Black.

ASSAILANT: It's hot ...

ANDRÉS: And these toys ...

MAN: The kids, they only come on weekends, I'm separated, free ... Don't think that I always invite whoever, the thing is I'm a special person, people interest me, their problems. When you spend the whole day seated in front of a desk you get isolated from the world. You live in this artificiality of telephone calls, business meetings. I've always been adventurous, whenever I travel I go right to the heart of the city, the sex shops, the dangerous neighborhoods, that's where the food is, life's brief, so you have to try everything. You understand me, you're also adventurers, you're born that way and there's no way to stop being so ...

ASSAILANT: It's uncomfortable here ... let's take off our clothes ...

MAN: You're better than I thought.

ASSAILANT: Hospitality pays.

MAN: Do you want to see some movies? But don't get scandalized …

(With the remote control he plays a porn video, the screen is offstage, we hear the audio.)

MAN: You're so far away, come here.

ANDRÉS: What do I do?

MAN: The same thing as on the screen, nothing out of the ordinary, I'm in the middle, and you're the grey-haired guy taking off his shirt, come on, do it, put it there, around your neck, and continue.

ASSAILANT: You never played Simon Says? It's the same thing …

(While they watch the video the MAN strokes ANDRÉS, the ASSAILANT interferes and that excites him.)

ASSAILANT: Why don't we take a shower, huh?

MAN: Not a bad idea, let's go.

ASSAILANT: It's great under the water …

ANDRÉS: No, water, no …

(They go to the bathroom; you can feel the noise of the shower. ANDRÉS falls to his knees.)

MAN: Tell your friend to come …

ASSAILANT: Hey man, hurry up …

ANDRÉS: It's the flood, it inundates the apartment, the walls break, and my body turns to salt.

(A fight is heard, blows, a heartrending scream, ANDRÉS levitates, the naked ASSAILANT enters, bathed in water and blood, waving the shining ring.)

ASSAILANT: See? It's gold.

ANDRÉS: And him?

ASSAILANT: Him? He's asleep, his problems are over … take a look around, whatever you find is yours.

ANDRÉS: Nothing here is of any use to me, just you …

(ANDRÉS launches himself at the ASSAILANT, they roll around.)

ASSAILANT: Are you crazy? Let me go.

ANDRÉS: Come out, I know you're here, why don't you appear? I'm ready to confront you, show yourself, spew forth.

ASSAILANT: Shhh, calm down, I don't want to hurt you, come with me and I'll take you to my den of iniquity.

SCENE V

MARÍA – GRANDMOTHER.

(MARÍA is waiting for the clock to toll eight, she sits in front of the window and begins to pray the rosary, but then she gets excited and throws ice cubes on her vulva.)

GRANDMOTHER: They're having tea again, all they do is drink and eat.

MARÍA: They must be hungry, señora.

GRANDMOTHER: Gluttons, María, they're pigs … Ay, Lord, what has your kingdom come to … What are you hiding there?

MARÍA: A rosary.

GRANDMOTHER: What have you gotten yourself into that you're going around praying at this hour? Take off those hairclips and wash your face, penance is for Holy Week. They've got the television on all day long, no wonder they're dazed … When will you come for me, Lord, when?

MARÍA: Maybe they're watching the Passion? They said they were going to broadcast it from Rome with the Pope.

GRANDMOTHER: You suffer the Passion, you don't watch it. Come on, take off your shoes and I'm going to wash your feet, you don't know how terrible it is to do this with my arthritis …

MARÍA: I don't like to take off my shoes …

GRANDMOTHER: Where did these ice cubes come from?

MARÍA: They fell, there; I've taken off my shoes …

(GRANDMOTHER washes MARÍA's feet.)

GRANDMOTHER: Humility isn't easy; tomorrow we'll keep silent. We have to purify this house, María, listen …

MARÍA: Are there mice?

GRANDMOTHER: It's Julia.

(They pray, MARÍA says good-bye to the Virgin.)

SCENE VI

In the Transvestite's House.

(The TRANSVESTITE is practicing a voice-over for his next show.)

ASSAILANT: I live with him or her, that's why I like it. If he were a woman we'd have problems, if she were a man she'd be a faggot. He isn't anything, she isn't anybody, or better said, I don't want to be with anyone. She thinks she's a chick, but when he showers and he gets a hard on he can't be. I don't like to touch her. Yes, he's useful, washes my socks, talks to me like a friend, how he gets in fights and gets cut up, tricks them and robs them like I trick them and rob them.

SHE: You're sick; you always kill them in the tub.

ASSAILANT: At least I don't stain my clothes that way.

ANDRÉS: Why under the water?

SHE: So he doesn't leave fingerprints, you crazy little thing.

ANDRÉS: He let you do it like he accepted it, resigned himself to be beaten for …

ASSAILANT: I was quick nothing more, I slipped a tender wave through his neck and then I turned him around, smashed his head against the side of the tub and drowned him in the water, what could be easier?

ANDRÉS: A baptism from hell, and his angel, his guardian angel who should have defend him ...

ASSAILANT: The angels are gone, they got bored over time ...

SHE: They got fed up with me fast, when I was born, I think.

ANDRÉS: They're winning, the Lord is weak.

ASSAILANT: What are you so worried about? Don't you read the papers? Ahh, why do some have rights and others not, when the soldiers opened up the commies' guts or drowned them in shit, did anybody say anything? Who told you that guy was good? Maybe it was up to me to punish him. Let's stop talking nonsense, no one here is good or bad, we just are, nothing more.

SHE: I couldn't do it, and you, what are you looking at?

ANDRÉS: Your eyes.

SHE: Everyone fixates on the same thing, and this is what I am, nothing more ... Listen, we could get a little bit of money from this guy, you want to?

ASSAILANT: Why don't you suck my dick for a while? I'm nervous.

SHE: You're always the same, I get excited, but I never find pleasure.

ASSAILANT: And you, crazy little one, what do you want?

SHE: Business, business, I know a rich lady, kind of strange yes, but she pays well, and I've got another, the only thing you have to do is go tell them stories, good money. Do you think I'm ugly that you look at me so much?

ANDRÉS: You're black.

SHE: Ay, my son, and I washed yesterday. Take a bit, so we can trust you *(Passes him cocaine.)* like this ...

ANDRÉS: But if I have a child it will come out contaminated, it will be a lost soul, I will procreate for the armies of evil.

SHE: Ayy, you've it all wrong. Listen, the old lady can't have kids by now and if it does happen she'll have an abortion,

Christ you're complicated. We do everything cooperatively here; if you want to stay we share everything, got it?

ANDRÉS: My body is for punishing and humiliating, do what you will ...

SHE: Listen to that, I like it, you're poetic, I can see you pretty as a woman you. I've also got one who likes guys but dressed as women, with us you can be rich.

SCENE VII

MARÍA – ESTEBAN.

MARÍA finishes praying her rosary.

ESTEBAN: Andrés left good teachings in this house.

MARÍA: I prayed before.

ESTEBAN: He hasn't returned?

MARÍA: He's preaching, I think he's preaching, every time I go out I look through the churches, perhaps he went to the country. The Señora went out to sell aprons, so she could feel poor ...

ESTEBAN: He could leave some sort of sign; I need to talk to him.

MARÍA: Can I serve you tea ... On the fourth floor they're having their snack, they never miss it ...

ESTEBAN: Some of us want to be heroes, others saints, it seems that we all need to die with some halo on our head.

MARÍA: I want to have a house and someone who loves me, nothing more.

ESTEBAN: I'm going to sell my soul to the devil ...

MARÍA: Don't do that, for god's sake, don't' even joke about it.

ESTEBAN: You have to write a letter in blood, then burn it on a moonless night and shout Lucifer ... Lucifer ... I'm HIV positive, María, a doctor told me and it's the same as being possessed, but no one can cure me, let me serve you, sit down like the Señora.

(MARÍA illuminated, seated in front of the window, while ESTEBAN serves her and waits on her.)

MARÍA: Such beautiful things are happening to me, I think I'm going to die.

GRANDMOTHER: They can hear your screams from the elevator, how dare you? And when I'm doing penance? Go look for your friend Andrés who was so good here. He fed Vivaldi and then he went to his meditations. Do you want an apron?

SCENE VIII

ANDRÉS and THE CLIENT.

THE CLIENT: Sit down, here's a little cup of tea, how young you are.

ANDRÉS: Not so much, I'm 26.

THE CLIENT: 26 years old, the same age as my Marcel, if it hadn't been for the accident.

ANDRÉS: Your son.

THE CLIENT: He liked music so much, he'd play the radio loud, and he was going to form a band with his friends. Do you like music too?

ANDRÉS: I sing sometimes.

THE CLIENT: He was going to be a doctor, he would have treated my hypertension, and he'd be taking care of me. You look sad, tell me what's going on.

ANDRÉS: My mother died and …

THE CLIENT: No, she's alive, it was your father who died abandoned and suffering. You like my neck? Touch it. Careful, you're choking me. Let go!

ANDRÉS: I wanted him to feel me.

THE CLIENT: Well, come here, put your little head here, poor child, I would have given you everything, you'd have your furnished room, full of records, we would have traveled, to the best hotels …

ANDRÉS: Cars, drinks, cigarettes, everything …

THE CLIENT: And love, lots of love, now I walk alone through the shops, I make meals and invite my friends, we always talk about the same thing, sicknesses, betrayals, but you, Marcelo, you fill my life, you know, I'm going to buy you a guitar, the black one. How you've grown, child, soon you're surely going to get married, tell me, are you still going out with Macarena … ?

ANDRÉS: No, I'm not going out with anyone.

THE CLIENT: Why, Marcelo? You're a good boy, more than one girl would like to have you at her side. Ay, what a difficult life, you can help me.

ANDRÉS: That's what I'm here for.

THE CLIENT: You were always so good, Marcelito. I want to give you everything, lie down on the bed.

ANDRÉS: Is this good, or should I turn around?

(The CLIENT lifts her skirts and urinates on ANDRÉS' face.)

THE CLIENT: Turn around, open your mouth … Feel how it burns, Marcelo, Marcelito, why did you leave me? The only thing that comes out now is urine, never another child. Why? Why?

ANDRÉS: Wake up; I'm here in front of you … How many have you possessed?

THE CLIENT: What's going on with you? Keep calm, Ayyy.

ANDRÉS: Leave this body, free her.

THE CLIENT: Let go of me, you're crazy, who sent you? Don't come back …

ANDRÉS: I'm in the middle of Lucifer's kingdom, I get lost in his labyrinths and he hides himself behind the possessed, his realm widens and you don't help me stop it. What more can I do …

SHE: We're going to lose this client if you go on this way.

ANDRÉS: I have to find your master, the one you don't even know, because you don't yet realize …

SHE: Ay, you made me break a nail; you're making me shiver. You're giving me crazy thoughts, kid, here, take this and behave yourself …

SCENE IX

The Apparition.

MARÍA – ANDRÉS.

MARÍA covers herself with ashes, looks at her watch, it's eight o'clock. Begins to pray.

MARÍA: It's just turned eight, God save you María, full … *(MARÍA sees ANDRÉS.)* ANDRÉSito, ANDRÉSito, how are you? Nothing much has happened since you left, the Señora has us on a vow of poverty. I put the cream on that you gave me every morning, but just a little, so that it lasts, the lady in front left with the little guy and the gentleman arrived with a blond who waited for him in the taxi.

ANDRÉS: María, I have confronted the angels of evil but they escaped, I will continue my battle. The Lord has given me signs, when I invoke Him I rise several centimeters off the ground, I know now that I am achieving the yearned for halo.

MARÍA: See you later, take care … Now and in the hour of our death, Amen.

SCENE X

GRANDMOTHER – MARÍA.

MARÍA finishes her rosary, the GRANDMOTHER enters furious, carrying menstrual pads and VIVALDI.

GRANDMOTHER: You whore, you whore, look what I found, how many knitting needle abortions have you carried out, you wretch, and in my own house …

MARÍA: Don't hit me, señora, I didn't want to stop up the toilet so I threw my menstrual pads out with the ground meat. How could you think I'd do such a thing, with a fetus?

GRANDMOTHER: Ay, the arthritis is cramping my whole body. Hurry, break me some eggs, what pain, my god. More, María, more.

(MARÍA breaks eggs over the GRANDMOTHER's body.)

GRANDMOTHER: Let's go out front, we have to purify this neighborhood. Come on, María, and make sure you bring the aprons.

Sequence Five—Homecoming

SCENE I

In the Church.

ANDRÉS – LADY – ESTEBAN

The LADY approaches the coffin, takes a candle from her bag, lights it. ANDRÉS enters.

LADY: Nobody's come to see him. Did you know him?

ANDRÉS: No, but now he isn't alone.

LADY: When they can't see me I light candles, these electric bulbs aren't up to the task. Like the word says: you have to mourn them with candles, take one and don't get caught …

ANDRÉS: I help them with their farewells, I look into their faces and I can relive their final moments. He was a postman, his fondest hope was to buy himself a bicycle, when he got one he was happy, because he got home earlier, but he wasn't greeted with joy, a little while later she left him, and he, when he finished delivering in Independencia, went to bars and dedicated himself to alcohol, this brought him further torments and nightmares accompanied his drunkenness, little by little he decided to leave, until he was run over yesterday. But he will be redeemed because while the carabineros tried to revive him, the only thing he worried about was whether the letters were stained with blood.

LADY: Halleluia, praised be … Halleluia …

ANDRÉS: Esteban, how good to see you. *(They embrace.)*

ESTEBAN: Yes, she called me on the phone, I heard her distinctly, pure, I was happy, she asked me how I was, I wanted to run to her … she told me that she felt a debt to me, that no one was to blame … everything lit up, I told myself that she'd realized where her love lay, she told me that she'd called Cristián as well and that she hoped I'd understand ... And then she dumped me. That's how I knew that at least, if we couldn't have shared love, the plague united us ...

ANDRÉS: *(Hugging him.)* It's a cross, a marvelous cross ... The Lord has placed you in my path, to be found. I will infect myself like you, we will cure the sick and together we will cross the heavenly threshold.

ESTEBAN: We're not in the Middle Ages, telling you about it was enough for me, I'm going to live it all, enjoy every day ...

ANDRÉS: This is my obligation, that's what I'm here for, to console the afflicted ...

ESTEBAN: When I'm afflicted I'll call you ...

ANDRÉS: Admirable and glorious Saint Rocco, special protector of the afflicted and those infected with the plague ... The magnanimous multitude acclaims you, full of joy, free us, pious Rocco, from the contagious plague. The sick and infected implore your protection, plead for your healing, the more they prostrate themselves you free them from dangerous sickness. Wondrous saint, have pity on us.

SCENE II

The Miracle of the Canary.

MARÍA – ANDRÉS – THE GRANDMOTHER.

MARÍA, desperate, runs from one side to the other, begins to fill some bags in a disorderly fashion.

MARÍA: You came back! And I have to leave, before she catches me.

ANDRÉS: Where are you going?!

MARÍA: She's going to kill me, he's gone, and I couldn't do a thing ...

ANDRÉS: Take it easy ...

MARÍA: I did it to make things better; I wanted to give her a surprise.

ANDRÉS: María, María.

MARÍA: I went to clean the cage, to brighten up her day, and the canary flew away.

ANDRÉS: Come, Saint Francis will help us … *(They kneel, pray.)*

(The GRANDMOTHER enters singing, with the cage and VIVALDI inside.)

GRANDMOTHER: María, pick up the birdseed that's scattered all over the kitchen.

MARÍA: It's a miracle, you are truly a saint.

GRANDMOTHER: You're back, Andrés, your room's clean, the bed's made. But we've taken a vow of silence and poverty here …

ANDRÉS: I'm enlisting in the army, Grandmother.

GRANDMOTHER: Pilots, sailors, salt of the earth, your mother didn't like them, obey, be a man like the best of men, and don't forget to confess to the chaplain and go to company mass, they're so beautiful, make your helmet shine, wash your underwear and always pray to the Virgin so she protects you from bullets and sabers. Our Lady of Montserrat protected Saint Ignatius. She'll do the same for you.

SCENE III

ANDRÉS – CAPTAIN.

The CAPTAIN brings a folded uniform, ANDRÉS undresses and dresses himself like a soldier.

CAPTAIN: You, get dressed, ten seconds: one, two, three, four …

ANDRÉS: I'm finally a Roman, I will persecute the Christians. I will have to violate the fifth commandment, destroy the lives of the sons of God, I will be the best soldier in this army and even if I have to drive my lance through the King of the Jews himself I will do my duty, I only hope that in that instant, Lord, you will give me a sign and stop my hand as you did with Saint Paul.

CAPTAIN: *(Bringing a prisoner.)* Guard him and make sure he doesn't move. *(The prisoner makes a gesture, asking for a cigarette, ANDRÉS hits him with his rifle butt.)*

ANDRÉS: It's a tooth, he lost a tooth.

CAPTAIN: You hit them with the rifle butt by the ear, to stun them, not in the jaw.

ANDRÉS: I made a mistake, he moved just when …

CAPTAIN: There are no excuses here, only victories or defeat … I like the way you look; you can see you're a soldier. He's a sure thing, dry; he hides civilians' weaknesses and wears a carcass of steel. With an army of men like you, this country would be great. At attention, sure … Remember, this isn't a hand, it's a talon … and a heart doesn't beat here but a drum that resounds and marks time to march, I hear it and know who you are, I recognize a man at arms … You will come with me tonight.

ANDRÉS: I will obey, my captain.

CAPTAIN: In the darkness bats and rats are trapped. Firm, discreet, think on this … They're not made like us, they cover themselves in stolen carcasses, if you open their skulls you'll find nothing but worms.

ANDRÉS: I'll try to …

CAPTAIN: In battle there are no words.

(Truck headlights light up a point; mark a red cross on the ground.)

ANDRÉS: I feel my feet sink in the mud, my hands sweat and turn into black claws, I see my Captain with a hunchback and his mouth has no lips, from his gums emerges a bifurcated tongue that wipes his forehead, his gigantic eyes shine like headlights. I have finally arrived at the center of darkness …

(A WOMAN enters, she wears a white tunic, song rises to heaven and an aura surrounds her body.)

ANDRÉS: My nostrils are filled with a heavenly fragrance, it's the odor of sainthood, and an aura illuminates her body. Martyrdom is reserved for her and I will have to be the one to strike her, I wait for the signal, your light blinds me. The ray that will destroy this living center of Hell … You stopped the hand of Abraham, and Paul's sword, now show your divine power.

CAPTAIN: Present arms, aim …

ANDRÉS: She has been crowned; her pupils contemplate the heavenly choir of angels that will receive her. Gabriel brings her a purple cloak; one second more and she will be on the right hand of God the Father.

(The rumble of shots is heard, celestial music fills the space, ANDRÉS throws down his rifle and kneels in front of it. Two angels take her in their arms and carry her to heaven.)

ANDRÉS: Blessed are you among women.

CAPTAIN: Halt … halt … halt …

(ANDRÉS escapes.)

Sequence Six

SCENE I

GRANDMOTHER and MARÍA purify the street with holy water.

MARÍA: Should I scrub the sidewalk too ...

GRANDMOTHER: Everywhere, María, everything needs to be purified ... Most holy prince of glory and powerful Archangel Saint Raphael, prince of doctors, health to the sick, light to the blind, joy to the afflicted, custodian of travelers, guide to pilgrims, master of perfection, protector of virtue, exalter of alms, fasting and praying, I beg you most pious prince to help me with sicknesses, to accompany me on the roads and to defend me from the devil, I also plead with you to grant me what I ask for as well ... consider my petition. Give salvation to this neighborhood, its people and its animals. All for the greater glory of God and my soul, amen. Repeat, María ...

SCENE II

ANDRÉS' Ritual.

ANDRÉS – ESTEBAN – MARÍA – GRANDMOTHER.

Anointing him with oil and ashes.

ANDRÉS: They've begun to pursue me; I've begun to conquer them. They will come looking for me.

ESTEBAN: For me too.

ANDRÉS: Believe in him and you will be healed.

ESTEBAN: The only thing I believe in is the virus growing in my blood.

ANDRÉS: I will be with you and I will care for you, accept these holy oils.

ESTEBAN: I always thought your fifties was a good age to die, I didn't want to see myself old and wrinkled, now I'd like to live to eighty and contemplate life, I look through the window and love the sun's rays, I'm fascinated by the way my body moves, I see people run to their jobs and distressed before shop windows, and it makes me envious.

ANDRÉS: I know you are He: among the sick, those who suffer, you will find me.

ESTEBAN: I lack energy, my lungs burn me, I'm tired, and you're bothering me.

ANDRÉS: Offer up your pain.

MARÍA: They're going to come, they've been to the house twice, but don't worry, everyone's talking about you, they know about the miracle of Vivaldi, and they say they've seen you float and that you communicate with the dead … and I, who tried to abuse you. Several wait for you outside.

ANDRÉS: I killed a saint; I'm not worthy of anything. I'll go towards them as so many others have done for their faith.

(MARÍA takes out some scissors and cuts off a piece of his shirt.)

MARÍA: Let me cut off a little piece. Don't worry; I'll take care of him.

ANDRÉS: María, there's Esteban. Esteban, there's María.

(The GRANDMOTHER, half-naked, enters. Egg whites slip down over her body.)

GRANDMOTHER: The arthritis has taken over my entire body, I can't go on, Lord, I won't move from here until you come to look for me, bring the hammer, María, and strike hard. Strike hard, María.

SCENE III

Testimonials.

1ST TESTIMONIAL: He brought me these clothes, they were new, he sat down beside my sick mother and prayed, he put his hands on her forehead and mother smiled, it was the only time she talked again. She felt his purity and that relieved her burden. Blessed be he.

2ND TESTIMONIAL: I lived in egoism, envying my neighbors because they could buy more than me, jealous of Jaime because he could keep sinning with another woman, resenting the TV spots where others had yachts and perfumes. That's how I lived, bitter, forgetting that this isn't my mansion or my kingdom. Now I'm at peace because ANDRÉSito laid his hands on my forehead and I found the spirit. He was sent, yes, he was.

SCENE IV

ANDRÉS sits on a metallic seat, like the electric chair, with electrodes attached to his skull. MARÍA, ESTEBAN, the GRANDMOTHER nailed to the wall, and the Witnesses, are all in scene.

ANDRÉS: *(Singing.)* The Lord will care for me, I have nothing to fear … *(Electric shock.)* The Lord is my shepherd, I have nothing to fear … *(Electric shock.)* The Lord … Bring the Holy Father, the commission of the saints; let them testify to the miracles. I want to see the bishop, let them bring the bishop from his seat … On this site will you build His Church … *(Electric shock.)*

DOCTOR SANTOS: Andrés, speak, Andrés …

ANDRÉS: They have me seated in the dock like Christ, they nail on the crown of thorns and cover me with this ridiculous cloak, I can do no more than give my thanks to the Lord for bringing me to the threshold of martyrdom. Continue, continue so that I will see the eternal light. Write, pagan, write what I have to tell you, from these words will be born a legend, and from this tongue bathed in saintly gold will be born the story of the path to sainthood. Today I am reborn and from today on thousands will follow me, the hour has come to retake the road to eternal glory. Glorious angels, sing.

(ESTEBAN dies and while canticles fill the space, ANDRÉS' mother enters with a cake and three candles.)

MOTHER: Blow out the candles, Andrés, and make three wishes.

THE END

Ecstasy's Saints:

SAINT LUCY: A virgin of Syracuse who went with her mother Eutychia on a pilgrimage to the tomb of St. Agatha at Catania, Sicily. When her mother was miraculously cured there, she gave all her money to charity. Her pagan suitor, the Consul Paschasius denounced her as a Christian and she was ordered to be placed in a brothel, but the four oxen who were to drag her there refused to move. To save herself from shame, she plucked out her eyes (her attribute) and sent them to Paschasius on a plate. Another version is that she was condemned to death in 304 during the Diocletian persecutions, her teeth and eyes were pulled out, and her throat cut with a knife or dagger (another of her attributes). The lamp which she carries may be a pun on the Latin accusative form of *lux–lucem*, "light" and *Lucia* (Lucy).

SAINT ANNE: A rich lady of Bethlehem, married to St. Joachim, and the mother of St. Mary the Virgin. Childless for twenty years, and grieved because her husband was not allowed in the Temple because he lacked a son and had retired in sorrow to his sheepfold, she put on her bridal attire and sat in the garden with her servant Judith, watching with envy the sparrows feeding their young in a laurel tree. An angel appeared and told her to hasten out to meet her husband as her prayer had been answered and she would bear a child. She met Joachim at the Golden Gate as he returned with his flocks from the pasture. There they kissed and in due time she bore Mary, whom she dedicated to the service of the Lord.

This legend is not scriptural and resembles the story of Samuel (1 Sam 102). It is first found in the *Book of James* and was popularized in the *Golden Legend*. It was linked with the doctrine of the Immaculate Conception of St. Mary the Virgin, to explain how she came to be born without taint of original sin. Thus a dove is sometimes shown kissing Anne's lips and the closed Golden Gate before which she greeted Joachim symbolizes non-human conception.

Anne, represented as a middle-aged matron, became the pattern of perfect motherhood because of the saintly way in which she educated Mary, teaching her to sew and to read. At the hour of her death, Jesus (either as an infant or as a young boy) was at her bedside to comfort and bless her. She appeared (until this representation was condemned by the Council of Trent) in a group of three, St. Mary on her lap, and Jesus on Mary's. But later, Holy Family groupings more frequently showed St. Mary, the Christ-Child and St. Joseph.

The cult of St. Anne began in the East. A church was dedicated to her in Jerusalem and another in Constantinople during the reign of Emperor Justinian I (483-565). It spread to the West at the time of the Crusades when her head was brought to Chartres and her veil, said to have been brought to Provence by St. Mary Magdalene, was venerated as a relic. St. Bridget of Sweden also brought back relics of St. Anne from her pilgrimage to Jerusalem, and her Order, the Brigittines, had a special devotion to the mother of St. Mary the Virgin. Her feast day is 25 July in the East and 26 July in the West.

SAINT GEMMA: MARÍA Gemma Umberta Pia Galgani (March 12, 1878–April 11, 1903) was an Italian mystic, venerated as a saint in the Roman Catholic Church since 1940. She has been called the "Daughter of Passion" because of her profound imitation of the Passion of Christ.

Gemma was the fifth of eight children born in the hamlet of Borgo Nuovo in the provincial town of Capannori. Her father, Enrico Galgani, was a prosperous pharmacist. Soon after Gemma's birth, the family relocated north from Borgo Nuovo to a large new home in the Tuscan city of Lucca in a move which was undertaken to facilitate an improvement in the children's education. Gemma's mother, Aurelia Galgani, contracted tuberculosis. Because of this hardship, Gemma was placed in a private nursery school run by Elena and Ersilia Vallini when she was two-and-a-half years old, and was regarded as a highly intelligent child. Sent to a Catholic boarding-school in Lucca run by the Sisters of St. Zita, Gemma excelled in French, arithmetic and music. She was allowed at age nine to receive her first communion. At age 20, Gemma developed spinal meningitis, but was healed, attributing her extraordinary cure to the Sacred Heart of Jesus through the intercession of Venerable Gabriel of Our Lady of Sorrows (later canonized a saint), and Saint Marguerite Marie Alacoque.

According to a biography written by her spiritual director, the Reverend Germanus Ruoppolo, Gemma began to display signs of the stigmata on June 8, 1899, at the age of twenty-one. She stated that she had spoken with her guardian angel, Jesus, the Virgin Mary, and other saints—especially Gabriel of Our Lady of Sorrows. According to her testimonies, she sometimes received special messages from them about current or future events. With her health in decline, Ruoppolo directed her to pray for the disappearance of stigmata; she did so and the marks ceased. She said that she resisted the Devil's attacks often. Gemma was frequently found in a state of ecstasy. She has also been reputed to levitate.

In early 1903, Gemma was diagnosed with tuberculosis, and thus began a long and often painful death. There were numerous extraordinary mystical phenomena that occurred during her final illness. As one of the most popular saints of the Passionist Order, the devotion to Gemma Galgani is particularly strong both in Italy and Latin America. She is a patron saint of students (said to be the top of her class before having to leave school) and of pharmacists.

SAINT FRANCIS: Founder of the Order of Friars Minor (Franciscans), born c. 1181 in Assisi, son of a rich cloth-merchant, Pietro Bernardone. He was christened Giovanni, but was called Francesco (Francis) either because the name belonged to his mother's side (her surname was Pica and her family were Provençal), or because his father traded in France. At first a carefree, dissipated youth, he was moved by his experiences as a prisoner-of-war in Perugia and a serious illness which followed, to devote himself to the care of the poor and of lepers. One day he exchanged his rich clothes for the beggar's cloak worn by one of his former wealthy acquaintances who had been reduced to poverty. That night he dreamed of a magnificent palace filled with fine garments and superb arms, all marked with a cross. At first he thought that it meant that he should become a soldier, but the voice of Christ told him, "These are the riches reserved for my servants, and the weapons which I give those who fight for me."

While praying in the ruined church of St. Damian, Francis heard the crucified Christ order him to repair it. He sold some of his father's goods and offered the proceeds to the parish priest, who refused the money. He hid in a cave to escape his father's anger, was thought to be insane, and was taken to the bishop, before whom he tore off his clothes to reveal a hair shirt. The bishop covered him with his cloak, as a sign of his acceptance into the religious life. Disowned and disinherited, Francis lived in a cell near the church of Santa MARÍA degli Angeli, a chapel in which (the Porziuncola) became the place where he used to meet a group of twelve followers, among them St. Clare, daughter of a noble family, and later founder of the Poor Clares. Once, on his way to Siena, Francis met three poorly dressed maidens who all resembled each other and who greeted him with the words, "Welcome, Lady Poverty!", before they vanished. Francis symbolically took Poverty as his bride. This did not free him from the temptations of the flesh, but he repressed them by rolling naked in the snow and throwing himself into a thorn bush. Roses sprang up where drops of his blood bespattered the earth.

Wishing to found a new Order, the Brotherhood of Poverty, Francis went to Rome in 1210. Innocent III (1198-1216) only gave his permission for it to be established after he had had a vision in which he saw the church of St John Lateran (the Pope's church as Bishop of Rome) tottering and being propped up by Francis and St Dominic (whose Dominican Order was also constituted at that time).

In 1219, Francis went on a missionary journey to the Holy Land where he attempted to convert the Soldan of the Saracens by proposing an ordeal by fire. The Imams refused to accept his challenge to walk through the pyre and emerge unscathed. Back in Italy, he encouraged the growth of his Order through his example, living in poverty, weeping for the sins of the world, and spending much of his time in prayer and contemplation. His belief in the kinship between men and nature enabled him to perform many miracles, preaching to the birds who acknowledged his message by flying away in the form of a cross, and taming the wolf which ravaged the town of Gubbio by persuading him to sign a treaty under his dictation.

While on a retreat at La Verna in 1224, he prayed that he might feel in his body the agony of Christ on the Cross and was rewarded with the stigmata, purplish marks on his hands and feet recalling the wounds inflicted by the nails at the Crucifixion. He also had a vision in which he heard music made by angels. After patiently enduring great suffering in his last days, he asked his companions to place him on the earth and he died (1226) intoning, "Bring my soul out of prison, that I may praise thy name" (Ps. 142 (141): 7). His last request was that his body should be buried with the remains of criminals at the Colle d'Inferno, outside the city walls of Assisi, but his fellows buried him in the church of San Giorgio. St Clare and her nuns came out to bid him farewell as the cortege passed their convent of St Damian. It was said that when his tomb was opened his body was found standing upright, his eyes still open in contemplation. He is depicted in brown Franciscan habit, exhibiting the stigmata or gazing on a skull. His chastity is denoted by a lily and his devotion to prayer by a crucifix. He was canonized in 1228.

SAINT ROSE OF LIMA: The first saint to be canonized (in 1671) in the Americas. Born in Lima, Peru, of poor parents in 1586, she supported them by her embroidery, needlework and by cultivating flowers for sale. She refused offers of marriage, and at the age of twenty became a tertiary of the Third Order of St Dominic (Dominicans). She lived austerely in a hut in her garden and was rewarded with mystical experiences. Her severest mortifications were the wearing of a crown of thorns and sleeping on a bed of broken glass. It was said that the Vatican was showered with roses as a sign that she should be made a saint.

SAINT MARTIN OF PORRES: Born in Lima, Peru, in 1579, his father was a Spanish gentleman and his mother a colored freed-woman from Panama. At fifteen, he became a lay brother at the Dominican Friary in Lima and spent his whole life there as a barber, farm laborer, almoner, and infirMARÍAn among other things.

Martin had a great desire to go off to some foreign mission and thus earn the palm of martyrdom. However, since this was not possible, he made a martyr out of his body, devoting himself to ceaseless and severe penances. In turn, God endowed him with many graces and wondrous gifts, such as, aerial flights and bilocation.

St. Martin's love was all embracing, shown equally to humans and to animals, including vermin, and he maintained a cats and dogs hospital at his sister's house. He also possessed spiritual wisdom, demonstrated in his solving his sister's marriage problems, raising a dowry for his niece inside of three day's time, and resolving theological problems for the learned of his Order and for bishops. A close friend of St. Rose of Lima, he died on November 3, 1639 and was canonized on May 6, 1962. His feast day is November 3. He is the patron saint of interracial harmony and barbers.

SAINT GABRIEL: The second in rank of the archangels, one of the seven angels who stand ever-ready to enter the presence of God and be his messenger to humankind.

He interpreted for Daniel the vision of the Ram and the He-Goat (Dan 8:1-27) which foretold the destruction of the Persian Empire by Alexander the Great (356-323 BC), and explained the prophecy of the seventy-two weeks (Dan 9:1-27) which promised the freeing of Israel from captivity and the approach of the Messianic age. According to tradition he announced to Jaochim and Anna the impending conception of St Mary the Virgin and told Zacharias that he would become the father of St John the Baptist (Lk 1: 13-20). His supreme task was as angel of the Annunciation, when he was sent to tell Mary that she was the woman chosen to bear Jesus. In this episode he may be shown wearing an alb or a dalmatic and carrying a herald's baton (or a scepter); a lily, symbolic of Mary's virginity; or an olive branch, signifying peace between God and humankind through the Incarnation. He may also display a phylactery, or scroll, with the words of the angelic salutation, *Ave Maria*, "Hail, Mary", or *Ave Maria, gratia plena, Dominus tecum*, "Hail, Mary, full of grace, the Lord is with you." In early representations, Gabriel and Mary are shown standing, or Mary takes up a pose of humility, indicating thereby her acceptance of the divine will. Later, as the cult of the Virgin developed, Gabriel kneels to acknowledge her as Queen of Heaven, or Queen of the Angels. Although not named, Gabriel is also assumed to be the angel who announced the birth of Samson to his mother, and the one who brought the glad tidings of the birth of the Messiah to the Shepherds. According to tradition, it was Gabriel who comforted Jesus during his Agony in the Garden of Gethsemane.

Gabriel watches over childbirth and, since 1921, is the patron saint of television and telecommunications. With St Michael, he guards church doors against the Devil. He is also revered in Islam because he dictated the Koran to Mohamet.

SAINT ROCCO (ROCH): A saint invoked for protection from plague, cholera and other infectious diseases. Born in Montpellier, France, in 1293, his wealthy parents died when he was twenty, leaving him their money, but he was

converted to a religious life, sold all his worldly goods
for the support of hospitals and the poor, and set out on
a pilgrimage to Rome (hence he is depicted in a pilgrim's
garb and carries a staff). At Acqua Pendente he found the
city ravaged by plague and spent some time there nursing
the sick. He was infected at Piacenza (a plague spot is
shown on his bared leg) and would have died had not a
faithful dog (shown as his companion) brought him food
each day from his master's table. When he returned to
Montpellier he was so emaciated that he was unrecognized
and thrown into prison as a spy. He spent five years in a
dungeon where an angel comforted him. Before he died in
1327 he wrote an account of his life. When the manuscript
was discovered he was rehabilitated and buried with great
honors by his repentant fellow-citizens.

OUR LADY OF MONTSERRAT: The mountain named
Montserrat rises 20 miles northwest of Barcelona, in the
region of Catalonia, which takes its name from the Spanish,
Catalan for "sawn mountain" probably because its rock
outgrowths seem to be the teeth of a saw from a distance.
These most unusual lofty cone-shaped jags are almost
perpendicular. The highest cone rises to a height of nearly
4,000 feet, while the circumference around the entire base
of the mountain is measured at about 12 miles. The church
that contains the miracle-working statue of the Madonna
and Child sits about halfway up the mountain. Blackened
by candles that burned before the statue day and night this
particular image dates back to at least the twelfth century.
S. Ignatius of Loyola made an annual pilgrimage to
Montserrat, as have a million or more pilgrims every year
in modern times.

According to tradition, the miraculous image was first
known as La Jerolimitana (the native of Jerusalem), since
it is thought to have been carved there in the early days
of the Church. The statue was eventually given to St.
Etereo, Bishop of Barcelona, who brought it to Spain.
In the seventh century, when Saracen infidels invaded
Spain, the Christians of Barcelona heroically defended it

for three years until defeat appeared imminent. Knowing that they could hold out no longer, they decided to take their treasured image of Our Lady to a secret, safe place. Quietly, with the knowledge of the Bishop and the Governor of the city, a group brought the statue to Montserrat, placing it in a small cave, April 22, 718. A complete account of the miraculous image, the cause of its removal and the place of its hidden security were recorded in the archives of Barcelona. Even though the location of the statue was eventually forgotten, the people of Barcelona never forgot the holy image for almost 200 years. Then, in 890, shepherd boys from Monistrol, a village at the foot of Montserrat were sent to discover the treasure. While tending their flocks that night the shepherds were surprised by lights and the sound of singing coming from the mountain. When this happened once again, they reported the situation to their priest, who looked into the matter. He, too, heard the singing and saw the mysterious lights, so he reported this to the Bishop, who also witnessed the same occurrences. At last the statue of Our Lady was discovered in the cave and brought out and placed in a small church that was soon built; this little church developed into the present church that was completed in 1592.

Although not located on the peak of the mountain, as are the sanctuaries of Monte Cassion and Le Puy, the monastery is situated high enough from the surrounding area to make one think it safe from attack. Yet the monastery sustained considerable damage during the Napoleonic invasion. Additional harm was inflicted during civil wars and revolutionary disturbances. The treasured image of the Madonna and Child was hidden during these times, but was soon restored to its place of honor when the church and buildings were quickly repaired. The Autonomous Government of Catalonia spared these buildings during the Spanish Civil War of 1936-1939.

Benedictines settled in the monastery hundreds of years ago and still maintain the sanctuary and provide hospitality to the steady stream of pilgrims who go there. The number of historical figures connected to the sanctuary or who have visited it, include one of its hermits, Bernat Boil, who accompanied Christopher Columbus to the New World, thus becoming the first missionary to America. One of Montserrat's first abbots became Julius II, the Renaissance Pope for whom Michelangelo worked. Emperor Charles V and Philip II of Spain both died with blessed candles from the sanctuary in their hands. King Louis XIV of France had intercessory prayers said at Montserrat for the Queen Mother, and Emperor Ferdinand III of Austria made generous financial gifts to the monastery. All the kings of Spain prayed at the shrine, as did Cardinal Roncalli, who later became Pope John XXIII.

Some of the Saints who visited there were St. Peter Nolasco, St. Raymond of Penafort, St. Vincent Ferrer, St. Francis Borgia, St. Aloysius Gonzaga, St. Joseph Calasanctius, St. Anthony Mary Claret and St. Ignatius, who as a knight was confessed by one of the monks. After spending a night praying before the image of Our Lady of Montserrat, he began his new life and the founding of the Jesuit order. A few miles away is Manresa, a pilgrim shrine of the Society of Jesus. The shrine holds the cave wherein St. Ignatius Loyola retired from the world and wrote his Spiritual Exercises.

Leo XIII declared the Virgin of Montserrat the Patron Saint of the Diocese of Catalonia. The statue has always been one of the most celebrated images in Spain.

SAINT IGNATIUS OF LOYOLA: Founder of the Society of Jesus (Jesuits), born Iñigo (Latin *Ignatius*) at Loyola in the Spanish Basque country c. 1491. He was wounded during the French siege of Pamplona and spent his long convalescence reading many devotional books, after which he decided to devote himself to the service of Christ. He made a pilgrimage to Jerusalem, humbly studied Latin with schoolchildren in Barcelona, took his degree in the University of Paris and gathered around him a small company of followers, including St. Francis Xavier, who vowed to become missionaries. These formed the nucleus of the new Order, which was approved by Pope Paul III (1534-49) in 1540. Its members were dedicated to the promotion of the Faith, particularly in education and in overseas missions. Ignatius was canonized by Pope Gregory XV (1621-3) in 1622, the year of his death. His *Spiritual Exercises*, much used in religious retreats, was aimed at training the soul in the way of perfection. His remains are in the church of the Gesù in Rome. There is no contemporary portrait of him but his death mask survives. He is depicted bearded, in Jesuit habit (black with a high collar and a small tonsure on the back of the head); or in Mass vestments, holding the book of the Rule of his Order; with the Jesuit motto "*Ad Majorem Dei Gloriam*" ("To the greater glory of God"); the sacred monogram HIS (adopted by the Jesuits) inscribed on his breast. A dragon at his feet symbolizes his victory over sin and his casting out of devils. He is also shown healing him on his way to Rome saying, *Ego vobis Romae propitious ero*, "I will stand by you on your way to Rome", and an angel showed him a tablet with the words *In hoc vocabitur tibi nomen*, indicating the name of the Order.

SAINT PAUL: The Apostle of the Gentiles, supposed author of the New Testament epistles which bear his name, some of which are certainly his. His name was Saul, born at Tarsus in Cilicia, and thus "a citizen of no mean city" (Ac 21: 39). He was of Jewish parents who had also the advantage of being Roman citizens, a fact which would later give him the right to be sent to Rome for trial. He was brought up as a strict Pharisee and studied in Jerusalem under Gamaliel. His hatred of the new Christian sect caused him to take part in the stoning of St. Stephen, the first martyr (Ac 8: 1-3). He heard the young deacon pray for his executioners and this led to the great event in his life, his conversion, which took place when he was on the road to Damascus, "breathing out threatenings and slaughter against the disciples of the Lord". He was blinded by a light from heaven and heard a voice saying, "I am Jesus whom thou persecutes: it is hard for thee to kick against the pricks" (the goading of conscience) (Ac 9: 6). He was cured of his blindness in Damascus by Ananias, a Christian, who was told in a vision to visit him. He was baptized, took the name of Paul, and retired to the desert to meditate. He had previously sought ferociously to drive Christians out of the synagogues, but he returned to Damascus to preach Christ with equal vigor. Strict Jews "took counsel to kill him" and watched the city gates, hoping to capture him, but Christian disciples let him down from the walls by night and he escaped to Jerusalem. There it was necessary for St. Barnabas to vouch for him because the Apostles could not believe that Paul was the same man who had previously ill-treated them (Ac 9: 1-31). It was agreed that Paul's field of activity should be among the gentiles. He came into conflict with St. Peter at Antioch over the question of the circumcision of gentile converts, which the Church in Jerusalem insisted on, but which was finally resolved in Paul's favor (Gal 2: 11-14).

The vivid account of Paul's missionary journeys given in the *Acts of the Apostles* ends with his preaching the Gospel in Rome for two whole years while awaiting his trial. The 2nd-century *Acts of Paul and Thecla* adds further details that may have basis in fact. Paul (his name means "little") is described as small of stature, with a bald head and crooked legs, his nose somewhat hooked, his eyebrows meeting, but his face full of friendliness, "for now he appeared like a man, and now he had the face of an angel", a description which influenced his representation in art. His conversion of St. Thecla at Iconium caused his imprisonment, from which he emerged to have many other adventures. He was thrown to the wild beasts in the stadium at Ephesus but he was protected by a lion that he had baptized, and was saved by the onset of a violent hailstorm. The account ends with Emperor Nero ordering Paul's execution. When his head was struck off, milk spurted over the executioner's clothes. Paul returned from the dead to tell Nero that he was alive in God.

St. Peter and St. Paul are depicted together as the founders of the Church of Rome. They were said to have been executed on the same day and are shown taking leave of each other, or being put to death together. St. Paul's attribute is the sword that cut off his head (this was his right as a Roman citizen). It is also a reference to the "sword of the spirit" (Eph 6: 17). His severed head bounded three times, and at each point where it touched the ground, three fountains (*Trei fontane*) gushed forth. He returned from the dead to give back to Plantilla, a Christian follower, the veil that she had given him to bind his eyes before his execution. In art St. Paul is usually shown holding an inverted sword, but he may hold a book or scrolls to represent his epistles. When twinned with St. Peter, he stands for the Church of the Gentiles and St. Peter the Church of the Circumcision. Paul's emphasis on justification through faith caused him to be considered by Protestants as their champion. Thus St. Paul's Cathedral, London, is in some ways intended to contrast with St. Peter's, Rome, the Church of the Counter-Reformation.

St. Paul's statement that he was "caught up into paradise, and heard unspeakable words, which it is not lawful for a man to utter" (2 Cor 12: 4) was elaborated in the apocryphal *Apocalypse of Paul* into a vision of the torments of Hell, which was so vivid that it influenced the representation in art of the Last Judgment. He himself was afflicted with a mysterious illness, "a thorn in the flesh, the messenger of Satan to buffet me, lest I should be exalted above measure" because of the mystical vision which he had been granted (2 Cor 12: 7).

SAINT RAPHAEL: One of the three archangels named in the Bible (Tob 12: 15), the others being Gabriel and Michael. He is also one of the seven angels who stand in the presence of the Lord. As his name means in Hebrew, "God heals", Raphael was said to be the angel who stirred the waters of the Pool of Bethesda. As he protected Tobias on his journey, he is the model of the guardian angel. He is also the protector of travellers and pilgrims and is thus sometimes depicted as a winged wayfarer with staff and scrip (or wallet). When he carries a fish, the reference is to his adventures in company with Tobias. A jar of ointment recalls his cure of Tobit's blindness (Tob 11: 7-8) and indicates that Raphael is the patron of apothecaries.

LONG LIVE THE REPUBLIC: THE THREE ANTONIOS

Characters

ANTOINE GREMEY

ANTOINE GRAMUSSET

ANTONIO DE ROJAS

JULIANA

MANUELA

FERNANDA

THE BOY

SARAVIA

MANUEL DE OREJUELA

ADRIANNE

SERAFINA

THE SLAVE

THE GOVERNOR

THE JUDGE

CONSTABLE

ROUSSEAU

The play is based upon the historical facts known as the case of *The Three Antonios* during the colonial period in Chile, when two Frenchmen and one Chilean conspired to establish The Republic.

To further their cause they wrote *The Polpaíco Manifesto* (1785), a declaration similar to the *Declaration of the Rights of Man* (1789), published in France right after the French Revolution.

JULIANA and The BOY emerge from the earth. They look, they chase each other, they run between ditches and columns ... They are stopped by the sound of an aria ... ROUSSEAU emerges.

THE BOY: You're dying, Rousseau. What eternal roots your tongue sowed, what beautiful horizons your eyes wove, leave me your shadow so that I can bask in your aura.

ROUSSEAU: Bury me, Flavio, bury me. Don't let my hands touch steel; don't let my feet drag through the dust ... seal my eyes with melted lead, cut out my tongue and burn it completely.

THE BOY: It's too late now, Rousseau ... It's already too late ...

ROUSSEAU: Sing then, Flavio, sing one of my operas. Sing that I've confused everything I thought, that power was like music, and liberty a poem ... If I've been wrong, Flavio ...? How many torments draw near! ... How many libertarian passions shipwrecked on the reefs ... Flavio, tyranny's reefs are stronger ...

THE BOY: The Frigates have already raised anchor, Rousseau ... and your ideas are blazing in their masts. It's already too late ... Rousseau ...

ROUSSEAU: Stop them, Flavio! Stop them! They'll realize ... they'll come to realize that I was only a poet. Flavio, if democracy grows old like my body, and the people, it's heart, no longer has the passion to beat ... Man is the heart of the state, but he has to beat, to beat ... Who will make him tremble? ... Poetry, Flavio ... I've written nothing more than a farce ...

THE BOY: We're arriving, Rousseau.

ROUSSEAU: Sing, Flavio ... the Supreme Being calls me and reason no longer serves me ... Sing! ... Sing! May they pardon me ...

(Allegory of ROUSSEAU's death. A shooting star passes and a noise shakes the sky. On a sailing ship off the coast of America ANTOINE GREMEY and ADRIANNE tremble.)

GREMEY: Rousseau has died ... Adrianne ...

ADRIANNE: I know, Antoine. Let's kneel and pray the Lord takes him to his bosom ...

GREMEY: Here, Adrianne, we'll scatter his ideas across these coasts we're approaching and from these lands those sitting comfortably in the thrones of injustice will be made to tremble.

ADRIANNE: The sea ... Antoine ... The sea is red.

GREMEY: It's the heat, Adrianne, the heat of the New World ...

ADRIANNE: Beloved husband, keep quiet in these Spanish lands.

GREMEY: They don't belong to Spain; they belong to the men who inhabit them.

ADRIANNE: Antoine, when will we stroll beneath the grapevines again?

(Allegory of being received in America ... Music, Carmen Miranda dances or negro songs.)

GREMEY: Listen, Adrianne ... listen, the torrents of these lands, the shouts of its people, listen, Adrianne ... The New World receives us, its waterfalls bathe our foreheads, its rivers sate our thirst, its forests embrace us, the mountains unleash a thousand rocks like cannon fire ... The New World receives us, Adrianne ...

(A storm is unleashed, the ship shakes, MANUELA FERNÁNDEZ enters wildly clutching a clock, a black woman, her SLAVE, follows her.)

SLAVE: Ayy, mother mine we're goin' to drownnn! Baby Jesus protect us ... Ayy, we're goin' drownnn, Saint Martin of Porres protect us ... Ayy, Virgen of the condemned, protect this po' negro ...

MANUELA: Be quiet, woman ... Ayy, my clock fell. Shut up, you stupid nigger, if you don't, I'll sell you.

SLAVE: Ayy, mamacita, don't sell this poor negro to someone else ...

MANUELA: You, Monsieur, don't you want a screaming nigger ...?

GREMEY: Madame, I'm a Humanist ...

MANUELA: And for just that reason she'll be useful to you. You French are always conducting strange experiments ... Aren't you?

ADRIANNE: The sea is blue, Antoine ...

GREMEY: Come here, child, soon these lands will be yours and no man will have the authority to subject you ...

SLAVE: Master, this negro won't scream anymo', I won't scream anymo' ...

MANUELA: *(Stroking her clock.)* It's gone, the storm is gone. This is the only thing that strikes the hour in Castile as it does here ...

ADRIANNE: We've brought ... *(She looks at her hands and cries.)* ...

MANUELA: Ayyy, Monsieur, tell me about the court. Is the Countess of Paris still so loose with her skirts? And His Majesty, this little fat one you have, so refined, those ballets in Versailles must be marvelous!

ADRIANNE: Madame ... Look at the dolphins.

(The action stops to observe the dolphins passing. During all the following scenes the frigate remains onstage. Between sea trunks and ropes suspended in the space, this creates a series of parallel pictures. ANTOINE writes with his pen, ADRIANNE folds fabric, The SLAVE fans Manuela ... The ship moves ... ANTONIO DE ROJAS sends his books to the Viceroyalty of Chile.)

ANTONIO: More than three hundred, Serafina, obtained during three years of arduous searching. Mathematics, Latin, Astronomy, Engineering, and man's fantasies. They sent me this from St. Petersburg.

SERAFINA: I'll wear their names like hair ribbons; I'm also a jewel, Antonio ...

ANTONIO: This is the Armada that will fight ignorance in the Indies.

SERAFINA: Let me sail and fight with them ...

ANTONIO: They leave tomorrow on the Aurorita and in six months they lay down their roots in Valparaíso … Wrap them well. Dampness will destroy them as much as tyranny.

SERAFINA: You're leaving and I'll be left sewing banners …

ANTONIO: Careful with those, they're prohibited. This is Rousseau, an old man they call an Anti-Christ, a demon's abortion.

SERAFINA: Antonio, look at my lips …

ANTONIO: I suffer to think of them falling into the hands of some ignorant cleric, not to mention those devoted hypocrites who know more than all the devils in hell … We have to protect these good friends …

SERAFINA: Don't leave me in Spain … Take me to the Indies …

ANTONIO: Read, Serafina, read others since honey isn't made for asses …

SERAFINA: My honey isn't for asses either. Read my letters, Antonio …

ANTONIO: They're not interested in this foolishness, for that they have their books that from the first page on give them a hundred, two hundred days of indulgence.

SERAFINA: Antonio, bind me and keep me on your most precious bookshelf.

ANTONIO: We'll change the covers, so they won't suspect. These boxes are worth more to me than if they were filled with silk or gold dust.

SERAFINA: Turn me into a book; stick me in your boxes …

ANTONIO: We won't see each other again, Serafina, your Indian returns to his jungle …

(SERAFINA desperately rolls about in the books.)

SERAFINA: Antonio … I too am liberty!

JULIANA AND THE BOY

JULIANA: Keep reading, child, keep reading …

THE BOY: I'm not done; I've still got the Third Antonio's story to go ...

JULIANA: And the "Reina del Mar" that doesn't appear. Child, don't you see two black chimneys, don't you see the smoke over the waves ...? And that noise ...

THE BOY: They're planes, aunt ...

JULIANA: They say they painted them red ... take me to the beach with my bracelets; we'll look for messages. *(JULIANA puts her hands in a pool of water.)*

THE BOY: What are you talking about ...?

JULIANA: They're shouting outside, if voices had power few of us would have tongues. But let them shout, it's nothing more than air, only puffs of air.

THE BOY: It's the Frente Popular, aunt.

JULIANA: Bring me my hat, so he finds me like I was when he left, my rings, child, my rings.

THE BOY: Where are you going ...?

JULIANA: To the shore, don't you see, child, don't you see their black chimneys on the horizon ...? It's the "Reina del Mar" ... Here comes Antonio ... Wave to him, wave to him so he sees us. Show him the open box, the one he promised me he'd fill with envelopes ... What are they shouting for ... ! Why are they shouting?

THE BOY: They're for Ibañez, aunt ...

JULIANA: As if opening your mouth and emitting sounds was enough ... if that were only enough ...

THE BOY: Should I continue reading, aunt?

FERNANDA'S VISIT

FERNANDA can't look up, she carries an empty cage in her right hand.

FERNANDA: Let's go in, no air for us, Saint Ermengilda ...

JULIANA: Sweets from the Augustine nuns.

FERNANDA: One, to fill you with love.

JULIANA: Let's pray the rosary.

FERNANDA: I just finished praying it, aunt.

JULIANA: When will the frigate arrive? Manuela is bringing us a harpsichord.

FERNANDA: Harpsichord?

JULIANA: Music, Fernanda, music like they have at court ...

FERNANDA: What beautiful hands Doña Manuela has. It makes me sad, aunt ... when I come from the novena they look at me and laugh .

JULIANA: With envy, child, with envy ...

FERNANDA: They say an Indian bewitched me, and that's why I can't raise my eyes ...

JULIANA: Those who look at the ground can see what's hidden, Fernanda ...

FERNANDA: Yes, I see their footprints. I was watching, aunt, who was here wearing English boots?

JULIANA: He's a fine-looking young man, full of gallantry, his name is Antonio Rojas, and he'll be at the Tertulia ... Fernanda.

FERNANDA: I'm scared, aunt, after what happened in Chillan, these foreigners scare me.

JULIANA: The Irishman ...?

FERNANDA: Yes, they say that he climbed under Riquelme's sheets in the dead of night and took away her honor ...

(Thunder and trembling.)

JULIANA: The Republic has given birth to one of its men ...

(FERNANDA and JULIANA pray.)

"Your fecund mother died in her eighth month and three days later they opened her, on the side with a steel point, from the bloody wound they took your prodigious self ...

Be his protector and guide Ramón Nonato Glorioso ..."

ON THE FRIGATE

SLAVE: Today was bornn ... today was boorn ... the one who will liberate this poor Negress ...

MANUELA: We've arrived ... We've arrived, finally we have arrived ... how beautiful, don't you like it, Monsieur Gremey ... The Viceroyalty of Chile ...

GREMEY: It's beautiful, señora ... very beautiful ...

ADRIANNE: There are grapevines, Antoine ... there are grapevines ...

MANUELA: Countess, from now on, Monsieur Gremey ... I bought the coat of arms of a Countess in Spain.

GREMEY: Pardon me, Countess ...

MANUELA: You'll be enchanted by Santiago once you get to know it, it's not like Paris, but we soon will be ... Monsieur.

ADRIANNE: There's hunger in Paris.

MANUELA: Hunger! How can they be hungry when they even eat snails ...? What a relief, I haven't been able to let go of it *(The wall clock.)*, the way the frigate has been moving ... I've also brought a harpsichord, Monsieur ... They're going to be green with envy ...

(Music, the din of arrival.)

MANUELA: Julianaa ... Fernandaa ... Look, even the Judge is here. Yoo-hoo. Come in my calash, Baron Gremey.

GREMEY: The gifts the Lord has blessed me with won't increase because I'm a Baron.

MANUELA: Voila le Chili!

(Choreography that demonstrates the colony, music ... Some plant, others beat wet clothes against the ground ... The characters on the frigate remain frozen on the stairs while the following scene proceeds.)

JULIANA AND THE BOY

THE BOY: The Frente Popular won, aunt ...

JULIANA: I know, child ... I know, but read, read ... read about the City of Caesars ...

THE BOY: And the Third Antonio ...

JULIANA: Yes, the third ...

THE BOY: And Antonio Gramusset on the banks of the Mapocho began to build a machine that would make his fortune, the destiny he'd been denied.

ANTONIO GRAMUSSET AND MANUEL

GRAMUSSET: I've worked lands, dug mines and nothing, Manuel, riches have gone up in smoke, but with this machine, my fingernails will turn to gold. I'll go to Lima and live like I've deserved.

MANUEL: No, Antonio, come with me on the expedition, we'll conquer the City of Caesars, and there we'll dress ourselves anew in the smoothest silks, our palates will enjoy dishes never seen, look how we're acclaimed, feel how the nymphs bathe our feet in rose perfume ... It's happiness, Antonio, we'll take your machine and we'll build it out of steel and gold like an obelisk in the midst of the Andes.

GRAMUSSET: Help me with this ... you'll have your city and I my riches.

(FERNANDA and ANTONIO DE ROJAS meet.)

FERNANDA: The English boots . . .

ANTONIO: Are you looking for something? Can I help you? ...

FERNANDA: My aunt says I'll be able to see what's hidden like this ...

ANTONIO: Are you going to the plaza?

FERNANDA: It's fish market day.

ANTONIO: I've got a hidden soul; perhaps you'd be able to see it?

FERNANDA: What are you suffering from, señor?

ANTONIO: From seeing you ... remembering Spain, from Ignorance ...

FERNANDA: It's late; the sun no longer illuminates your boots ...

(FERNANDA takes off and runs into JULIANA who's going to see ANTONIO GRAMUSSET's invention.)

JULIANA: Fernanda. Let's go to the river to see Antonio's machine.

GRAMUSSET: Look, Manuel, they're coming to see it ... Keep working you Indian idiots or we'll never finish.

JULIANA: Explain your invention to us, Señor.

GRAMUSSET: Look. On this spot we'll erect two towers taller than two hundred feet ...

JULIANA: What! ... Taller than the towers of the Iglesia de la Compañía, Monsieur Gramusset ...

GRAMUSSET: That's right, now that the Lord has sent us science to use and make this kingdom one of the most powerful in the universe ... They'll fuse wheels taller than what transports your calashes ...

FERNANDA: Who will be able to move them, Monsieur ...?

GRAMUSSET: Four reins made of double leather will connect them to five mules, that walking in a circle will make the wheels turn ..., and thus by the art of hydraulic science we will remove the water inundating our mines and their treasures will be within our reach ...

JULIANA: You'll be rich, Antonio ...

GRAMUSSET: Yes, and I hope that our glorious monarch will bestow upon me its exclusive use in all of his colonies ...

FERNANDA: You'll have to dig deep, Señor ...

JULIANA: Don Antonio, come tomorrow, we'll introduce you to another Frenchman.

(GREMEY's arrival and JULIANNA's welcome.)

MANUELA: Look, Santiago du Chili ...

ADRIANNE: They aren't wearing shoes; they're bathing in the ditches.

MANUELA: Degenerate races, poor people ...

ADRIANNE: There's a gallows in the plaza.

MANUELA: To scare the indigenous, nothing more ...

GREMEY: And this smell?

MANUELA: The filth, Monsieur ... I'll leave you with Juliana; she's only a creole, a mixture, Monsieur, a mixture ...

GREMEY: I'll teach them French, Madame.

MANUELA: The poor thing doesn't know what to do so they notice her.

JULIANA: Welcome, Señor, Señora, I've been waiting for you impatiently, here's your home, your student *(She presents FERNANDA.)* ...

MANUELA'S LESSONS

MANUELA: Julianaaa, I've got so much to tell you, let's see, where did I leave that clock ...

(Choreography to the sound of a minuet.)

First, forget about chickpeas and dried beans in your shoes ... You walk like this ... your hand here ... the fan like that ... you walk like this, your little foot here, your little mouth there, the fan here . . . the hand there ... Greeting like this ... greeting ... like this ... Ayyy, I'm exhausted.

THE MEETING OF THE TWO ANTONIOS

JULIANA: Antoine Gramusset ... Antoine Gremey ...

GREMEY: From Bordeaux, Monsieur.

GRAMUSSET: From Rheims ...

GREMEY: Tell me what's happening in the New World.

GRAMUSSET: Tell me what's happening in the Old World.

MANUELA: And you, sir, have you found your citadel?

MANUEL: Soon, señora, soon.

MANUELA: Countess, it seems you're not up to date ... Uyy, these two have already become friends, one of them is bewitched and the other one makes me crazy with his yellow and green sea ...

ADRIANNE: If you like I can teach you some weaving patterns and the letters ...

FERNANDA: Thank you, Señora, but we don't have wool or printing presses here ... You have scales on your feet!

GRAMUSSET: Did you come to make your fortune, Gremey?

GREMEY: I'm here to teach.

GRAMUSSET: You'll have your academy, I'll finance you. I'm going to buy a palace in Rheims and you'll have all the vines from Bordeaux.

GREMEY: I see three heads on pikes.

GRAMUSSET: It's a country of Indians, Gremey, and let's not forget that the barbarians destroyed Rome.

GREMEY: They're whipping them!

GRAMUSSET: They'll have burned the bread ... I'll have the best carriages and silks in France ...

GREMEY: A France without carriages or silks is coming – we'll be free ...

GRAMUSSET: Only riches will make us free, Antoine ...

WOMEN EMBROIDERING

The embroidering women, hypnotized, advance towards the horizon in ecstasy.

JULIANA: Look at Antonio, the way he moves his arms, the French are handsome.

MANUELA: I'll tell you later ...

ADRIANNE: Antoine's the only one I know.

FERNANDA: What color are his shoes?

MANUELA: They tickle your ears ...

JULIANA: Are they friendly and sincere ...?

FERNANDA: Do their boots shine?

MANUELA: They squeeze, Juliana, they squeeze.

ADRIANNE: Antoine's the only one I know.

MANUELA: The neck fascinates them ...

FERNANDA: Do they wear buckles or laces?

JULIANA: They feel your anger and your happiness.

MANUELA: Tongues that run on and on.

FERNANDA: Do they wear worn heels?

MANUELA: They die for breasts.

ADRIANNE: The only one I know is Antoine.

FERNANDA: And their soles, what are their soles like ...?

MANUELA: They take you by the wrists, they cover your mouth, they lift you up and let you go, they whip you, they whip you, and they bite you ...

(They repeat monosyllables from their speeches.)

THE OBSESSIONS OF THE MEN

MANUEL: Come to my city and each of you shall have his dream.

GREMEY: What city are you talking about?

GRAMUSSET: The gold is slipping away from us.

MANUEL: You'll find it in the middle of the Andes.

GREMEY: A Republic in the middle of these mountains. Manuel. Your walls are made of marble.

GRAMUSSET: I'll glove my hands in deerskin ...

GREMEY: No more subjects, only free men ... Manuel. Your temples are made of worked stone ...

GRAMUSSET: Six black horses for each one of the calashes.

GREMEY: The community will elect its representatives.

MANUEL: The lands are so healthy that sickness is unknown.

GRAMUSSET: Silver jars and aromatic water to bathe my body.

GREMEY: No more subjects, only citizens ...

MANUEL: Whiter than Athens, greener than Babylon.

GRAMUSSET: Featherbeds and leather couches.

GREMEY: No one will be opulent enough to buy another, nor miserable enough to have to sell oneself.

(A chorus of men and women repeats one of their sentences, the chorus fades as the music begins ... Individually they dance "el cuando" or some other colonial dance. FERNANDA's warning interrupts the dance.)

FERNANDA: There's a dust cloud coming this way ... I'm scared ... Did you step in a puddle, señor?

ANTONIO: Your hairdo is pretty.

MANUELA: This one's a good catch, Magistrate of Lampa, Cavalry Captain, and all those noble titles ... Don Antonio, what a surprise, how strange that we never saw each other at court ...

JULIANA: Señores, Antonio Rojas, Antoine Gremey and Antoine Gramusset ...

THE BOY: Aunt, the three Antonios have come together.

JULIANA: I know, child, I know ... The "Reina del Mar" stopped ... and they've lit the lights. Are they dancing, child? ... And these wails, why are they wailing?

THE BOY: The President committed suicide.

JULIANA: That is why they stopped him, that's why ... Give me my bracelets; I have to pick up Antonio's button. Your button, Señor ...

GRAMUSSET: My gratitude, Señora ...

JULIANA: Give me your livery and I'll fix it for you.

ANTONIO: Welcome to our lands and I hope you come not to conquer but to extol the knowledge and learning that has been denied us for so long.

GREMEY: Latin and verses fertilize our spirits; I am no more than a humble laborer.

THE ARRIVAL OF THE TRAITOR SARAVIA

SARAVIA: Monsieur Saravia at your service … I admire French culture, Monsieur Gremey; I even have a French ancestor. Marivaux, … Racine, philosophy, the porcelain … so many things, no? …

MANUELA: I brought a miniature from Sevres with me …

GREMEY: What a pleasure, señor, we could get together for readings …

SARAVIA: In any case, the tedium of the colonies coarsens one. They say that the classics are all the rage, I've got Plato here, logic isn't simple.

ANTONIO: You won't be alone in Chile, Gremey …

GREMEY: What a pleasure to meet you, I sense that you have faith in thought …

SARAVIA: Of course, Gremey, faith in both God and Man, in a short time this kingdom will be talked about, have no doubt …

GREMEY: I don't doubt it, Señores.

SARAVIA: It will be the richest in all the Indies, isn't that so, Don Antonio?

FERNANDA: What beautiful feet you have, Countess …

MANUELA: Seriously? Well, one has to take care of oneself since they're the only thing you can show …

(They leave.)

GREMEY: Did you hear, Adrianne? Did you hear how reason echoes in these lands? …

ADRIANNE: Crickets, Antoine, crickets ... they stick to the walls ...

GREMEY: They're the candles and the lime ... Adrianne.

ADRIANNE: Take your apron; it's what you came for ...

GREMEY'S CLASSES

Two boys roll in the mud, others climb the wardrobes ... Music.

GREMEY: La nuit ... la nuit: l'aube ... l'aube ... la n, et la u, nu ... la n, et la u, nu ... You don't know how to write, you don't have ink, you don't have shoes ...

ADRIANNE: They'll learn, Antoine, they will learn ...

JULIANA: Have patience, señor; life isn't easy in our kingdom ...

GREMEY: I'll get used to it, señora, I'll get used to it ...

JULIANA: Bien sür.

GREMEY: Very good pronunciation, señora.

(They laugh happily. Saravia passes with his fighting cocks.)

SARAVIA: Come to the fight, Gremey, come, one of these will beat the governor's ...

GREMEY: Thank you, but I should persevere.

SARAVIA: Don't fatigue yourself, come see my roosters. Then I'll talk to the rector of Carolingian Academy so that you can give your philosophy courses ...

GREMEY: I'm grateful, señor ...

SARAVIA: We're here to serve, Gremey, come, come ...

(FERNANDA runs, they throw mud at her, she falls.)

JULIANA'S TALE

JULIANA: Fernanda, in order to know and to count, bread and flour for the Augustinian nuns, flour and bread for the nuns of Saint John, tea and orchids for the beggars, rice and flour for our Lord ... Fernanda, in a kingdom far, far away lived an enchanted girl, she was reviled, and her hunchback caressed an evil fairy's breast ... To hide her injury she hid between the brambles. One fine day she met a shepherd who smiled at her.

SHEPHERD: Come with me to look for something bright,

Come with me and be my guiding light ...

JULIANA: Since everyone maltreated her because of her hump she didn't believe the shepherd was talking to her. And she closed her eyes thinking that the verses he recited were meant for her.

SHEPHERD: Come with me, we'll play on the beaches,

Come with me to pick peaches.

JULIANA: When she heard him she bolted, but she got caught in the thorns. The shepherd looked at her and taking her by the arm showed her his flocks ...

FERNANDA: She, scared, threw herself into the river and the shepherd followed her ... The river's torrent carried them both along. And if you go to the river now you will hear their words of love since the Lord has united them ...

I'll go ... I'll go ...

(FERNANDA leaves at a run, while MANUELA passes in parallel with her slave.)

MANUELA: How boring, nothing happens here ... At least the Indians could invade us.

GRAMUSSET AND GREMEY CONSPIRE

GRAMUSSET: It's going slowly, it's going very slowly. The iron doesn't arrive, the Governor doesn't respond. I'll be old, Antoine, I'll be old before my hands turn to gold.

GREMEY: There's discontent, the creoles complain.

GRAMUSSET: They've raised taxes.

GREMEY: England has declared war on Spain.

GRAMUSSET: What if we made your Republic, Antoine? ... Let's build your Republic.

GREMEY: You're delirious.

GRAMUSSET: I'm serious; let's destroy the monarchy.

GREMEY: It sounds like a dream, we can't Antoine, and the two of us can't do it alone.

GRAMUSSET: What are we here for, Gremey? Why did we cross the seas? We didn't leave our France just to come here and sink in the mud.

GREMEY: But the two of us can't do it alone. They have canons, soldiers.

(SARAVIA passes by on his way back from the fight.)

SARAVIA: What a battle, Gremey ... What a battle! These are my heroes, Gremey; I'll give them the best grain.

GREMEY: They're birds, señor.

SARAVIA: The Governor won't sleep tonight. I'm sorry, Gremey, the rector wouldn't accept you as a member of the Academy. He's afraid of the sciences. But we'll keep trying, isn't that right, my swaggering beauties?

GREMEY: It's the only Academy. I had hopes.

SARAVIA: Come celebrate, Gremey ... come.

GREMEY: Reason will illuminate their minds ...

GRAMUSSET: The creoles will follow us – have no doubts.

GREMEY: I'd forgotten that this is why I came – I'd forgotten it.

GRAMUSSET: We'll declare Independence and then we'll establish the dictatorship.

GREMEY: No, Gramusset. Only the order of free men.

GRAMUSSET: As I said, a dictatorship, while we organize the new order.

GREMEY: That's not the way it's written, Gramusset.

GRAMUSSET: As you wish, I know nothing of philosophy – you make the proclamation.

GREMEY: And if they denounce us, Antoine? What if they denounce us?

GRAMUSSET: They won't be able to. It's like my machine, Gremey. We're going to build a great pyramid, each of us will look for a supporter and he will connect with another, without informing on the one before, and then that one with another and another and another until we'll be thousands, Gremey, thousands. But we won't know them and they won't know us, but we'll all act as one.

GREMEY: For the Republic ...

GREMEY ANNOUNCES

GREMEY: *(Announcing.)* Adrianne, I've been chosen, the Lord and men desire the establishment of equality and reason in this land ...

ADRIANNE: I have to go to France ...

GREMEY: I will build a Republic, a model for the universe, nations will follow us, and we will be the guiding star ...

ADRIANNE: I have to go with them to Versailles.

GREMEY: Man, Adrianne ... will reconstruct paradise. Happiness, Adrianne. Happiness will be for all.

ADRIANNE: The women are surrounding the palace, Antoine; I have to go weave the garlands. Look, Antoine ... Look, the sky is blue ...

MANUELA AND THE NEGRESS

MANUELA: Well, it's blue ... Isn't it terrible, Don Antonio? The amount I paid for this Negress and now they authorize free trade with the Congo! Just imagine! ... Prices will fall! ... Shut up, you screeching nigger ... She's well fed, not calloused, look ... Turn around, you ... she sings too ... I'm taking her to the plaza to see if I can recoup something ... going for 300, the little black bitch ... for 300, healthy with all her teeth *(MANUELA cries)*, she knows how to clean and iron, for 300.

SLAVE: Mistress, don't sell this po' Negress...

THE CONSPIRACY

GRAMUSSET and MANUEL.

GRAMUSSET: Prepare your expedition, Manuel, saddle the horses; we're going to build a Republic.

MANUEL: I don't understand you.

GRAMUSSET: The Republic will meet the City of Caesars...

GREMEY and ANTONIO DE ROJAS

GREMEY: I don't know what you think; I only wanted to confide in you ...

ANTONIO: It's wonderful, Antoine, wonderful! You can count on me and my friends. More than one regimental captain is tired of obeying drunken, uncultured generals.

JULIANA AND GRAMUSSET

(JULIANA strolling with wildflowers.)

JULIANA: You seem distressed ... and your building has stopped ...

GRAMUSSET: No, Madame, I'm happy. These machines will sprout like wheat; hundreds of frigates will pile up in the ports to ship them off to every capital in the Indies.

JULIANA: If you've got another livery lacking buttons ... I could ...

GRAMUSSET: Don't worry yourself, Señora, soon I'll have so many uniforms that when their buttons fall I'll give them to orphanages.

JULIANA: You're strange; you wash with your own hands.

GRAMUSSET: That's the way to strengthen the skin and to converse with you ...

ANTONIO DE ROJAS AND GREMEY

ANTONIO: Don Antonio, you've made me breathe again.

JULIANA AND GRAMUSSET

GRAMUSSET: Don't you want to be president of a nation? All these Spaniards would have to do you reverence and sit in the last row.

JULIANA: I govern my house, that's enough for me, Don Antonio.

GRAMUSSET: No, you're intelligent, come; let me tell you a secret ...

JULIANA: Child, where are you? I need you to read to me. They're going to declare Independence ... And the "Reina de Mar", you can't see it anymore.

ADRIANNE: They're writing the White, the Blue and the Red ... I have to go to France – I have to go ...

FERNANDA: Lines of wagons, naked feet, and this dust ... I can't see: I can't see ...

THE THREE ANTONIOS AND MANUEL

ANTONIO: A false message will give the alarm ...

GRAMUSSET: It will say the English are bombing the port.

MANUEL: They'll gather in the Governor's house to deliberate.

GRAMUSSET: That's where we'll take them. Others will disguise themselves as monks and incite rebellion.

GREMEY: They'll say that outside the Republic there is no salvation ...

GRAMUSSET: Others will take possession of the treasury.

MANUEL: We'll loose their horses and take their calashes ...

GREMEY: The revolution will take place without anyone losing a single strand of their property, nor a single drop of blood from their body.

ANTONIO: Come to my hacienda in Polpaíco, there the muses will guide your pen ...

THE DECLARATION OF THE RIGHTS OF MAN OF POLPAICO

Fires illuminate the horizon, with torches, music, and the declaration an epic procession takes place offstage.

MANUELA: What a smell, what can they be burning.

SARAVIA: It's guano; the wind brings the smell from the farms.

MANUELA: I'm going to asphyxiate ... it isn't your roosters ...?

ADRIANNE'S WARNING

ADRIANNE: We're nude and full of wounds; sea monsters devour us, Judas' thirty pieces of silver laugh at your pen.

GREMEY: The Supreme Being guides my hand, Adrianne. He desires his sons' liberty. We'll be both apostles and martyrs.

ADRIANNE: Stop your pen, Antoine ... Stop it ...

JULIANA AND THE BOY

JULIANA: What's happening to you, child? What's happening to you?

THE BOY: My hands, aunt ... my hands ...

THE WOMEN MEET

ADRIANNE: Let's prepare the garlands ... we'll make them like the ones for the grape festival.

FERNANDA: How are they woven?

ADRIANNE: I'll teach you.

JULIANA: Teach me too.

MANUELA: Ayy, they're preparing for the festival of Saint James the Apostle.

THE WOMEN'S SONG

For Santiago del Nuevo Extremo, I will embroider a flower to plant my love throughout its streets.

For gentlemen and poor men this flower I will weave, to leave dawn's sigh in their eyes.

What do you embroider, señoritas? If only you could know.

Jasmines and pearls for yesterday's dreams.

Tears and smiles for the festival of life.

What do you embroider, señoritas? If only you could know.

Garlands for an afternoon that will light all brows and your own.

For this afternoon that you weave I will also work.

For Santiago and its people you will also govern.

Garlands on one door will touch those on another and as they touch each household, love

will be received.

On that day happiness will shelter us all together and man will obtain it without my

painful laments.

The Republic will bring us this garland's gifts.

What are you embroidering, señoritas? If only you could know.

GRAMUSSET — MANUEL — GREMEY

GRAMUSSET: You're sure they're lost?

GREMEY: They got lost somewhere on the road from Santiago to Polpaíco.

MANUEL: The wind took them.

GREMEY: We have to find them or we'll be discovered.

GRAMUSSET: Were they signed?

GREMEY: No, but if they're found …

GRAMUSSET: What are you worried about? No one's going to find them.

MANUEL: Let's go back now ...

ONE THE EVE OF—FAREWELLS

ANTONIO: I want to give you a present.

FERNANDA: My gentleman.

ANTONIO: Remember me when you touch it.

FERNANDA: I'll always remember you, señor. Your footprints are in the corner of the hall.

GRAMUSSET — JULIANA

GRAMUSSET: Señora, I came to thank you.

JULIANA: A little bit of anise.

GRAMUSSET: Señora, I'm a foreigner and you've been so cordial that I feel like I'm back in the aroma of Rheims ...

JULIANA: You exaggerate, some anise?

GRAMUSSET: You'll have rubies and emeralds to adorn your neck.

GREMEY — ADRIANNE

GREMEY: They're filling the trunks.

ADRIANNE: They're ripping up the stones in the streets of Paris.

GREMEY: My eyes can't rest, they'll come looking for me ...

ADRIANNE: My beloved husband, talk to me.

GREMEY: Dear Adrianne, I don't want to leave you.

ADRIANNE: Keep everything ... call the calashes. They're meeting in Versailles. The King hasn't spoken. It's time to leave ... it's time to leave.

GREMEY: I didn't sign it, they can't find me, and I didn't sign it.

SARAVIA: Come, Antoine, let's go to the bullring ...

GREMEY: I should finish some lessons ...

SARAVIA: I've found some pamphlets that will interest you.

GREMEY: You found them ... Along the road?

SARAVIA: Proscribed writings, we could go to my cellar and I'll show them to you ...

GREMEY: What are they about, Señor?

SARAVIA: A book of luxuries you can't even imagine ...

GREMEY: I think I understand you.

SARAVIA: Men of reason always understand each other ...

GREMEY: Would you like to see men of reason govern these lands?

SARAVIA: Not only these lands, but the entire Universe.

GREMEY: I'm happy to hear you say so. Let me share a proposal with you ...

SARAVIA: Tell me, Antoine – tell me ...

FERNANDA'S FEAR

Carrying a giant rock–she throws it into the well in order to see her reflection.

FERNANDA: Mother of God, who always squashes lizards and demons with your feet ... I'm afraid of them, how many reptiles will surge out of the depths when you move without being careful?

THE BOY: Fernanda, tell Juliana to wait ...

FERNANDA: Who's speaking? I can't see your footprints ...

THE BOY: Two pages have disappeared; tell her two pages have disappeared ...

SARAVIA: Magnificent! Antoine, it's a perfect insurrection! Let's proceed immediately, why wait any longer? Let's proceed! ...

JULIANA: Child, child ... my bracelets... I can't see well, it looks like they're makings signals to us ...

SARAVIA: We'll all participate, Gremey, my relatives, my friends, even my roosters!

GREMEY: Calm down, Señor. And keep quiet.

(ADRIANNE sings her farewell.)

ADRIANNE: We're going, Antoine, we're going. We're taking the garlands, we're taking the looks, we're going, Antoine, we're going ... To the festivals in Paris.

THE DAWN OF THE CONSPIRACY

GREMEY: They sleep, but tomorrow they will awaken free.

ANTONIO: There will be Academies, Libraries, and Institutes ... Manuel, I will be the Colonel of the Princess Regiment and offer the City of Caesars to the Republic.

GRAMUSSET: Think of how many machines will be needed, so many ...

GREMEY: We'll have to clean ditches, organize the market, open the registers, and count the citizens ...

MANUEL: Soon, friends, soon ...

SARAVIA'S DELIRIUM

SARAVIA: Yes, yes, prepare the insurrection. The governor prisoner, no more flag processions, no more Royal Audiences. No more cockfights, or court parties, only equality, equality...

MANUELA: Saravia ... Saravia ... have you heard the latest? The English fleet is sailing into port; they're going to invade usss ...

SARAVIA: Rumors, Countess ... rumors ...

MANUELA: The English are such gentlemen, but doesn't it make you nervous? ...

SARAVIA: It's beginning, it's the plan, the Frenchmen's plan; it's their plan ...

MANUELA: Ayyy, they aren't French. Saxons, Saravia ...
Saxons.

SARAVIA: I'm afraid of the noose. My lands, the whips ...

MANUELA: Now, now, you ... "Good Morning", and they'll
treat you well ...

SARAVIA: It's the insurrection, Countess, Gremey and
Gramusset's plan ...

MANUELA: Nooo, not here in the kingdom, noo, didn't I say
they brought something? ...

SARAVIA: They've confided in me and I don't know ...

MANUELA: But who ordered them to do the things they think?
Go to the Royal Audience immediately and tell them
everything. I don't want to see you hanging in the plaza ...
go ... go ...

SARAVIA: But, Countess ... but ...

MANUELA: But what? ... Or do you want slaves to rule us? ...
Look at how my hands are shaking ...

SARAVIA: Thank you, Señora. You've saved me from the abyss.

MANUELA: Creoles in the Palace ... Nooo ...

SARAVIA'S BETRAYAL

GOVERNOR: Are you sure, Saravia? My ears have never heard
such a black and infernal ruse. Just listening to you makes
me grind my teeth, Saravia.

SARAVIA: Excellency, nothing more than my fealty and
obedience to our Sovereign brings me to your feet ...

GOVERNOR: You have saved yourself from Hell, Saravia, and
from terrible agonies. Leave and fear no more.

(Winds and earth whip the blackness.)

JULIANA: Fernanda, close the shutters, put out the candles ...

FERNANDA: It's going to quake ... It's going to quake ...

JULIANA: I don't know, I don't know, but I don't want the light of this night entering my house.

GREMEY'S CAPTURE

GREMEY: Adrianne, it's been so long since I've been in your arms ...

ADRIANNE: Antoine, Antoine, your hair is wet.

CONSTABLE: Antoine Gremey, leave your wife and come with us.

GREMEY: Who are you? ...

CONSTABLE: You're to be judged, but neither heaven nor earth will pardon you.

GREMEY: I didn't write it, Señores. My hand was guided by reason and the wishes of our Lord. Don't you understand that God is free and desires the same for his children?

CONSTABLE: Silence, blasphemer!

ADRIANNE: You'll always take my hand, Antoine, always, come on, let's stroll beneath the grapevines ...

GRAMUSSET'S CAPTURE

GRAMUSSET: Set me free, I've done nothing! Let me go, I tell you ...

CONSTABLE: You deny what is sure as fire.

GRAMUSSET: Nothing your tongue spits is true. Let me go, I tell you.

CONSTABLE: You deny it, Antoine? If that's so nothing will save you.

GRAMUSSET: You're stopping my construction, the future of the kingdom.

JULIANA'S DESPERATION

JULIANA: Fly Manuel, Fly Antonio de Rojas, Fly Antoine,
  so that this dawn is covered with veils and the "Reina del
  Mar" is seen no more.

THE TRIAL

GOVERNOR: You have plotted to destroy one of the most
  precious jewels of the Royal Crown. You should be grateful
  for the ground that protects you.

GREMEY: My writings betray me. Oh, my perfidious pen.
  Adrianne, forgive me.

JUDGE: Silence, Antoine, silence. The forces of evil possess you.

GREMEY: And you found them. The wind took them from me
  on the road to Polpaíco, and you found them.

GOVERNOR: Don't deny the hell you meant to establish.

GRAMUSSET: You're making me lose time. I don't understand
  a thing you say.

GREMEY: Reading them didn't convert you. You read them and
  didn't feel as if the horizons opened and the trees of your
  land grew larger, or the clouds laughed. You didn't feel it.

GOVERNOR: Silence, Gremey, you're mad.

JUDGE: Confess, Antoine Gramusset and we'll put an end to this.

GRAMUSSET: I have nothing to say to you ... Let me go ...

GREMEY: It was my thought alone, Señores, no one else. Let
  him go free, it's my ink, my hand, and my pen.

GRAMUSSET: You've heard him. Let me go free, you're
  stopping my construction.

GOVERNOR: Burn his construction.

GRAMUSSET: My invention, Señores, you can't, you can't ...

JUDGE: You'll see the flames from here, Gramusset.

GOVERNOR: Cover his lands with wagons of salt ...

GRAMUSSET: I beg you, don't kill God's earth.

GREMEY: Take all my worldly goods, deport me to France, but let me go die in Bordeaux ...

JUDGE: You'll die in the public square, in the light of day and the opprobrium of this kingdom.

GRAMUSSET: I know nothing, I've done nothing, I'm innocent I tell you ...

GREMEY: Permit me a pen ...

JULIANA: How will we clothe ourselves in Paris, child? ...

GOVERNOR: Put them on the first frigate to Lima, they'll take charge of them there ...

JUDGE: What? What about their punishment? ...

GOVERNOR: Do you want to make them martyrs and sow the word "Republic" throughout the Colonies? No, Señores, this never happened and you will swear your silence.

JUDGE: And the others ...

GOVERNOR: Don't think you can try Rojas and the creoles won't mutiny. They'll keep quiet for their own good.

(GREMEY and GRAMUSSET, boarding the frigate.)

GRAMUSSET: We embark, who knows for what island. Good-bye riches, good-bye Juliana.

GREMEY: Adrianne, in these lands looking at us will one day tremble those who rock in the thrones of injustice.

GRAMUSSET: We're no more than two prisoners on a miserable frigate. In Lima, Gremey, in Lima we'll escape ...

GREMEY: Flight, Gramusset ...?

GRAMUSSET: In Lima I'll have my riches and you your Liberty.

FERNANDA: Antonio's footsteps are disappearing – they're disappearing.

MANUEL: Antonio, they've taken the Frenchmen prisoner.

ANTONIO: I know. I'm going to Polpaíco to work my lands.

MANUEL: I'm going to my city. I'll descend with their golden armies and set them free, Antonio, I'll set them free.

JULIANA AND THE BOY

THE BOY: They're boarding the frigate, aunt.

JULIANA: I know, child, I know. We'll go to Bordeaux to receive them.

FERNANDA: The ground's covered with seaweed, the sand turns to foam … Good-bye, Antoine …

THE BOY: Page 289 is sad.

JULIANA: There isn't sadness, at most pains that disappear.

MANUELA AND THE NEGRESS

SLAVE: Don't hit this po' Negress, don't hit me.

MANUELA: Idiot, stupid, it's your fault those poor little ones drowned. It's your fault.

ON THE FRIGATE

GREMEY: Let's get rid of our clothes, they're the only things that sink, Gramusset …

JULIANA: Let's get rid of our clothes, child, and go to the festivals in Paris.

GRAMUSSET: You're right, Gremey, you're right. Leave them to the ocean's depths.

THE BOY: What did the Three Antonios look like, aunt? I can't find their portraits …

JULIANA: Let's go to France, that's where they should be. The "Reina del Mar" will take us.

GREMEY: Let's go to Paris, Gramusset. Where the Republic is being born.

(ADRIANNE enters dressed in white.)

ADRIANNE: Come, Antoine, come. We have to go to the Bastille and free the prisoners and look for powder for our rifles.

THE TAKING OF THE BASTILLE

Musical choreography. Everyone clambers up the grand stairs and picks up palm branches. The ANTONIOS edit decrees they throw into the air. The women descend carrying the symbols of the revolution: the triangle, the lead. The noise of the guillotine begins. The Three ANTONIOS climb up on its base. The women knit.

JULIANA: The public insults them. They try to speak to them.

ADRIANNE: They don't see, they don't see, liberty has blinded them …

JULIANA: They'll let them tear up the paving stones.

FERNANDA: They'll put laurel wreathes at their feet.

JULIANA: We've got a minute for the Republic not to succumb—now we have three seconds …

(The Three ANTONIOS are guillotined.)

ADRIANNE: The grapevines are drying, Antoine …

EPILOGUE

JULIANA: Take me to the rocks, child, the "Reina del Mar" is sinking. Antonio, Antonio, you'll find your riches …

THE BOY: They're shooting the patriots, aunt …

JULIANA: Look, look how the smoke of their chimneys is snuffed out, the people in their boats shout, the sea embraces them, child, the sea will protect them.

THE BOY: Should I continue reading, aunt? …

JULIANA: There are no more stories, child, at least not for me. Others will continue writing but you, stay here, you stay here so you can read them.

THE BOY: And that September morning, and that September morning …

THE END

GORDA

Characters

PANCHA

GORDA

THE LIFEGUARD (JORGE)

A YOUNG MAN

THE VOICE

Set description:

The stage space encompasses both the interior and the exterior settings of the play. Downstage, the beach with a small strip of land – the Lifeguard's place. Upstage, a balcony with a beach chair, framed by the curtains of an apartment with sliding glass windows, at the back a fragment of a bed.

The Voice parallels the characters' actions.

THE WOMEN

Strong sun, noises of the sea and people on the beach, music from a radio.
PANCHA speaks from beneath white sheets.

PANCHA: Ayy, Gorda, please, turn off the radio, close the
curtains, this dawn sun overwhelms me, it makes my
eyelashes twitch, it wrinkles my skin, I'll get zits, herpes or
who knows what. Have you ever seen anything worse than
the sun at 10am?

(GORDA slowly closes the curtains.)

THE VOICE: Gorda approached the sliding glass windows and,
with her big round eyes, her lips painted red, sketched a
small smile of satisfaction. Jorge turned his back to her
and his red elastic bathing suit made the roundness of
his buttocks and the narrowness of his waist stand out;
when he turned his head, Gorda timidly raised her hand,
knowing that, from the beach, she was nothing more than a
silhouette, a shape camouflaged by the folds of the curtain.

PANCHA: Gordita, the curtain, please, I'm exhausted, those
brutes left me worn out, coke cut more each time, it
seemed to me that they were snorting anesthesia or
amphetamines, you used to wake up feeling marvelous and
now it's like you'd snorted sulphur … Ay, I don't know.
Come here, you're going to die when I tell you, Gorda,
you can't imagine how much fun I had, I got in some car,
suddenly I was in a jeep with those big wheels, surrounded
by some seventeen year old boys. I couldn't believe it,
they treated me beautifully, it was marvelous, and I felt like
Cleopatra attended by four slaves. What more could you
want? On the whole, before you're eaten by worms, better
to be eaten by Christians …

(PANCHA has a coughing fit.)

THE VOICE: Gorda closed the curtains, and sat on the edge of
the bed. Pancha's stories, whether they were true or not,

were at least entertaining … When it reached 10PM she brought Pancha her glass of orange juice.

(GORDA enters with the orange juice.)

PANCHA: You've outdone yourself, Gorda, I'd better get up … Ay, I don't know what to wear … Let's see, the shirt with the mini skirt, nothing doing, or lycra with Bermudas, no, too aerobic, the matched set and ready …

(GORDA opens the curtains and sees JORGE who takes shorts and a shirt from a bag, fastens his sandals, and, sipping a drink, looks at the horizon …)

THE VOICE: She imagined he was looking at her, that he felt her solitude, her need for companionship and, uniting her gaze towards the horizon with his, they absorbed the ting-a-ling of Valparaíso's lights together.

PANCHA: Ay, Gorda, someone's at the door, go open it.

(GORDA lets in a young man, tan, with a wide smile.)

YOUNG MAN: Hi, is Pancha ready? Tell her to hurry up; they're waiting for us, nice place …

(GORDA disappears and then spies on them.)

PANCHA: Hi, where's Felipe?

YOUNG MAN: Who cares about Felipe? You look fantastic.

(They embrace and begin to get excited.)

PANCHA: Okay, let's get going or we never will … Loreto … Bye … See you later …

THE VOICE: Gorda sat in the armchair, hit the remote control, and watched the evening programs thinking of Jorge, about his diet, about the day he was going to take her in his arms …

(She sleeps. Daybreak, PANCHA enters.)

PANCHA: Divine, Gorda, … divine … It was divine. Ayy, bed looks so good, I'll tell you everything tomorrow.

(GORDA, carrying a coffee, sits on the balcony … she looks at the horizon waiting for JORGE to arrive.

When he enters the sun brightens, she takes off her shirt, puts on a straw hat, lies back in her beach chair and, contemplating him, paints her nails, reads magazines … the two of them seated watching the horizon. PANCHA wrapped in the sheets.)

PANCHA: Ayy, Gorda, bring me some mineral water … You're so loving, thanks.

THE VOICE: Thus, the day went by, him on his lifeguard's podium, she on the seventh floor balcony … And she, adjusting her chair, thought …

GORDA: This is quite the summer.

THE VOICE: When it was 5pm *(She looks at her watch.)*, she put on her sandals and a long, flowery dress and went down to walk among the rocks and the breaking waves …

Gorda And The Sea

She's on the beach, washing her face with seawater, looking for mollusks … jumping from steep rock to rock. Music.

THE VOICE: At the highest point she stopped and, wrapping her dress around her legs, tried to guess which of the hundreds of tiny figures was Jorge.

GORDA: If I threw myself in the water, and let myself be gulped down by the marvelous oscillation of the waves, he would see me, he would run to save me, he would take me in his arms and I'd feel the warmth of his breath, and I would revive and thank him for his bravery. I'd invite him to tea and make him the apple küchen I do so well. And I'd ask Pancha to do us a favor and leave us alone for the afternoon.

In The Apartment

PANCHA: Gorda, you're finally here, I was very upset, where could she be? I couldn't find you anywhere ... Ay, but Gorda my big bird, tell me something, look at me, here ... Do you see? My eyes are blue! Caroline lent them to me. Don't they look great?

GORDA: They're beautiful on you, Pancha.

PANCHA: And what have you been up to? Tell me, I came down out of pure boredom, I didn't feel like doing anything, but then this stupendous guy, much better looking than the one who drove you crazy in that video clip, laid a towel at my feet, I was so nervous, I was so not dressed, well, I'll make it brief, we ended up talking about everything, and now he's probably desperately waiting for me in Charlies, I'm super late ... kisses, Gorda, don't open the door for anyone.

Gorda's Illusion

She turns on the radio, wildly dances to reggae ... JORGE appears.

JORGE: Let's sit down.

(JORGE takes her by the hand.)

GORDA: He's going to tell me that this is the unmistakable heat of love.

(JORGE kisses her. Worn out, GORDA hugs a pillow ... then she pulls at the rolls of flesh around her waist, gets depressed.)

THE VOICE: She's been told she writes well, perhaps if she wrote some letters to Jorge, he would realize that there was someone else who shared the same feelings. She opened her writing pad and began what would be a long correspondence with her lifeguard.

GORDA: "You might find it strange to get this letter, you don't know me, and I'm sure that for you I'm nothing more than one of the thousands of grains of sand you contemplate on a daily basis, I don't want you to think that I'm fresh or forward, but tell me, when you look at the sea, do you always imagine the land on the other side of the horizon and do you think that there are other young people like us there, who are thinking about us? When you receive this, and if you agree, wave it, I'll see you, pardon me once more."

He probably gets hundreds of letters, he'll think I'm ridiculous, he'll think I'm crazy, what can I offer him?

THE VOICE: Conquering all her fears, with the greatest sense of daring in her entire life, she gave the missive to a boy who ran along the coast ... At 3p.m. Jorge waved a letter in the air.

(A suggestion: when GORDA finishes writing the letter, she makes a gesture with it in the air, the same gesture the lifeguard makes with the letter ... GORDA is overjoyed.)

THE VOICE: She felt like a beauty queen being crowned, she heard the hurrahs, the acclamations, and she could only hide her face in her hands.

The Second Missive

GORDA: "Jorge, you can't imagine the happiness you produced for me with a gesture that for you is surely so small, but when you raised your hand, it was so important for me, I've always thought, as I observed you opening umbrellas and planting them in the sand, that you feel like a magician planting wonders in a desert plain, if this is true, raise your hand please."

THE VOICE: At 4pm Jorge once more waved a paper in the air. Gorda was unable to do anything more than kneel, raise her head to heaven and declaim …

GORDA: Thank you Lord, My God, for giving me the happiest moments of my life.

THE VOICE: Serene now, sure that an unmistakable union had been established, she wrote her third message, revealing her first feeling.

GORDA: "Jorge, I hope you won't get scared or think I'm a witch, since I've discovered your thoughts twice now, but I was so sure … Before I introduce myself, if it's not too much trouble, I'd like your response, when you see so many bodies burning in the sun, turning themselves black, doesn't it make you think of a gigantic grill and the smell of the tanning lotion or boiling oil? I love you, your unknown friend."

THE VOICE: At 5:30pm Jorge got up and waved the paper in the air for more than a minute, trying to discover the author of these unusual messages.

GORDA: Ayy, Loreto, pinch yourself! So you know you're not dreaming.

THE VOICE: When she wrote her fourth missive she no longer enjoyed the same feeling of ecstasy, only a heavy weight on her chest.

GORDA: "Jorge, you have given me the most marvelous moments of my life, I will no longer ask you to wave your arm, I will no longer bother you with my writings, I know that we love each other and want this to last forever, in another moment you will meet me."

THE VOICE: Gorda took a pin and pinned the missive to her chest, she turned off the radio, straightened Pancha's bed, opened the sliding glass windows wide, extended her arms and ran through the apartment, the armchair, the pillows, her bag, the little lamp, the chair on the balcony and Pancha's towels paraded before her …

(Beach sounds, the sea. A flash of light blasts and ignites the scene. GORDA lies dead, smashed against the street with her hands open and her missive on her chest. The LIFEGUARD stands up on his podium, euphorically blowing his whistle.)

THE VOICE: A gigantic roar runs across the beach, as the center of the local volleyball team makes the winning point.

THE END

THE OPERA CLEANERS

Characters

OLD ROSA

MARITZA

THE CLEANER

LOLO

SAMUEL

The action takes place on the stage of the Opera Theatre,
then in the street, and in the young men's apartment.

First Sequence

In the Opera Theatre

The Cleaners stand in a line at the edge of the stage, each with their bucket and their mop.

Maritza's Performance

THE CLEANER: The three of us entered in a line, each of us with her bucket and her mop, and all at once we began to mop the stage, I knew that we wouldn't go three meters before Maritza would let her utensils fall and, gathering up her skirts, untying her bun, she'd begin to tap her heels like a flamenco dancer, believing herself to be the Great Martita of Lima.

> *(MARITZA leaves the stage and returns with a black mink, lowers her neckline and starts zapateando and singing cante jondo, she exits and then re-enters to receive her applause.)*

OLD ROSA: That's enough nonsense – we have to get home.

THE CLEANER: Maritza's the one something will happen to, she's saying good-bye.

MARITZA: Ayy, I'm tired, I don't know how the artists do it, and for such a long time.

OLD ROSA: This isn't a nightclub. Stop, since you don't know the difference between an artist and a … I better shut up, keep mopping, this has to shine tomorrow … Come over here, mijita, and let's show her what an artistic scene looks like; the one that the Spaniards did.

> "Stop looking at the plain …
> His horse is no longer there …
> It's the light of absence that makes you
> Cry so much."

THE CLEANER: "What are you saying?
> That I should stop watching?
> Leave my sad glance behind

… That I'm waiting in vain
For him to arrive …
You don't treat love with disdain,
Like straw does a wheat field."

OLD ROSA: "I see a mortal armament shining
Between your skirts … No, no
… don't do it, not even by accident."

THE CLEANER: "Let this iron pierce my heart
That can endure no more …
Death announced itself to me today,
Arriving at a gallop …"

OLD ROSA: "Pay no attention …
To the voices that want to do you harm."

THE CLEANER: "What do you know of love
… and it's fatal design?
Leave me alone, let go …
I will accompany him …
It's my last regret …" *(Stabs herself with the knife.)*

OLD ROSA: "My sister, what sadness, what solace.
But what do I see? … There he comes
… his silhouette galloping across the mountain
… Love that shouldn't be there shining in his eyes …"

MARITZA: Killing yourself for a guy, the same old story … I'd
get myself a lollipop and then ciao … Gallop … gallop …
so much that you can't anymore and then ciao …

OLD ROSA: I don't know what you're doing in this sacred
space … You lack breeding and knowledge. Dear God,
what kind of a country have we become?

MARITZA: You're such a know-it-all … Of course, maybe
you come from a well-heeled family … I've got plenty of
culture, just not your kind, old woman.

THE CLEANER: Calm down, Maritza, we should all go
together today, you haven't heard the radio, there are
more bad guys in the street every day.

MARITZA: Mijita, what I need is for one of these bad guys to appear and give me a buzz, because with the guy I've got at home I don't know if I've got a cunt or not.

OLD ROSA: Look at you, indecent snot-nose, how can you use that vocabulary? Haven't you realized yet that we're in the Opera? We're not cleaning motels.

THE CLEANER: And Maritza confronted her for the first time and told her this and that.

MARITZA: Look here, old lady, I've had it up to here with your stupidities, with your education about the Opera. They must have drained all the blood out of you that's why you're so afraid.

THE CLEANER: Now it became clear that she was saying good-bye.

(They continue cleaning, OLD ROSA throws a bucket of water and it grazes MARITZA.)

OLD ROSA: You were on my part of the stage. Okay, now, hurry up, I've got a delicious potato stew waiting for me at home.

(OLD ROSA hits her with a mop; they rip each other's aprons.)

THE CLEANER: I don't know why I kept quiet, but I went towards the lip of the stage, almost at the edge, and I began to sing.

(She sings 'Madame Butterfly', it's as if she's hallucinating, the others stop fighting and begin to rock, The CLEANER keeps singing.)

OLD ROSA: Ayy, my God, it looks like she's possessed.

MARITZA: What are you talking about, possessed. Hey, have you gone crazy?

THE CLEANER: Let's hurry up – it's getting late.

(She faints; MARITZA brings some water from her bucket and revives her.)

OLD ROSA: What's wrong with her? I hope she doesn't have any symptoms.

MARITZA: Shhttt … I've never seen you like this.

THE CLEANER: Don't worry – I'm fine. I picked up my things, hung up my apron … Maritza fixed herself up and fixed herself up and Old Rosa put up with the tears.

OLD ROSA: Ay, why should I care about this, it's someone else's sorrow … perhaps this is what it means to get old and begin to lack love for real.

THE CLEANER: And then it felt like my blood pressure rose again, and I said "Maritza, let's go together."

Second Sequence

In the Street

THE CLEANER: So we were in the street with me checking to make sure we weren't hit by a car, or a microbus would have to slam on its brakes, and Maritza kept talking and talking.

MARITZA: You know this can't go on like this much longer, you just see what happens when I get that old woman alone. When the ballet dancers came last time she wouldn't let me clean the dressing rooms. What does she think – that I was going to offer myself there?

LOLO: Two beautiful ladies, you ... yes ... Come here, come, what are you two doing?

THE CLEANER: And she let go of my arm, and she moved and he moved, and the young man looked her up and down.

MARITZA: Ayy, I thought you were Rolo – you look a lot alike.

LOLO: If you like Rolo we're all right ... You're coming from the Theatre.

MARITZA: I work in the show ... little things, you know ...

LOLO: Artists have it good, you can see it; you can see how sensitive you are ...

MARITZA: Thanks ... But, listen, I can't get over how much you look like Rolo.

LOLO: And Rolo is as much a guy as I am.

MARITZA: Don't flatter yourself ... and what are you doing?

LOLO: Checking out the calendar here ... Thinking of inviting my parents to the opera as a gift. I bet that you're in the ballet.

MARITZA: Well ... yes.

LOLO: You can tell by the good leather you're wearing ...

MARITZA: Just like I do in the dance.

OLD ROSA: Don't lose your opportunity, bitch … *(To herself.)* And the other idiot waiting for her … Maybe when I get on the bus I'll sit next to a cultured gentleman reading something and he'll ask me: "Do you like to read as well?" And I'll take advantage of the moment to tell him about the novels I have at home … That I belong to the municipal library and discover a different author each week … And I'll ask him if he'd recommend what he's reading. And then he'll realize who he's talking to and he'll say, "Look, I was just reading about two strangers who meet on a journey" … He'll realize besides that I'm intellectually attractive … Him in his marvelous suit. He'll say to me: "It's my lucky day, I couldn't drive due to smog restrictions, that's why I'm on the bus. And that's how I got to meet you" and everything will continue giving … He'll tell me that he separated two months ago. And that books help him deal with the solitude. It's atrocious not have anyone with whom to watch the news. And I'll take advantage of the moment to tell him that I've got a delicious potato stew at home. Why do only the whores on TV get to have luck?

LOLO: You must know María Callas.

MARITZA: No, I've only worked here a little while. She must have been here before I arrived.

LOLO: Don't worry about it … But let's not keep standing here … You're so entertaining … Let's go to my place.

MARITZA: You're also very nice … Let's go, then.

LOLO: I'll give you a present there so you can see how nice I am. Tell your friend to relax, take it easy, no need to be so emotional.

MARITZA: She's just super shy … but she'll have to wake up.

THE CLEANER: And they kept talking, but, since I couldn't leave her alone I drew near and said … "Hey, Maritza, we should go. It's getting late."

LOLO: What's your hurry? Let's go to my apartment, I live with a friend, we'll have some coffee, listen to some music, and all of a sudden we'll dance.

MARITZA: We'll do it all … This bastard has taken my heart. Come on, silly, maybe the other one will be just as good.

THE CLEANER: And, since I had to take care of her, I went with them …

Third Sequence

In the Apartment

THE CLEANER: So the three of us found ourselves in an apartment with beautiful wallpaper, big flowers with a rose colored background.

MARITZA: Your place is incredible; Lolo, but you need a screen, the naked light bulbs are really ugly, I'll give you one, if you want ...

THE CLEANER: He brought three glasses, all of them different, and filled them with malice and Coca-Cola.

LOLO: The two of you are great ... Cheers ... *(His cell rings.)*

LOLO: Yes, better come at once ... they're ready, tipsy, hurry up, I've got them on the grill, yeah, ethnic types, I found them in the center itself ... yours is a bit annoying ... I'm sure she's never felt it ...

MARITZA: We're in luck, girl, we've fallen into the real shit, a couple of decent guys, not like that Peruvian who's always bothering you, we could both end the night with hot guys. This is a good drink Lolito ... you're so loving.

LOLO: Come here, then, so you can see just how loving I am.

THE CLEANER: He got a bit vulgar as he put his hand on her thigh and, I think he grabbed her intimate part. So I started to look at the parquet, which was very cracked ... When I raised my gaze, he was licking her neck and opening her blouse. It's a good thing they knocked because who knows what would have happened. Since I'm shy I looked out the window and saw that since the sky was still calm nothing disgraceful had happened, as long as we got to daybreak Maritza would save herself from the premonition.

LOLO: Hey, I told you I'd introduce you to my friend, I'll leave the two of you alone.

THE CLEANER: How are you? Pleased to meet you.

SAMUEL: What's your name? They call me Samuel.

MARITZA: Loosen up, girl – go for it … ciao.

SAMUEL: Come here, nearer, take a look … you can see the Entel Tower.

THE CLEANER: This would be a great place to spend New Year's Eve … I commented … Then he rubbed up against me with his body and I realized that this was what the priest talked about … I was faced with temptation for the first time. And there in front of me, the false lights of the desert.

SAMUEL: The lights are beautiful.

THE CLEANER: As I thought to myself, these lights in the night are idolatry.

SAMUEL: Hey, you're a quiet one … that's the way I like my girls … with an interior life … you understand … You let yourself enter the panorama … If it penetrates you then you start to think … So many people in so many buildings … So, you work at the opera.

THE CLEANER: His eyes were black and received the bright filth of the city … I felt his breath … hot … expanding from the gullet of the dragon. Yes, I work there … in … cleaning …

SAMUEL: Relax, we're here to have a conversation, two people who want to get to know each other … Everything's cool … Do you like this poster? … I understand that you don't want to talk; I'm also an interior sort of person … Do you see these vials I have? … In this one I keep my cut fingernails, the other one is all my own hair, it used to be down to here … And this one is full of all the cockroaches I find … Well, now, my pants are about to burst.

THE CLEANER: I had no idea what he was talking about. I did notice that he seemed educated, I thought he told me something about some vials so I asked … "Do you study medicine?"

SAMUEL: No, but my parents would like me to. Besides, you'd be able to stick your fingers wherever you want, and I'm very curious.

THE CLEANER: I was petrified, I couldn't move, and so as not to seem rude I said ... "Uyy, your parquet floor's all cracked."

(The CLEANER's feet begin to move by themselves, she begins to zapatear and then she faints.)

VIOLATION

SAMUEL takes off her skirt, opens her blouse ... rapes her.

THE CLEANER: When I opened my eyes I was on the ground, they'd taken off my skirt and an icy liquid ran from my place of sin ... that's when I knew they'd abused my person, violated the secret that I'd guarded for so many years for the one who deserved my love, and my sadness was so great, that my entire body cried, tears shed through my pores, my brain shook and I thought of my mother and the parish priest ... "Why, why have you forsaken me, Lord? Why have you let evil possess my body?" My eyes crept out from under my eyelids and swung over all my limbs, the table, the glasses, everything trembled with my dishonor, but a lightning bolt hit my forehead and calmed me, and I realized that they hadn't touched my soul, only the flesh, the body destined to turn to dust, and I asked my Lord for forgiveness ...

(The CLEANER gets up, gets dressed and hears noises in the next room.)

That was when I remembered Maritza, the two guys, and my premonition.

(She runs down the hall and stops, petrified.)

They had Maritza there, crucified on the bed, the one with the longer hair was choking her with his member, and she was blue, unable to breathe. The other sunk his teeth into the birthplace and stuck a viper's tongue inside of her.

(The CLEANER runs towards the other side of the stage and returns gripping a knife like a sword.)

And I grabbed the biggest knife, which was nothing less than Archangel Gabriel's sword, and I buried it in his neck, that of the first demon eating her entrails. The other one, spitting pus from his penis and wailing like Lucifer, tried to attack me, but He guided my hand and I drove the sword through his chest.

(MARITZA enters, naked, covering herself with a shirt full of blood. The CLEANER embraces her.)

THE CLEANER: I saved you – Maritza – I saved you … Praised be our Lord.

THE END

LEGUA'S GYNECOLOGIST

The Confession

Talking to a member of the audience.

I should tell you that this situation makes me just a little bit nervous, even though I'm Catholic, I didn't get used to ventilating all the little stupidities that occur to one from your first communion on, like everyone surely, but we're not going to talk about fools and madwomen, how charming their antics can be, are we? Pardon me, my breath is bothering you, no, no, don't turn away, I'll try to talk like this, more to one side, can you hear me? One can see that you're a sensitive person. Ummm ... what an odor. I'm sure that your stench is what attracted me. It's really exquisite, you know, these days it isn't usual for people to bathe, let alone go out perfumed ... This is what assures me that you know how to keep quiet. Really. *(Coughs.)* This cough is driving me crazy, bronchitis. The smog. *(Coughs.)* Don't worry – it isn't contagious. You live here. Or don't you? The smog is appalling ... Tell me *(Coughs.)* No, don't look at me; it's just that I don't dare, could I touch your shoulder? ... It would give me a little more confidence, this way I'll give myself the idea that we're already acquainted, that you are this person in whom I wanted to confide. But, lamentably, he's not here ... I've lied, I've lied in such a terrible manner, that my lies have created realities, you understand, fictions that have become facts. They tell me about virtual reality! Nonsense. I created a world for them. Full of sadness and memory. Today you are giving me the opportunity to unburden myself; I'll do it so well, that it will permit me to walk tranquilly, to say the least. And you will feel that you've carried out a humanitarian action, something positive and that is very comforting. ... I'm a doctor; I bet you'd already guessed, since we recognize each other from Legua. Gynecologist, strange, have you noticed my hands are always damp? Curious ... No, don't think I'm going to tell you a tale about getting all excited

297

and that now I feel guilty and all the rest. That's too obvious. Besides, I'm a professional.

I pay attention to everything, I know their mucous membrane forward and back, I'm aware of who's doing well and who's not ... In reality, as soon as they enter a world's decided. But when they are girls, crippled, dark, heading towards black, with their complacent smiles filled with yellow teeth, with rolls of fat under the breast. Then ... I really can't stand them. They arrive early, then they have to go to work, frightened, with their inflated wombs, trying to be friendly, modulating. You know ...

"Just so the kid pops out healthy, doctor" And a cheap cologne .... I can't tell you. The fingernails, listen, atrocious, between black and violet, with skin full of bruises. And then they put on this face of cheap pride, asking "will it be a little man, doctor?" ... They don't understand a thing you tell them ... then they repeat ...

And then I feel like I'm fulfilling my obligation, I'm discovering my purpose in life, in this chain of human perfection. Imagine if all these fetuses generate more fat men and women, dark girls with yellow teeth and limited intellectual coefficients, people who will then vote for other badly dressed men, dark, stinking, and of low intellectual coefficient. And that's when I reaffirm my purpose and I know that it wasn't chance that made me a gynecologist ...

I look at them tenderly, I make the nurse leave, I take them by the hands, I play with their knuckles and look at them like a priest, and then, in a soft voice, I tell them. "The child isn't well, his little legs haven't formed, and the pharynx is extended, this means, señora, that there is no mouth." And I cry with them.

I console them, tell them they're young, there will be other opportunities, I put them to sleep, carry out the therapeutic abortion and I tie their tubes.

Sometimes they want to bury them, the old story of the little angels, I tell them they were already incinerated. And that they were nothing more than matter; they hadn't yet developed a soul. Sometimes they say they heard their cries. I say, yes, noises, the last agonies of the deformed. We embrace and leave the future in God's hands.

I only do this Tuesdays and Fridays, as part of the medical school's plan to help people in extreme poverty.

But today I had a small malaise, I doubted my actions, that's why I came to you, I sensed you'd understand, I even feel that you are silently grateful for my labor. Now I feel much better, I don't know how to thank you. Only people like you should have children …

THE END

WWW.OBERONBOOKS.COM

Follow us on www.twitter.com/@oberonbooks
& www.facebook.com/OberonBooksLondon

www.ingramcontent.com/pod-product-compliance
Ingram Content Group UK Ltd.
Pitfield, Milton Keynes, MK11 3LW, UK
UKHW031249020325
455689UK00008B/138